European Issues in Children's
Identity and Citizenship **1**

Children's understanding in
the new Europe

European Issues in Children's
Identity and Citizenship **1**

Children's understanding in the new Europe

*Edited by Elisabet Näsman
and Alistair Ross*

Trentham Books
Stoke on Trent, UK and Sterling USA

Trentham Books Limited

Westview House	22883 Quicksilver Drive
734 London Road	Sterling
Oakhill	VA 20166-2012
Stoke on Trent	USA
Staffordshire	
England ST4 5NP	

First published 2002

British Library Cataloguing-in-Publication Data
A catalogue record for this book is available from the British Library

1 85856 251 1

Designed and typeset by Trentham Print Design Ltd., Chester and printed in Great Britain by Cromwell Press Ltd., Wiltshire.

Contents

v

Series Introduction:
European Issues in Children's
Identity and Citizenship

Children's Understanding in the New Europe is the first volume in the series *European Issues in Children's Identity and Citizenship*. This series has arisen from the work of the ERASMUS Thematic Network Project called Children's Identity and Citizenship in Europe (CiCe). This network brings together over 90 university departments, in 29 European states, all of which share an interest in the education of professionals who will work with children and young people in the area of social, political and economic education. The network links many of those who are educating the future teachers, youth workers, social pedagogues and social psychologists in Europe.

The CiCe Network began in 1996, and has been supported by the European Commission since 1998. This series arises from our conviction that changes in contemporary European society are such that we need to examine how the processes of socialisation are adapting to the new contexts. Political, economic and social changes are under way that suggest that we are developing multifaceted and layered identities, that reflect the contingencies of European integration. In particular, children are growing up in this rapidly changing society, and their social behaviour will reflect the dimensions of this new and developing social unit. Identities will probably be rather different: national identities will continue alongside new identifications, with sub-national regions and supra-national unions. Our sense of citizenship will also develop in rather different ways than in the past: multiple and nested loyalties will develop, more complex than the simple affiliations of the past.

Those who will work with children and young people have a particular role to play in this. They will have to help young people develop their own relationships with the new institutions that develop, while at the same time being mindful of the traditional relationships known and understood by parents and grandparents, and their role in inter-generational acculturation.

This series is designed to discuss and debate the issues concerned with the professional and academic education of teachers, early childhood workers, social pedagogues and the like. They will need to understand the complex issues surrounding the socialisation and social understanding of the young, and to be aware of the similarities and differences in professional practices across Europe. They will need to work with young people learning to be citizens – citizens both of the traditional political entities, and of the developing new polities of Europe.

As the first in the series this volume is deliberately intended to raise a wide range of related issues. Future volumes in the series will be more focused, on particular forms and areas of social learning (such as the political and the economic), or learning at different ages and in different types of institution, or the contribution of historical and cultural understanding to social development.

CiCe welcomes enquiries from potential members of the network. These should be addressed to the CiCe Central Coordination Unit, at the Institute for Policy Studies in Education, University of North London, 166–220 Holloway Road, London N7 8DB, United Kingdom.

Alistair Ross
Series Editor

On behalf of the editorial committee: Tilman Alert, Márta Fülöp, Yveline Fumat, Akos Gocsal, Søren Hegstrup, Riitta Korhonen, Emilio Lastrucci, Elisabet Nasman, Panyota Papoulia-Tzelpi and Ann-Marie Van den dries

Chapter Synopsis

Chapter 1
Introduction: Children in the new Europe
Alistair Ross and Elisabet Näsman

Chapter 2
Sharing children's thoughts and experiences
Elisabet Näsman and Christina von Gerber
When economy, worklife and politics are discussed in relationship to children, children's own perspective is rarely heard. If the focus is on children's understanding, their learning and how their constructon of their own identity is based on experiences from these areas, the importance of the voice of children is obvious. This contribution presents experiences from three research projects where children were informants, projects concerning worklife, unemployment and economy, all social phenomena viewed with children's eyes. To share children's experiences and ideas is an ethically and methodologically complex issue. The interaction between an adult researcher and a child as informant can come about in different ways, in different contexts and be based on different ways of communication. We give examples of the multiple approaches we have used in order to reach various groups of children at home, at school or at daycare centres. Overall, however, we argue that the main issue at stake here is which perspective the adult has in the interaction with the children, an interaction which concerns power, respect and understanding. This calls for theoretical reflection put in action.

Sammanfattning:
Frågor om ekonomi, arbete och politik i samband med barn belyses sällan ur barns eget perspektiv. Om intresset ligger i barns egen förståelse, deras lärande och hur barns identitetsskapande bygger på erarenheter från dessa områden blir dock betydelsen av barnens egen röst uppenbar. Det här bidraget förmedlar erfarenheter från tre forskningsprojekt med barn som informanter, projekt om arbete, arbetslöshet och ekonomi sedda med barns ögon. Att ta del av barns erfarenheter och tankar är en både etiskt och metodologiskt komplex fråga. Mötet mellan en vuxen forskare och ett barn

som informanter kan ske på olika sätt, i olika kontexter och bygga på olika kommunikationsvägar. Vi ger exempel på den mångfald ansatser vi använt för att nå olika barn i deras hem, i skolan eller på daghemmet. Framförallt vill vi dock hävda att det här är frågan om vilket perspektiv den vuxen har i möte med barnen, ett möte som handlar om makt, respekt och förståelse. Det kräver teoretisk reflektion omsatt i praktisk handling.

Chapter 3
Towards an anti-developmental view of children's social and economic understanding
Merryn Hutchings

Developmentalism, and in particular the Piagetian model, has been the theoretical framework adopted by a large number of studies of children's understanding of the social world, and in particular by those focusing on economic understanding. This chapter considers problems that are implicit in this approach, explaining why I regard it as important to find an anti-developmental alternative. I consider some alternative stances, and review the potential of social constructionism as an anti-developmental approach. Finally, I consider what the adoption of this perspective would mean for the researcher. My intention is 'to stimulate a self consciousness about the word 'development'" (Morss, 1996, p.1).

A postmodern perspective enables us to look on developmentalism as one of the grand narratives of modernity, and to evaluate it as a story. Instead of concentrating on how accurate it is in describing reality, we can consider how and why it came into existence, and what effects it has had. We need to consider the nature and origins of developmentalism. Such change is seen as unidirectional, and generally involves the notion that adult thinking is more rational and complex than that of children. This is not seen simply as an accumulation of knowledge, but rather as a fundamental change in the quality of thinking. Development is thus towards a particular goal, logical abstract thought, though not everyone will reach this goal. Rational thought can be identified as a particularly western, masculine and middle-class value, which, in the nineteenth century was strongly associated with the concerns of government.

This chapter is concerned with the way that the developmental story continues to reverberate in research into the development of children's social and economic understanding. I will examine how the course of development has been defined; how norms have been constructed and used; and how those who do not meet the norm have been considered. Many of the examples I use refer to the development of children's ideas about work, which is central to social and economic organisation.

Chapter 4
Intergenerational differences and social transition: Teachers' and students' perception of competition in Hungary
Márta Fülöp

Present day adolescents, who began their schooling after the political changes of the late 1980s, could be the ideal builders of the new democracies and we might expect them to have political, economical and social concepts that, as a consequence of living in and directly experiencing the changed structure, reflect the ruling ideology of the new political system rather than that of the previous regimes. However, these young people are being socialised by their parents and teachers, who were brought up during the previous social system and became adults and working people in a completely different ideological system. If this is so, it is a very important theoretical and practical question as to how the parents' and teachers' ways of thinking change, and how their ideas are reflected in the young people's ideas. In other words, how effective is the intergenerational transmission of values when compared to the influence of the changed ideology of the political arena and the social reality that young people perceive around them in their everyday life?

This chapter consists of five main parts. The first three parts are theoretical introductions: the first reviews the literature on intergenerational transmission of values and conceptions of social, political and economical questions; the second the literature on social transition and social change and how they effect different generations; and the third examines these two topics in the context of societal changes in Central and Eastern Europe. The fourth and fifth parts are based on an empirical study carried out among Hungarian secondary school teachers and secondary school students. As competition is a key element of contemporary social change, the fourth part compares how teachers and students perceive the role of competition in present day Hungary. The fifth part discusses teachers' ideas about the role of the school in preparing students for future competition and the possible ways teachers and school can do this.

Chapter 5
Children's understanding of society: psychological studies and their educational implications
Anna Emilia Berti

From the sixties to the eighties, children's understanding of politics has been studied mainly within three different approaches: the Piagetian one, which fostered a search for stages of political understanding based on, and secondary to, Piagetian stages; the approaches of social representations and political socialisation, which stressed the importance of the information which children receive from home, school, and the media. Very few studies have been carried out within the the domain-specific approach, which nowadays has a leading role in educational and developmental research. In this chapter I present this approach first; I then summarise the main data on children's understanding of political notions, highlighting how these data can be interpreted within the domain-specific approach. Finally, I present some results from intervention studies on teaching political notions and discuss their theoretical and practical significance.

Tra gli anni '60 e gli anni '80 lo studio della comprensione del mondo politico nei bambini è stato guidato da tre approcci principali: quello piagetiano, che ha stimolato la ricerca di stadi dello sviluppo della comprensione politica basati su quelli piagetiani e da essi dipendenti, e gli approcci della socializzazione politica e delle rappresentazioni sociali, che hanno sottolineato l'importanza delle informazioni che i bambini ricevono da famiglia, scuola, mass-media. Uno scarso numero di studi si è invece richiamato all'approcio dominio-specifico, che negli ultimi vent'anni ha acquisito un crescente consenso nell'ambito della psicologia dello sviluppo e dell'educazione. In questo articolo, dopo una breve descrizione degli assunti che caratterizzano l'approccio dominio-specifico, presenterò una sintesi dei dati sulla nozioni politiche presenti a diverse età, dalla prima fanciullezza all'adolescenza, mostrando come possono essere interpretati all'interno di tale approccio. Infine, presenterò i risultati di alcuni studi-intervento sull'insegnamento di nozioni politiche, discutendone il significato teorico e pratico.

Chapter 6
Identity and pre-school education
Riitta Korhonen
This chapter clarifies how children's identity develops in early childhood and in pre-school learning. The development of identity belongs to a child's whole development and life, especially the emotional life. Identity can be defined in many ways, for instance from individual, social, cultural and ethnic viewpoints. A human being grows as a member of his or her own community and culture. Everybody has besides his or her own personal history at least a small part of cultural heritage (Keltinkangas-Järvinen, 2000). Cultural knowledge is important psychologically because if the person knows his or her background and roots it is almost the same as self-knowledge.

A child's home, parents and family are the basis for growing. Their other environments: daycare, pre-school, friends etc also have an important influence on a child's life. This view is from the ecological model created by Bronfenbrenner (1979).

The meaning of the learning environment in the institutional learning for a child's development is remarkable. A group of children confirms a child's cooperation, feeling of fellowship and friendship and other social skills. A child learns to be active in the group alone, without the support of his or her own family. The experiences of success, group coherence and confidence in relationships develop a child's personality and learning. A child has possibilities to accept himself or herself as a unique person. The respect a child receives offers him or her the possibility of having a happy and cheerful childhood. This is a good ground for the future and it is also a child's right. A child whose emotional life is in balance can learn to understand others and little by little also see and respect differences.

In pre-school education it is possible to focus on every child as a personality with different personal needs and create a rich, developing and active learning environment. In such an environment a child has the possibility to be a unique person and this will help to build personality and identity. According to the context a child has models in his or her own home, but the other important environment for learning and developing is a group in the pre-school with other children and teachers.

Tässä kappaleessa selvitetään lasten identiteetin kehittymistä varhaislapsuudessa ja virallisen oppivelvollisuuden kynnyksellä. Identiteetin kehitys on sidoksissa lapsen kokonaiskehitykseen ja lapsen elämään erityisesti tunne-elämän alueella. Identiteetti voidaan määritellä yksilön, yhteisön, kulttuurisen ja etnisyyden näkökulmasta.

Ihminen kasvaa omaksi itsekseen oman yhteisönsä ja kulttuurinsa jäsenenä ja hänen henkilöhistoriassa on myös osa kulttuuriperimää (Keltinkangas-Järvinen 2000). Kulttuuriin perehtyminen sisältää psykologisesti myös syvemmän merkityksen; oman taustan ja juurien tunteminen on lähes samaa kuin itsensä tunteminen.

Tässä tarkastellaan lapsen koko elämänpiiriä kontekstuaalisen oppimisteorian (Hujala 1998) pohjalta, jossa lapsen koti ja perhe muodostavat ytimen lapsen kehittymiselle. Lisäksi lapsen elinympäristöön kuuluvat muut ympäristössä vaikuttavat tahot lapsen elämässä. Näitä ympäristöjä voivat olla lapsen päivähoitopaikka, esiopetus, koulu ja erilaiset harrastukset. Tämä näkemys pohjaa Bronfenbrennerin (1997) ekologiseen malliin.

Erikssonin (1950) on esittänyt lapsen identiteetin kehittymisen pohjaavan perusluottamukseen ja siitä saatuihin kokemuksiin lapsen varhaisina vuosina. Aluksi lapselle tärkeimmät henkilöt ovat vanhemmat ja sisarukset ja myöhemmin muut lapsen kanssa toimivat aikuiset ja lapset.

Institutionaalisessa oppimisessa oppimisympäristön merkitys lapsen kehitykselle on suuri. Ryhmässä oleminen vahvistaa lapsen ryhmään kuulumisen tunnetta, yhteistyötaitoja ja lapsi oppii toimimaan omana itsenään vertaisryhmässä ilman oman perheensä malleja ja tukea. Onnistumisen kokemukset, ryhmään sitoutuminen ja luottamuksellisten suhteiden luominen edistävät lapsen kasvua ja itsetuntemusta, jotka ovat avainasioita sille, miten lapsi kokee ja hyväksyy itsensä oman persoonanaan. Lapsen kokema ja tuntema kunnioitus ja arvostus antavat hänelle mahdollisuuden onnellisuuteen ja huolettomuuteen, jotka ovat elämän peruspilareita. Tähän lapsella on myös oikeus omassa lapsuudessaan. Tunne-elämältään tasapainoinen lapsi oppii ymmärtämään muita ja vähitellen hän oppii myös kohtaamaan ja arvostamaan erilaisuutta.

Esiopetuksessa voidaan erityisesti kiinnittää huomiota lapsen henkilökohtaisiin tarpeisiin ja luoda hänen kannaltaan suotuisa ja lasta oikealla tavalla monipuolisesti aktivoiva oppimisympäristö. Esiopetuksessa lapsella on mahdollisuus olla ainutkertainen yksilö ja sen tukeminen edesauttaa lapsen oman identiteetin ja elämän rakentumista. Lapsi saa malleja ja vahvistusta omalle toiminnalleen. Omassa perheessään lapsi kuuluu yhteisöön ja lisäksi esiopetusryhmä muodostaa hänelle toisen tärkeän oppimisen paikan.

Chapter 7
Children's national identity and attitudes toward other nationalities in a monocultural society: the Polish example
Beata Krzywosz-Rynkiewicz

Taking into consideration the questions of nationality and religion, Poland is a relatively homogeneous country. 90 per cent of Poles declare Polish nationality and 95 per cent of them belong to the Catholic church. Does this mean that we can expect the problems of tolerance and acceptance to be less serious in a monocultural country whose citizens have almost no experience in dealing with representatives of other nationalities? Or maybe on the contrary, lack of such everyday contacts gives rise to strong stereotypes of and prejudice against others? What is this kind of prejudice connected with? Which spheres does it concern? Finally, does the sense of national unity allow people to remain open to other cultures, and is it conducive to the development of a spirit of community with the Europeans? Or does it create the atmosphere in which any 'difference' seems to threaten one's identity? At present, i.e. shortly before joining the structures of the European Union, those questions are of primary importance in Poland. The problem of keeping a reasonable balance between own national identity and acceptance for others will be soon faced by all Poles, regardless of their age and social status. However, to the highest degree it will concern young people – the generation whose attitude of tolerance is still at the stage of development. Those issues and questions constitute the object of our interest in the present chapter.

The chapter is divided into five sections. The first section is a short theoretical introduction. The second includes an analysis of the sense of national identity among Polish children, as well as certain cognitive and social categories associated with it. Section three is devoted to the problem of tolerance for others; it presents the results of research on the prejudices and stereotypes followed by young people in their perception of representatives of other nations. The results of investigations into the knowledge, acceptance and experience of Polish children concerning national and religious differences are also discussed. Section four deals with the role of school in modifying children's attitudes. It tries to answer the question of whether teachers are aware of the problem of tolerance (or lack of tolerance) and whether they are ready to make an attempt at conducting experimental classes aimed at increasing pupils' acceptance of others. Examples of behaviour modification programs are also provided, supported by the results of studies on their effectiveness. Section five examines the correlation between the sense of national ties and European identity.

Chapter 8
When students from Arles and Sparta meet:
social representations and identifications
Aigli Zafeirakou
This chapter describes an empirical study on the social representations of two groups of twelve-year-old students who participated in a school exchange between Arles in France and Sparta in Greece. The two groups visited each other's towns during a week in the spring of 1994. The students used drawings and texts to express their perceptions of their own town and that of the town they were visiting.

The study was inspired by theoretical insights about social representations and identifications, and uses qualitative and ethnographic methods. This chapter elaborates on two questions: firstly, what role does (and can) school education play in the way young students construct an image of their own town? secondly, how does the way a group represents its own town influence the way in which it tries to understand another town? The chapter also hints at some larger questions. Among what layers of representation does mutual understanding among students from different cultures work? How does understanding of the local and the distant relate? How do cultural interchanges across cultural borders affect mutual understanding, and how do they affect the educational project?

xv

Chapter 9
Youth and European identity
Emilio Lastrucci
This chapter is concerned with the development of a European identity in young people, conceived of as a special form of social identity, and with the relationship between European identity and national identity. This problem is analysed in two ways. The underlying analysis is based on a critical and comparative presentation of recent and relevant theories and models about the process of socialisation during adolescence, relating these to the construction of social identity and, more particularly, to the relationship between the development of historical consciousness and the process of political socialisation. This is set within a consideration of the findings of recent empirical research on socialisation, the formation of social identity and the development of historical consciousness (using especially the wide-ranging survey 'Youth and History', but also other more circumscribed inquiries in this area).

Chapter 10
Young men growing up: is there a new crisis?
John Schostak and Barbara Walker
Based on the authors' research with young people, this chapter explores in particular the experiences, understandings, explanations and hopes of boys in the context of the major social, economic and political changes taking place both locally and globally. By setting their dreams in relation to their realities, the impact on their sense of identity, agency and wellbeing is analysed in the context of social and personal expectations concerning 'maleness'. Is there a 'moral panic' about the apparent failure of boys relative to girls to succeed in education and employment? Or is there a 'real' crisis of 'maleness' going deeper than surface appearances? This chapter argues that in order to understand the experience of young people and boys in particular it is necessary to examine the differential allocation of resources to need, interests, and opportunities to develop talent to bring about the dreams, the hopes and the ambitions of young people.

Chapter 11
On the Development of Education for Democracy and Citizenship in the Czech Republic
Pavel Vacek
This chapter explores:

A) A broader social context and its influence upon education for democracy and citizenship and character education in the Czech Republic

B) Schools and their conditions for education for democracy and citizenship

Czech schools have the following advantages: a long educational tradition, sophisticated and stable school system.

Their disadvantages: social learning and education for democracy have almost no tradition (only since 1989), themes of citizenship, democracy etc. are not at the centre of attention of our teachers. If they do appear, then it is on a general level, not based on pupils' experience.

C) Outlooks of education for democracy and citizenship

Project topics orientated primarily towards this area (for example within projects supported by CiCe) have to be sensitive to the cultural and national differences of Central and Eastern Europe. These projects should be complex and flexible, dealing with both general and concrete issues.

K vývoji výchovy k demokracii a obačnství v České republice

A) Širší sociální kontext a jeho vliv na výchovu k demokracii a občanství a výchovu charakteru v České republice.

B) Školy a jejich podmínky k výchově demokracii a občanství.

České školství má následující přednosti: dlouhodobou vzdělávací tradici, propracovaný a stabilní školský systém.

Jeho nevýhody: sociální výchova a výchova k demokracii u nás nemá prakticky žádnou tradici (pouze od roku 1989), témata občanství a demokracie nejsou centru zájmu našich učitelů. Pokud se objevují, pak v obecné rovině, bez využívání zkušeností žáků.

C) Perspektivy výchovy k demokracii a občanství.

Témata projektů orientovaných primárně do oblasti výše zmíněných oblastí (např. v rámci projektů podporovaných CiCe) musí zohledňovat kulturní a národní odlišnosti zemí střední a východní Evropy. Tyto projekty by měly být komplexní a flexibilní, zabývající se jak obecnými, tak konkrétními otázkami.

1

Introduction:
Children in the new Europe

Alistair Ross and Elisabet Näsman
Institute for Policy Studies in Education,
University of North London, UK
Department of Thematic Studies, Linköping University, Sweden

The development of social understanding is both contextual and contingent: the development of individual identity can be seen as a reflection of the interaction of the various social groupings that exist at any particular moment. Children and young people's identity seem to develop within a particular social context. It can be argued that the current social flux, that is perhaps particularly a feature of contemporary Europe, is the consequence of major realignments, or of the major dispersal of social patterns.

Since 1945, in an accelerating manner, we have seen, perhaps especially in Europe

- the acquisition of substantial and unimagined material goods coupled with the persistence of major social inequalities

- the growing recognition of gender inequalities and substantial (though still far from complete) attempts to ameliorate these

- the end of the European empires of France, the United Kingdom, Portugal, Italy and the Netherlands

- major population movements (from the former colonies to the metropolis, across Europe, and others)

- the development of an international economy in which the majority of capital movements are speculative
- the development of global companies
- the development of a broad range of 'alternative' cultures (youth, gay, feminist, vegetarian and vegan, and many others).

The European Union has also developed from its inception in 1956, not simply by expanding its size, but also in its ambition and spheres of influence. Such major political change, though proceeding incrementally and step-wise, offers profoundly different social and political scenery in which young people are now socialised.

There have been other significant shifts in society over the past half-century. International travel has become more than commonplace for many Europeans: easier, cheaper, faster, and far more frequent. Many international borders in Europe have reverted to being merely lines on a map. The development of mass media has brought into our homes a culture that is partly shared and in common.

Changes of this sort will perhaps inevitably affect the way in which young people develop their views of the societies and communities within which they grow up, and consequently their own emerging sense of identity. What is happening in different parts of Europe? Are patterns emerging, commonalities across Europe, or are there major national or regional variations? Are these factors having such an influence on children/young people's social understanding, and if so, how?

This is not just a question of theoretical interest: there are some very practical consequences that will result from the answers to these questions. The states that comprise contemporary Europe (and much of the rest of the world) have professionalised much of the education and care of children and young people. How does the practice of these professionals reflect contemporary change and developments in society? Are our nurseries, social services, schools, etc. attempting to reproduce the social patterns of an earlier generation (one in which parents and teachers were themselves socialised), or are they able to socialise children into the contemporary nature of European societies – and prepare them for changes in these societies?

The chapters in this book address various aspects of these questions. We have drawn together a range of writers who approach these issues from very different perspectives – different disciplines, different cultures, different pedagogies. We are not attempting to present a rounded synthesis, a blueprint or a formula for the future, but to raise questions and issues that we believe students should be aware of, and should attempt to take account of in their future practice.

Firstly, how do we know what children think, understand and believe? Näsman and von Gerber consider the difficulties in collecting information and ideas from young children, illustrating their methods through case study material on children's understanding of unemployment. In doing this, they raise very significant ethical issues about researching young people's understanding, as well as the difficulties of getting a 'real' understanding of their ideas.

One important question is to examine how learning about society occurs. Naive developmentalists would have suggested, a generation ago, a series of stages of understanding that were largely determined by stage of development and chronological age. It was argued that all children, irrespective of culture and context, would pass through the same levels of understanding until they acquired a 'mature', 'adult' level of comprehension. Many studies have challenged this view, and we present here alternative new perspectives. On the one hand is the view that while the context of the social environment is critical, it acts to accelerate (or decelerate) the pace at which a child will move through the stages of understanding, and that what is taught – and how it is taught – is a major influence. On the other hand is the view that the notion of development is a suspect teleology, and that the social environment and context determine the direction and conclusion, as much as the pace, of changes in understanding the complexity of society. Both views agree on the impact of contemporary contingencies, and on the critical nature of the learning processes. Hutchings' chapter challenges the very idea of development in understanding, while Berti suggests that particular kinds of intervention can accelerate social learning and understand-

3

ing. Fülöp's stance is perhaps more conventional: she looks in particular at the rapid changes in Central and Eastern Europe, and considers the interaction between the changing social environment and more traditional intergenerational socialisation processes.

A series of contributions look at particular aspects of change in contemporary Europe, and attempt to identify the implications these have for children and young people and their learning about society. These have been ordered within this book in a rather eclectic manner: many of the chapters are based on case-study material, so we have sequenced the chapters to consider the youngest children first, and the oldest last – but the fundamental concerns of most of the contributors are not age-related, but issues that apply to children and young people of all ages in Europe today.

The development of identity starts at a very early age, and the preschool context is changing rapidly in Europe: pre-school provision is becoming more universal, and governments are playing a greater role in identifying the outcomes that they feel are desirable from such provision. Korhonen considers the consequences for children, and for the professionals who work with them.

Parts of Europe have always had diverse cultures living side by side, but this process has accelerated with recent migrations – refugees within Europe, and migrants from the former colonies. What is the impact on the social understanding of children growing up in areas that are now bicultural? Or in areas that are still largely monocultural, within a Europe of cultural diversity? How do processes of migration, assimilation and non-assimilation affect the developing identities of the children swept up in migration? The contribution of Krzywosz-Rynkiewicz considers this issue by focusing on children in a monocultural setting. Other forms of inter-cultural contact, particularly through exchanges, are considered in the chapter by Zaferiakou.

And, having come to the end of their formal schooling, what do young people think about the European idea, and about their own national identities? How do they match? There are considerable differences between the views and experiences of young people in dif-

4

ferent states. The outcomes of the Youth and History project, reviewed here by Lastrucci, show the kaleidoscope of responses, in which distinct trends and regionalities can be discerned. Gender roles have undergone – and continue to undergo profound changes. What are the effects of these on the developing identities of young people? Schostak and Walker examine the position of young men growing up, and the concept of maleness.

The major political changes that have occurred in Central and Eastern Europe since 1989, and their economic consequences, have been profound. Educational systems and their priorities have been addressed, but the ways in which learning has changed – or not changed – have affected the social psychology of learning. Vacek considers the particular problems that have been addressed in the Czech Republic.

There have been profound economic continuities and discontinuities in Europe. The nature of work and employment is changing: adult identity is often closely associated with work roles: what effect does the growth of unemployment, underemployment, and changing employment patterns have on the identity of children? What of the identity of child workers, and their conceptions of the local and the European economy?

5

2
Sharing children's thoughts and experiences

Elisabet Näsman and Christina von Gerber

Department of Thematic Studies, Linköping University, Sweden

It is essential that professionals who are working with children have the ability to share children's thoughts and experiences. Children's learning is now seen as a process in which children themselves are active and in which their experiences are of fundamental importance for the learning. Children reflect on and try to make sense of their experiences, not only in institutional settings such as schools, but in all the various contexts in which they take part. To any learning situation children bring understanding that they already have gained, and it is crucial for educators to be able to know what that understanding is. It is only children themselves who can tell us about this understanding.

In this chapter we describe the combination of different methods for communication with children that we have developed. We will also discuss the basic assumptions behind our approach. To have children as the focus of interest and to aim at promoting children's best interests are both kinds of child perspectives (Alanen, 1992; Näsman, 1995). In addition to this, our approach is to look at children's lives and conditions from their perspective and to see their communications as the core of the research. We will draw on experience from several projects in which we have looked, from the children's point of view, at parents' work, parents' unemployment and everyday life economy. Most of our examples are selected from a study of unemployment (Näsman and von Gerber, 1996; Näsman and von Gerber, 1998). The basic question is: 'How is it possible to get to know children's understanding and experiences? 'What does being 'a child' mean?' 'Getting to know 'the children's own world' is getting to know a large group in society and to understand a small part of the complex culture that we live in' (Doverborg and Pramling, 1988, our translation).

When we initiated our research project concerning children and unemployment some years ago, we found that very little had been written on the subject, and almost nothing that was based on letting children themselves communicate their thoughts and experiences. From a democratic point of view, this is a problem. As citizens, children ought to have a say in issues concerning themselves, a right that is clearly stated in the UN Convention of the Rights of the Child. Children's experiences of unemployment should, for instance, feed into political decision-making processes concerning unemployment. The lack of children's accounts in this area is, however, also a problem from a scientific point of view. If our understanding of society at large – and of children's lives and conditions in particular – does not include contributions from children as a social category of citizens, then our knowledge is incomplete and may lead to a bias in our understanding. Children as a category have a special status in the generational order of society (Alanen, 1992). They occupy a social position that gives them unique experience of and perspectives on social life and conditions. In research in which adults and children's perspectives are compared, it can be seen that children see and experience things in a different way from adults. Children's accounts are a necessary part of our knowledge of society.

This is not just a question of asking children. What we ask about is also important. Research concerning children is generally conducted from an adult perspective (Alanen 1992). Even research on children's understanding often focuses on issues that adults see as important, rather than the everyday life issues that children find important. Focusing on macro-economic processes in interviews with children on economic issues is an example of this.

The next problem is how we – adults – judge what children are able to tell us. The idea of children as 'not-yets' dominates (Quortrup, 1990). They are not seen as trustworthy to the same extent as are adults. Of course, children's abilities, personal experiences and cultural and social positions are in many ways systematically different from those of adults, but it is hard to maintain that the mechanism by which these kinds of things influence children's accounts are so very different from their effect on adult's accounts. For example, a biographical interview is always coloured by personal ability and experience, as well as by the cultural and social context of both the narrator and the listener (Holstein and Gubrium, 1995). Our basic assumption has been that even the youngest children are credible and important to listen to (Doverborg and Pramling 1988). This has often been demonstrated when both parents and children have given their separate accounts of a family situation. Even young children should be given the opportunity to speak for themselves: and what they say should not simply be used to analyse and measure their maturation level. Their accounts can also be used to inform us about important issues concerning their world of ideas, as well as about the society that they live in.

We focus on children, and we have their interests as the starting point in our work. We have chosen to work from the children's own perspective, which means that we have the ambition to interpret and communicate children's experiences and understanding to adult society: for instance, on the issue of unemployment. We believe that this intention will be of benefit to children, since through this they will appear as individuals who can be reflective and can act, and whose opinions are worthy of respect and consideration. Nevertheless, target groups of our research have been children and adults, particularly those adults who, through their work, influence the condition of children – for example, pre-school personnel.

Children's expressions, both about factual issues and about the values and emotions that they hold, are vital to our understanding of their situation. But to use children's descriptions of their situation as the only valid basis for an interpretation and critical evaluation of the adult version is questionable. Children's subordinate position may influence their conceptual framework, and encourage them to accept and transmit adults' worldviews and values, without adding their own personal reflections. To rely solely on children's own versions may therefore serve to contribute to their subordination. This is a very real dilemma. We build our research based on children's images of their reality, but we have also to put their answers, as well as adults' answers, under critical theoretical examination. We consider what children communicate as part of a social and cultural context and process. Our interpretation is based upon what it generally means to be a child, how a stereotype of a child is constructed and how adults and children interact with each another (Näsman, 1995; Holstein and Gubrium, 1995). One difference between children and adults – apart from size – is that children have not had time to experience interaction with other people as much as have adults. Adults often talk about children as being immature. We would rather consider every human being as constantly developing through experience – in other words, being engaged in a process which continues through the whole course of life. Three years' experiences of difficulties do not necessarily mean very much to a fifty-year-old. But to a child, these three years will constitute a much larger proportion of his/her life, and these experiences will accordingly have a much larger impact. But this is not only a simple question of quantity: experiences gradually become structured into relatively stable constructions of belief systems and worldviews. We must therefore consider how the impact of experiences that occur early in the lives of children will affect our interaction with them.

Adult interaction with children

The purpose of every act of communication is to make contact. What sort of contact we achieve depends partly on our own behaviour, and partly on the other person's experiences. Some adults are not careful in their contacts with children when they meet them in their daily lives. Children's experiences of poor adult–child relationships and interactions have, among other things, an impact on how children treat adults.

10

Habits and routines ease everyday life: they help us save energy in dealing with problems and handling the unexpected. Part of our daily routine is making interaction with other people easier. We usually spontaneously identify people we meet as being in particular social categories: child/adult, male/female, Swedish/immigrant and so forth: and we associate these categories with certain characteristics and patterns of behaviour. We thus often identify and treat people as types rather than as individuals. This usually makes our lives easier – but it may also cause problems by preventing us from discovering the person behind the stereotype. Children are one of those social categories that are connected with such established stereotypes. If communication with a child is to reveal something beyond what the adult already knows (or thinks s/he knows), it is important for the adult to try to treat the child as an individual, and not as a stereotyped member of a category. This may also be decisive for whether the child will be able to discover the adult as a person, rather than as a stereotypical 'grown-up'. So we argue that when interacting with a child it is consequently necessary to transcend the cliché through an awareness of the child's existence. We have to consider the child not as a child, but rather as someone that we cannot place. That gives us a new and different situation to manage, and someone new to get to know, and this in turn makes it easier for us to listen to what the child is saying.

Our sample of children

We have discussed children as a social category, but children are not all alike. It is important also to consider cultural and social diversity in understanding childhood. Our informants have been strategically selected to include diversity in terms of age, gender, social class, ethnicity, local context and, depending on the specific issues, for factors such as the employment situation and occupation of the parents. In all our projects we include both urban and country contexts. In the unemployment study each district was subdivided into categories based on the level of unemployment.

As well as sampling children, we have also sampled the social contexts in which children spend their everyday lives: home, daycare centre or school. We met some children in their homes, and while there also interviewed their parents. A larger number of children were visited in the context of their pre-school and school, where we also interviewed members of staff.

Another sampling principle was the length of time a parent had been unemployed. Some children had experienced unemployment in the family for a long time, others for a shorter period and some not at all. We also wanted to follow the process in an unemployment situation, so we returned to see the same children over a period of time. In the whole project we have met and interviewed approximately 500 children.

Methods of communication

We have used a combination of several techniques for communication with children in the sample. Some children were interviewed in groups, at pre-school in groups of two to three children, or at school in groups of five to six children. Boys and girls were generally interviewed in separate groups. The children in the families were interviewed individually, usually in their own room. The children were mostly interviewed without the presence of other adults. In pre-school settings, a child that seemed to be in need of support during the interview could also be accompanied by someone from the staff.

The interviews with younger children took 20 minutes, while those with older children lasted between 30 and 45 minutes. The optimal length of the interviews was decided on the basis of a pilot study. All interviews were recorded on tape, and then transcribed and analysed.

Children in school settings were also asked to fill in a form in which the answers were mostly standardised. We were present during this activity, and the children were encouraged to ask us when something was unclear. In every class several children asked about how to interpret a question or how to choose an answer when they felt they couldn't exactly fit the alternatives given. This task took at most forty minutes.

School children who were not interviewed were asked instead to write a short essay on the subject we gave them: *If someone in my family was made redundant...* They were told that they could write either about a fictional family or about their own, and that we were only interested in the content of what they wrote: we were not going to judge their writing skills. We collected 100 essays.

Finally, the schoolchildren were asked to illustrate a topic we gave them: we selected various topics, such as an unemployed person, an unemployed mother, or an unemployed father. Again, we told them that we were not going to judge their drawing skills, but that we were interested in the content of what they drew. They could make a simple line drawing, a comic strip or whatever form of drawing they liked. We got 350 drawings.

The questions we asked

Our intention with these children's accounts was to learn what children thought about unemployment in a family context. We were interested in the impact of unemployment on their social situation at home, at school and at pre-school. We wanted to know about some particular issues that were essential to complement some earlier research and for our theoretical basis, but we also wanted to leave wide scope for children themselves to raise the issues that they saw as important in this sphere, in order to avoid the trap of adultism. We made a list of topics for these thematic qualitative interviews, allowing for open answers. We constructed interview guides and questionnaires to accompany these. Pilot interviews with groups of children were used to make adjustments according to the children's comments.

The interviews and questionnaires followed the same structure. We introduced the interviews with some basic getting-to-know questions. We then asked questions of a general nature about the institutions they were in, to smooth the ground for further conversation within the group. After this we asked factual questions, which were used to lead into the more sensitive area of what conditions could be like at home. Part of our questionnaire was a child-oriented version developed from Aaron Antonovsky's questionnaire to measure a sense of coherence (Antonovsky, 1987). The adult and child form was also filled in by the families we interviewed.

Follow-up interviews consisted basically of the same questions, but we also added issues that the children had spontaneously informed us about in the first round. For instance, the young children were asked in the second year if they had played at being unemployed, and if so, how they had done this.

Listening and paying attention in an interview

It may seem obvious that interviewing a child implies attentive listening, but there are reasons to consider this issue more closely. To be attentive during an interview is a matter of being mentally present and of concentrating on the child, when the interviewer is an active contributor, as well as when the children themselves speak. In other words, to be attentive towards the child is a general attitude, and perhaps not that obvious after all.

Very often, when adults are with children, and meet and begin to talk to them, they expect the children to wait patiently and to keep quiet until the adults choose to move on or expect them to contribute. Adults may also talk to each other about the children as though they are not present. In interactions with children adults also have the attitude that the adult has the prerogative to define the situation, and that the adult is allowed to act, while the child is supposed to be passive but attentive. This phenomenon is illustrated in the book title: *Be quiet when you talk to an adult!* (Kildevang, 1990, our translation). Even though there has been a radical change in Scandinavia during the twentieth century towards a more democratic relationship between children and adults, there are still reasons to believe that children generally have many experiences of this kind of treatment (Dahlberg, 1993). This makes it probable that the child is prepared for this – or even expects it – in any meeting with a grown-up. In the kind of research we are describing, it is important that the interviewing adult does not fulfil this expectation, as well as that the adult considers the importance of these kinds of expectation in their interpretation of the interaction in the interview.

Paying attention to the child does not only concern the initial stage of the interview. It is important to focus attention on the child, constantly, and not to allow oneself to slip in to the kind of attitude where the questions are asked and the answers mechanically over-heard, whilst one's thoughts wander to other matters such as what the time it is, what to do after the interview or whether the tape will last. The tendency *not* to consider children as important individuals is a cultural dead weight that must be actively resisted.

We often talk about the importance of being confirmed by the other person in a conversation. To treat someone as if one did not exist is a painful form of degradation for an adult. There are four words that together are both the basis of and a recipe for any successful contact with children: *Listen, Appreciate, Understand* and *Speak*. To listen is the basis all contact. Listening attentively prepares the way for a closer contact. Listening and interpreting body language and facial expressions enable a deeper understanding: something beyond a shallow display of emotion. If a child experiences that an adult is paying this kind of attention, it means that they feel that they are treated with respect as informants and may feel sufficiently con-fident to participate actively, both in answering factual questions and by telling about personal experiences, values and emotions. It is only through this kind of attentive listening that an empathic inter-pretation is possible, and this in turn allows the interview to evolve into a mutual exploration of the child's world of emotions, values and perceptions.

Adult and child in our study
In an interview with children there are obvious differences in age, size, power and authority. We have already touched upon some aspect of power. We now move deeper into what the expression 'the child' might imply.

As an adult interviewer, having had children of one's own, it is very easy to fall into the role of parent: the former teacher may also easily revert to that particular role again. No matter what, an adult is always an adult when compared to (and by) a child. These two social posi-tions, adult and child, are defined in relation to one another, and there are several terms of contrast connecting the two that presuppose the devaluation and subordination of children. Expressions such as 'childish' and 'second childhood' imply a reduction of children's mental capabilities. The concept of 'child' is associated with play, fantasy, irresponsibility and lack of credibility, and children are ascribed as lacking a sense of reality and being inadequately relevant and serious. When a child is described as behaving with spontaneity, it implies that they are displaying a lack of self-control and social competence. The expression 'Fools and children tells the truth' suggests that children (like fools) cannot master the rules of the social life. Children's lack of experience is often wrongly interpreted as a lack of a capacity to understand. This tendency of adult thought is evident: children are not really anything in themselves, and are merely undeveloped adults. Where the adult is perceived as the norm, children become the imperfect (Quortrup, 1990; Alanen, 1992; Näsman, 1995).

During our study we were sometimes surprised by the children's knowledge, insights and capacity to express themselves. This is in itself an obvious expression of the underestimation of children, innate in our own adult perspective. Before we began the first year's interviews we, and others with us, were doubtful as to whether young children had any notion whatsoever of unemployment. But it turned out that in most of the groups we spoke with there were children who could give an explanation that was acceptable to adults, as for example 'that one doesn't have a job'. The very fact that we were interested in asking the children often made them enthusiastic and willing to achieve.

The researcher, the child and other adults

Adult interviewers do not usually contact children directly, but through other adults in the child's surroundings. In the case of this project, this was through parents and teachers. Because of shortage of time and the fact that we were working over a geographically widespread research area, we were unable to visit children before each interview to develop our own relationship with them. Our contact with the children was largely dependent on mediating adults, and how they positioned themselves in the triangular relation of child–researcher–parent or teacher. The conditions varied considerably. One teacher commented that we ought to have an assistant teacher with us, since it wouldn't otherwise be possible to interview the troublesome boys we had chosen. In one daycare centre the staff had thoroughly prepared the children for our visit, and handled the contact between the child groups and us in such a way that everyone was relaxed and eager to join in. But in another daycare centre we were treated as a disturbance to their activities and routine. In one centre several children were reluctant to participate (despite their parents' consent), and we had to remind the personnel that even though the parents had consented, participation was voluntary for the children. An active attitude was necessary on our part.

The triangular relation we formed with parents was different. Their motivation for letting the children participate in the study was frequently to allow themselves an opportunity to speak. How the contact with the children was mediated varied. Families prepared for the interview in different ways: for example, some parents had talked to the children about what they thought we were going to ask about. The different extent to which children had thought about unemployment in these cases corresponded to how much they had been prepared for talking to us.

In all the families the parents let us talk to the children in private and without questioning us about their answers.

We usually began by sitting with the whole family around the kitchen table for a time to tell them more about the project. This moment also gave the children the chance to see what we looked like and to become a little acquainted with us. We then began the children's interviews. The fact that these were usually conducted in the child's own room contributed to the ease of establishing contact. We initially often talked about things in the room which the child was eager to show us or to talk about.

Sometimes parents contributed to establishing a trustful atmosphere by clearly signalling that they accepted us, and agreeing that the child could talk to us in private. A few parents, however, talked to us as though the children were not there, or introduced the child to us in a degrading manner. In some families it was necessary for us actively to try to establish a relationship toward the child that was different from the one that the child had with his/her parents. There were also interviews in which even small children, in a sincere voice, demanded that their parents were not to know what the child had told us, and then gave us very thorough answers. In these varying interactions with children it was possible to distinguish a loyalty towards the parents, as well as a willingness to tell us something that they did not want the parents to know that they had talked about. We also witnessed parallels to what Christensen (1994) describes in her interviews with children who had parents who were alcoholics: how important it was for children to know that the parent accepted that the child would talk about his or her life. In those families where the parents did not emphasise a relationship of superiority towards their children, the child could freely tell us about difficult situations with the parent.

Individual interviews or group interviews?

In the school and pre-school situations the individual child was not important to us: we were interested primarily in the culture that the children developed together. Group interviews were therefore a very relevant and appropriate method. To be interviewed with one's peers may make the situation in which a child that doesn't feel at ease with an adult stranger more easy to cope with. We tried to encourage each child in the group to take active part, without putting pressure on anyone who was shy or taciturn. The fact that individual children contributed to the discussion to a different degree did not present any methodological problems for us, since our intention with this part of the project was to get answers from the group of children collectively, not from specific individuals. There is always a tendency within groups towards domination by particular individuals.

In thematic group interviews the children may themselves influence the structure of the interview. The interviews thus had different patterns of dialogue, which had to be considered in our interpretation. for example, some answers followed a pattern where one child gave a thorough answer, and the others plainly agreed by giving a simultaneous 'yes'. In other cases, the children caught on to each other's answers and through this developed a longer discussion. In other groups children who held different opinions argued with one another.

Not all children understood the questions, and this was especially so in the case of children who had recently come to Sweden. Some children helped each other understand by discussing the questions together. That the group reached mutual conclusions and answers in this way was again not problematic, since our purpose was to find out which concepts and ways of reasoning existed and how they could be developed within the group.

An interview is not like turning on a tap, in order to receive the water that is already in the pipe. The respondent forms a mental image of the meaning of the question, and of the kind of person who is asking it and adjusts the answer accordingly. The content of an interview is the result of the interaction between interviewer and interviewee. When the group reaches an agreed conclusion in a discussion this process may become clearer to us, so that we may more easily take their symbolic interaction into consideration in our analysis.

In the families, we interviewed the members individually. Our way of asking questions and following them up was adapted to the different individuals who were to be interviewed, but the interviews were all based on themes common to the family interviews and the group interviews. We asked questions in the same area of all the family members. Comparing answers gave us some validation of the answers concerning matters of fact, but the answers most importantly illuminated situations from different family member's perspectives; each individual expressed feelings and understanding and we obtained from the outside the other family members' understanding of that individual. For example, we asked both the unemployed father and his children about how he felt. We cannot judge who was 'right' when the answers were different, but that was not the objective. We could rather analyse what the differences in the answers meant to the family members, and what it was in that particular situation, and in the social position of the various family

19

members, that could contribute to an interpretation of the differences. We were aware of the existence of loyalties within the family, perhaps particularly common among children towards their parents (Christensen, 1994). We also considered that it is quite understandable to 'forget', or to avoid talking about difficulties. The answers of children in the family setting were put into perspective when analysed alongside the answers given by the child groups at school, the anonymously written answers in the questionnaires, the essays, and the drawings.

Our general impression was that most of the interviews – whether in groups or with individuals – were characterised by an open atmosphere and by a wish on the part of the child to contribute seriously with answers about facts and feelings, even in sensitive areas. They also informed us about what, according to social norms, is seen as socially unacceptable. From the basis of the family interviews we can conclude that parents in Sweden are open, and willing to let researchers explore sensitive matters in relation to unemployment and family relationships with a focus on children and children's perspectives.

Children's essays – drama and realism

When we asked the school children to write an essay on unemployment this offered another way for us to express our interest in the children's own thoughts and ideas. But to write is a skill that children have to acquire, and this ability varies. Writing essays is one of the tasks that schools use to evaluate a child's development and achievement. As researchers, we had to consider these circumstances. Our instructions emphasised that the children were welcome to let their essays be anonymous and that we were not going to judge their writing skills. We wanted to ease the pressure on children to prepare a 'good' essay, and to give them room to make associations on the subject. The majority of the children chose to hand in their essays anonymously.

Although we tried to mitigate the possible association of essay writing with a test, the problem remained that many children might experience writing itself as difficult. We must therefore consider that

20

this is not a way of communicating thoughts and feelings that does justice to all children. But at the same time, free individual writing makes it possible for a child to choose his/her own level, while in the interview the interplay within the group might affect an individual child. During the writing exercise the only influences are the child's inner thoughts: what the essay is like compared to those of others; what we, the researchers, might think about it, and so on. Some of the few children who did not hand in an essay thought about it for quite a long time before explaining to us that they didn't want to. After some attempts to encourage them, they were naturally allowed not to complete the essay for us.

We saw the essay as an important complement to the group interview. The fact that it was individual gave children who might find it difficult to compete in group interview situations an alternative possibility to express themselves. At the same time, writing essays is very different from answering questions in an interview, since it is possible for the child to turn directly to the adult without being disturbed or interrupted. On the other hand, the adult is completely dependent on what the child has written. To further the interpretation of an essay through an interview would certainly deepen our understanding of the essay, but it also presupposes that the identity of the author is known, and we had chosen to give the children the opportunity of anonymity.

Because of the way the subject was presented in the essay titles, we got another perspective of parents' unemployment in the essays. This is clearly shown through the breadth of genres that were adopted. Some children wrote stories which seem to be realistic descriptions of actual events in the children's own families. Others wrote stories in which dramatic events take place in an ordinary environment. Still others wrote fairytales, with a classical beginning such as 'Once upon a time...' and obviously fictions family names like 'the Frogs'. We also got some imaginative science fiction stories. This gave us the opportunity to experience the range between the grotesque joke, the political pamphlet, the sentimental romantic magazine story, everyday realism and a sober analysis of facts. To be able to understand what the children communicate in their stories it is necessary to interpret them within the context of the specific genre they have chosen.

Children's drawings as communication

Writing is not easy for everyone. To give the children in school yet another alternative to express their thoughts we asked them to make a drawing. Different classes and individuals were given different instructions. The intention behind the task was partly that the medium of a picture provides more opportunities to express thoughts that may be difficult to verbalise. We also thought that some children might feel more comfortable with this kind of communication. It is far more common for children to make drawings than it is for adults. To draw is also a common activity in schools: it therefore felt natural to ask the children to make a drawing.

We told the children that the drawing could also be handed in anonymously. But drawings are, however, easier for others to get a glimpse of than are written words or marks in the questionnaire. It is easy for other children in the classroom, or a passing adult such as the teacher, to get a glimpse of it. Judging by the choices of subjects by some of the children in our study who sat next to each other, they were obviously affected by each others' drawings. This drawing exercise therefore demands a greater privacy if it is to become the private communication to the adult that it was intended it should be (Nordström, 1996).

Many of the earlier discussions about the need to consider the child's individual development and experience also apply here. Drawing is a creative process that demands both mental abilities and technical skills. Drawing implies expressing oneself through pictures. Acquaintance with the styles and symbols of the different 'languages' of pictures may vary with each child. There were some drawings that looked like caricatures, some that were strips of drawings, drawings fitting into the 'princess tradition' and some realistic portraits of the children's own parents. Some were simple line drawings, while others were well developed and detailed. There were pictures of events in various places, such as the home, the workplace, the labour market office and the bench in the park. Some of them integrated elements of text. Our interpretation had to consider genres, styles and content in relationship to the image culture of the children (Aronsson, 1997; Nordström, 1996).

What we did not try: observation of play and body language

Essays, drawings, interviews and questionnaires do not cover all the possibilities of sharing children's thoughts. Children's experiences, beliefs and values are also expressed through the way they act. It is important to observe and to try to interpret their actions. To express thoughts through dramatisation – through play – is an important element of children's culture. One of our questions was whether the children had played at unemployment. If they said that they had, we asked them to describe in words how they had done it. In about a third of the groups children had played at unemployment, and were able to describe how they had done it. In one of the plays the mother had to stay at home and be unemployed because the children didn't want to be at home by themselves. Another group dramatised unemployment as sleeping. Rather than answering verbally, one girl preferred to demonstrate to us how they had played the unemployed through posture and facial expressions. She straightened up, stiff as a stick, and stared straight forward with a grave expression. The physical dramatisation expressed her empathic relation to the feelings of an unemployed person.

The children's physical dramatisation corresponded to the postures seen in the drawings. It was not only the action that was important. The body has many possibilities of showing expression. We want to draw attention to the body as a medium for expressing thoughts and emotions. The children's own conceptions support this opinion.

The major advantage of observation as a method is that it gives even very young children, who haven't learned how to write and who has difficulties both with speaking and drawing, an opportunity to express their thoughts and feelings. Body language is the main means of communication between very young children, and they learn how to do this early in life (Feldman, 1982; Iverson and Goldin-Meadow, 1998).

Conceptualisation

None of the methods we have chosen in itself fully covers or reveals children's opinions about unemployment, or of their own situation. Although the essays and drawings express more fantasies and emotions than the answers in questionnaires and interviews, there are some factual comments in these too. Individual and group interviews also result in rather different kinds of stories. Using multiple forms of expressions increases the possibility of each child finding the best way to express personal thoughts, experiences and feelings. When these different forms of expression are used to illuminate each other, the picture we get become more broad, deep and diversified.

How should we approach the issue of how children conceptualise their everyday world? Although some of the explanations of children's cognitive development in terms of developmental steps reached by Piaget and other classic investigators, maintain their validity, new research has revised these and has demonstrated their limitations and inadequacies (Stern, 1991; Sommer, 1997). It is generally understood that children's conceptual development passes from the concrete, close and self-centred to the abstract, distant and role-taking. This is a widely recognised general idea, although today we also know that this development is not fixed directly to the child's age but varies according to the child's individual experience. 'Physical development is usually characterised as dependent on maturity, while intellectual development is, to a far wider extent, related to experience. The experiences that a child has had time or opportunity to gather are of significance to its way of thinking' (Doverborg and Pramling, 1988).

The development of the small child's ego begins with its first interactions with what we call the outer world. This is a lifelong process. The development of the self is constantly influenced by the interaction between the child and its surroundings, and by identification that is rooted in imitating parents and siblings. An active relationship with the outer world, a striving to understand and cope with it, is fundamental to man and his development of an ego and of a world-view (Antonovsky, 1987, Bratt, 1977). Any communication with children must take this into consideration. Research into children's cognitive and social ability is to some extent guided by differences in age – among children as much as between an interviewer and a child. But we must bear in mind that new research may require us to change our present understanding of this (Stern, 1991; Sommer, 1996).

The consequence of this for the interview situation is to avoid standardised and multiple-choice questions, and instead let the interview become more of an exploration. This will allow for a successive adaptation to the child's experiences and cognitive development. Otherwise there is a risk that the interviewer will in some cases underestimate a child, and thus get less information than would otherwise have been possible. On the other hand, if the interviewer overestimates the child, then the child's possibility to develop his or her thoughts during the interview will have been limited. An open and explorative approach is advisable in investigating the kinds of issue raised in our research.

Empathy

Children have a gradually developed capacity to take the role of someone else and understand his/her thoughts, feelings and actions. It is the same ability to role-taking that constitutes the interviewer's understanding of the child.

It used to be held that children do not develop what is known as empathic ability until later in childhood: this has been seriously questioned by later studies of infants (Lamer, 1991; Sommer, 1997). We define 'empathy' as the ability to get insight into and to interpret other peoples' feelings. Empathy has both a cognitive and an emotional aspect (Lamer, 1991). Children exhibit empathic reactions early in life. Again, they gradually develop their empathic abilities through their experiences, rather than in relationship to their age. Even very young children in pre-school environments can be seen to perform pro-social actions such as consoling (Vikan, 1987).

This empathic ability of children was displayed in our study through, for example, stories about unemployment within their own families. They described how their unemployed mother or father felt, and how that affected them emotionally. Other children were able to describe hypothetical situations, such as what they thought a child or a parent might feel if the parent was made unemployed. Those feelings were more dramatically expressed in some children's essays and drawings. Emotions, symbolised by a single or a series of signs, were prominent in the children's drawings. Distress, anger, emotional emptiness and so on were clearly depicted. Big, dripping tears creating small puddles were an obvious signal. Prickly hair, frowning black eyebrows and flashes around the head clearly indicated anger. Posture and hairstyle were also used as symbols for emotional status.

The combination of oral and written stories with drawings produced rich material for an analysis both of the width of children's emotional spectra and of their ability to make empathic interpretations of children and adults in situations of unemployment in the family.

Ethics

Up to this point we have looked at interaction with children from an instrumental perspective. Our aim has been to access their understanding. But it is now important to consider ethical aspects of these research techniques.

Ethical rules of research usually emphasise that the participants in a study must give their informed consent to their involvement. It is also a condition that the results of the research must not be harmful to the participants. These two fundamental rules raise particular questions when children are the subjects of and participants in a research project. We will here summarise some of the ethical comments we have made, and go beyond this in considering the way we have conducted our research. One intricate and fundamental question concerns the relationship of power between the researcher and the informants.

In our group interviews we drew our sample from children who wanted to participate, provided that they also had their parent's consent to be involved. When we returned for a second visit to the same setting we chose different children, since we wanted to be fair to the children, and there were always more children wanting to participate than we were able to talk to. But against our explicit intention of selecting the children ourselves, there were sometimes occasions where the teacher tried to influence us to choose someone that they considered to be 'more suitable': for example, a child with an unemployed parent. As mentioned above, some teachers also tried to dissuade us from choosing particular 'troublesome' boys. This kind of influence was unacceptable and required us to take active countermeasures.

For ethical reasons, we never asked for children's personal experiences of their parents' unemployment, either in the questionnaire or during the group interviews. In the group interviews we asked general questions, and in the questionnaires we limited personal questions to less sensitive areas. The essays and drawing exercises gave them the choice as to whether to be personal or not. The children were always able to decide for themselves whether they wanted to tell the group and us about personal matters. That many chose to do so is a result to be analysed.

All our questions about the areas we wanted to cover were direct, but we avoided initiating particular sensitive topics in the individual interviews. We never asked explicitly about drug use, child abuse or other criminal activities, but sometimes children voluntary told us about such things. The reasons for our approach were based both on ethical considerations and on our research strategy. To ask about criminal acts could be regarded as offensive, since it could have been interpreted that we thought that such behaviour was plausible in the child's case. This reasoning applied even more to questions about child abuse. Such information must be sought elsewhere.

In the course of an interview the interviewee becomes known as an individual to the interviewer. This is not necessarily the case using other techniques: the essays, drawings and questionnaires were all handed in anonymously if the child chose to do this. Nevertheless, in all classes there were some children who wanted us to put their names on the essays and drawing.

One of the so-called 'interview effects' is that of asking leading questions. Questions are seen as leading when the way a question is asked by the interviewer hints the kind of answer s/he expects. This problem is assumed to be more significant in an adult–child interviewer relationship, in which the child often perceives the adult as an authority. When our interviews were conducted in pre-school/ school settings, where one of the adults present also represented a formal authority, this risk is even greater. To let the children's answers be affected by their feelings of subordination in this manner would have been against our basic philosophy.

One technique to avoid leading questions is always to ask questions that point in two directions. 'Do you feel good about it or do you feel bad about it?' 'Do you want to go to school or would you rather stay at home?' 'Do you like ice-cream a lot, pretty much, not very much or not at all?' This way of asking questions is often very different from everyday language. When we phrased our questions in this way with young children, they showed a clear tendency to choose the last alternative mentioned. They seemed to have problems with keeping several options in mind. We had instead to phrase questions more openly, and then to examine it more closely through several steps, for example starting with 'What do you think about?'

The potential issue of imposing adult authority was also handled by our emphasising that there were no 'correct' answers in our study, and by stressing that we wanted to know what the children them-selves thought. Once again, we note that it is important to pay attention and to listen to responses. There is also an ethical consideration in taking care about the level of expectation of children's abilities. To underestimate a child's ability could be seen by the child as offensive, while making high demands of their ability might cause them to have a sense of insufficiency.

Which ethical claims concerning children's rights to influence research are reasonable? To what extent should the interviewer influence the interview? This is not simply a matter of leading questions, but also about who will control the whole process of the interview. We initiated these interviews out of our desire to talk with the children. This is already a form of control, but it is balanced by the children's participation being voluntary. It was our responsibility to make the interview meaningful both to us and to the children. The entire interview involves certain obligations: for example to sit still during the process. It was our responsibility towards the children to use the time efficiently and not to let it continue longer than necessary. Placing too much stress on achieving the results we wanted may, on the other hand, increase the pressure on the children and make them feel stressed. We tried to give scope for the children to answer in the way they wanted, and to concentrate on the areas in which they seemed to be interested, while at the same time trying to encourage them to stick to the subject area. Because we had a genuine interest in the associations they made in relation to our areas of questioning, we generally had no problems with letting them develop their answers in the direction that they wanted. The general tendency was that the children's answers were significantly shorter than those of the parents.

Our experience was that the children generally found our questions interesting and engaging, and that this contributed to their openness about their personal situation and experiences. It is important that most of the group answers to our questions included personal experiences of a parent's unemployment, and even comments that told about conflicts and personal feelings and could therefore be considered as sensitive. Both positive and negative experiences were spontaneously given to us. After the interviews the children were able to listen to their taped interview, and they generally wanted to do this and appreciated it.

The children's concentration during the interviews, and their readiness to answer and discuss our questions, indicated to us that the children saw the interviews as something positive. When some young children simply didn't answer a question and just kept quiet, this was not only a clear indication that the question did not motivate an answer, but also that the child did not feel under pressure to give an answer. Some young children didn't want to participate or got tired after a while. Occasionally a child would suddenly leave and begin to play instead. All such signs, indicating that the child no longer wanted to participate, were taken seriously and they were allowed to leave.

We mentioned above that the environment in which the interview takes place influences the interaction between children and interviewer. When children are responding at school, the interplay can easily be influenced by the school's demand for achievement, attendance and subordination to the teacher. In such an environment it is important to demonstrate a detachment from the teacher's role, in the same way as it is important not to be seen to side with the parents when interviewing children in their family home. When the children are expected to talk about something that might be sensitive it is important to try to find a location that they find safe. The child's own room is generally such a place.

We thought that it would be an advantage for everyone to conduct the individual interviews in the families' homes, and this was the case in practice. We did not feel that the parents thought that we were intruding into their private sphere. The children willingly let us in to their rooms.

We were going to return to re-interview the children in their families, daycare centres and schools after a year. We concluded our first session with them by expressing our gratitude and asking everyone if it was all right if we returned the following year. All were positive. We asked how we should keep in contact and prepare for our return. We wanted through this to further emphasise how important the children were to us, and that we would be thinking about them during the time we were away. Details such as sending a Christmas card, with a picture of us, to each of the classes, families and daycare centres proved to be important, especially to the younger children.

A sense of coherence

Facing difficulties that must be solved is a normal part of everyday life. Stress is a natural part of life. To cope with stress within the family, children may either interpret and manage the situation by themselves, or they may rely on their parents to maintain control. Structure and routines in everyday life contribute to making life seem safe and predictable, and this is something that enables children to develop their ability to understand and cope with situations. Aaron Antonovsky (1987) claims that children who in their daily life are facing normal reasonable challenges, and who trust their parents' competence and responsibility, getting positive feedback from those close to them, will experience these challenges as intelligible, meaningful and possible to handle. They will experience a sense of coherence. This sense of coherence enables people to cope with intense stress without impairing their health. But exposing children to too much stress during their early years will prevent them from developing a self-confident view of their lives and their ability to cope with stress.

What are the implications of this for communication with the children in the context of our study? There is an ethical demand that follows from this point. Even though our interview or interaction with the child was a brief moment in their life, it should contribute to the child's development of this sense of coherence. These theoretical aspects thus make it even more important that the adult listens attentively, tries to relieve him/herself of stereotypes, and avoids being too controlling. This may also be seen as a demand that the child shall not be simply treated as a 'vessel of information' to be emptied by the interviewer (Holstein and Gubrium, 1995). The interview should contribute to the development of the child's story about his/her self and his/her world, thus increasing the child's ability to comprehend and manage his/her life. To be able to ask a child, with the parents' consent, about problems that society might consider shameful, may break the secrecy that is in some families a more or less explicit strategy to cope in their relations with the outer world. This could come as a relief to some children, and give them an opportunity to deal with their experiences of family problems through interaction with others.

The interview must inspire a sense of meaningfulness, by confirming the value of the child's search for an understanding of his/her environment and self. To ask for a child's own thoughts is in itself a confirmation that the child is noticed, and that the child is an individual who can take action and handle his/her situation. This will contribute to enabling the child to comprehend their environment. Communication that contains all of these elements will give the child the knowledge that it is possible to develop a sense of coherence in their life.

3

Towards an anti-developmental view of children's social and economic understanding

Merryn Hutchings

Institute for Policy Studies in Education, University of North London, United Kingdom

Introduction

Developmentalism, and in particular the Piagetian model, has been the theoretical framework adopted by a large number of studies of children's understanding of the social world, and in particular by those focusing on economic understanding. This chapter will consider in some detail problems that are implicit in this approach, explaining why I regard it as important to find an anti-developmental alternative. I consider some alternative stances, and review the potential of social constructionism as an anti-developmental approach. Finally, I consider what the adoption of this perspective would mean for the researcher.

My intention is the same as that of John Morss, in his book, *Growing Critical: Alternatives to Developmental Psychology*: 'to stimulate a self consciousness about the word 'development'' (1996, p.1). He explains:

> We should, I think, worry about that word and its effects. We should be on our guard against the implications of the developmental attitude to people's lives and hopes. It treats others as behind or below ourselves, but destined to follow in the same path. The

search for anti-developmental alternatives must therefore be seen as an emancipatory project. (p.1)

A postmodern perspective enables us to look on developmentalism as one of the grand narratives of modernity, and to evaluate it as a story. Instead of concentrating on how accurate it is in describing reality, we can consider how and why it came into existence, and what effects it has had. Burman (1994) points out that by looking back at the origins of developmental psychology we can see how the various movements from which it arose and in which it participated have 'set the terms of developmental enquiry that reverberate even now' (p.9). She points out that it:

> '... participated in social movements explicitly concerned with comparison, regulation and control of groups and societies, and is closely identified with the development of tools of mental measurement, classification of abilities and the establishing of norms.' (pp.9–10)

We need, then, to consider the nature and origins of the grand narrative of developmentalism. Morss defines it as 'the production of, and reliance on, explanatory statements concerning general regulation of natural changes in the human life-span' (1996, p.51). Such change is seen as unidirectional, and generally involves the notion that adult thinking is more rational and complex than that of children. This is not seen simply as an accumulation of knowledge, but rather as a fundamental change in the quality of thinking: 'Development, as distinct from learning, ... is not a question of knowing and remembering, from less to more, but of knowing and understanding differently' (Furth, 1980, p.11).

Development is thus towards a particular goal, logical abstract thought, though not everyone will reach this goal. Rational thought can be identified as a particularly western, masculine and middle-class value, which, in the nineteenth century was strongly associated with the concerns of government. The working classes were believed to be at a lower developmental level, 'further from reason and intensely threatening because of that' (Walkerdine, 1993, p.456). Primitive peoples presented a similar threat, and were considered to be less developed than westerners because the development of the species was seen in the same terms as development of the individual. In this way developmentalism was closely allied to imperialism and the hierarchy of racial superiority (Burman, 1994). Burman points out that the nineteenth century child was equated with the 'savage' because both were irrational and undeveloped. Women were also believed to be incapable of reasoning; indeed Walkerdine (1994) points out that it was considered dangerous for women to reason because it might damage their reproductive capacities.

These characteristics of the developmental story still, as Burman put it, 'reverberate' today, and this chapter is concerned with the way that they have done so in research into the development of children's social and economic understanding. I will examine how the course of development has been defined; how norms have been constructed and used; and how those who do not meet the norm have been considered. Many of the examples I use refer to the development of children's ideas about work, which is central to social and economic organisation.

The factors that bring about development

Piaget worked and wrote over a long period of time, with considerable changes of emphasis, but his original concerns are still influential in the shape that developmental research has taken. He was not concerned with children's understanding of the social world; his main interest was in the development of thought that resulted from physical and logico-mathematical experience, or action upon objects in the world. There have been considerable debates about how far his theory is applicable to understanding of the social world. Some consider that cognition in this area must lag behind physical cognition (e.g. Furth *et al.*, 1976), possibly because in making sense of information received through talk children may not be 'in a position to use the most advanced instruments of their intelligence' (Berti and Bombi, 1988, p.6). Others argue that understanding of the social world develops earlier because of the interactional context (e.g. Hoffman, 1981; Dahlberg *et al.*, 1987). Jahoda (1979) distinguished between learning about social relations and social institutions; he argued (1984) that the rules and norms of the latter are not generally articulated, and so are harder for children to grasp.

Piaget identified four factors involved in mental development: organic growth and maturation of the nervous and endocrine systems; an internal mechanism of equilibration; physical and logico-mathematical experience acquired in actions upon objects; and social interaction and transmission; all four factors are seen as necessary for development and no single one would be adequate on its own (Piaget and Inhelder, 1966/1969). In his earlier work he saw social interaction as an intrusion which muddied the picture of the child's own original thinking, and attempted to distinguish the child's original convictions from all previous adult influences such as parents and the interviewer (Piaget, 1926/1929). But in later writings he considered that exchange of views could speed up development in older children, but younger children's talk was seen as too egocentric for real communication to take place (Piaget, 1964/1967). However, it is widely considered that he underestimated the importance of the social dimension in the construction of know-ledge (e.g. Donaldson, 1978; Tizard and Hughes, 1984; Wood, 1988; Schaffer, 1989; Meadows, 1993).

Piaget's neglect of the social arose from his contention that language reflects or represents thought, and does not contribute to develop-ment (1923/1926). Many subsequent theorists have instead followed Vygotsky (1934/1986), believing that 'language ... structures and directs the processes of thinking and concept formation' (Wood, 1988, p.29); in this view social interaction must play a much more significant role in development.

Piagetian theorists investigating children's economic and social understanding have taken up Piaget's ideas about physical and social experience in various ways. Furth (1980) indicated that his interest, like that of Piaget, was in the child's original convictions; comments in which children repeated what they had heard other people say were considered of no interest unless the idea had become a part of the child's overall understanding, in which case it became a 'spon-taneous conviction' rather than simply a 'verbal memory'. In contrast, Berti and Bombi claimed that they were extending Piaget's theory by considering those experiences that are verbally mediated: 'the greater part of the information available to children about work, the means of production, or buying and selling comes through adults' conversation and the mass media' (1988, p.5).

However, in much of their analysis they seem to lose sight of the importance of social interaction. For example, in discussing the understanding of production held by children living in contrasting economic environments, they refer only to the possibilities for the children to observe production processes.

This lack of attention to social interaction as a factor promoting development has led to one of the key problems with research into children's social and economic learning; a very limited concern with the social and cultural environment in which children live, and their social experiences. Indeed, some theorists regard experience as a hindrance to development: Linton (1990), examining the relative importance of cognitive growth and experiential learning in the development of children's understanding of supply and demand, profit, interest and income differentiation, found that: 'Children's experience if anything tended to impede rather than promote economic understanding, with eight-year-old children regarding the store's till as the terminal part of the process' (p.100).

Thus the older children's greater understanding was not 'a product of their greater experiential involvement' (p.101) but rather resulted from cognitive development.

In contrast, other researchers argue that the economic ideas that are generally understood earliest by children are those of which they have had greater experience. For example, Danziger (1958) pointed out that children's understanding of exchange develops much earlier than understanding of production. He suggested that the lower level of understanding of production is due to the children's lack of first-hand experience in this area; they generally have more experience of shops, which allows understanding of exchange to develop earlier.

Structure and content of thought

A characteristic of Piagetian cognitive developmentalism is an emphasis on *how* children think rather than *what* they think: 'the content of thought is accorded less attention than its generalisable structure' (Burman, 1994, p.154). Piaget's main interest was in the process by which experience is assimilated into existing structures and by which these structures are adjusted to accommodate the new ideas.

Following Piaget's lead, many of the studies of children's social and economic thinking have focused on the structure (sometimes referred to as the framework) of thought. For example, Furth (1980) stated:

> The word 'thinking' has been used deliberately rather than 'knowing' to make clear the direction of this investigation. In this study the concern is with the general theoretical framework that children use in making sense of societal events, rather than with particular information that they may or may not have about particular societal content ... the study is not looking for known and remembered information, but at the theoretical framework by which information is taken in and becomes part of a meaningful whole. (p.4)

Furth argued that environmental experience is important in providing the raw material from which understanding can be built, but saw children's thinking and behaviour as 'primarily a product of their developing minds' (p.10). He drew on the analogy of a child learning to speak; the child's specific environmental experience is crucial in determining which language will be spoken (the content), but it is less obvious why the child acquires the mastery of any language at all (the framework). His research interest was in how children develop the framework of thought about the social world. He saw this as an interpretive system which allowed children to link, and thus make sense of, the different social and economic events they experienced; the example of such a framework he set out is of understanding the flow of goods and money in the various transactions centred around a shop. It is not entirely clear why this is assumed to be a part of the framework of thought rather than the content; exchange through shops is not universal to all cultures, and it is not easy to see how this parallels his analogy of language learning. Nor is it clear why Furth assumed that this understanding resulted from the development of more logical thinking and resolution of cognitive conflicts; it is surely equally plausible to assume that it might be the product of specific experience (e.g. as a shopkeeper's daughter) or of social interaction between adults and children. Again, we see the lack of concern for children's social and economic environment.

When researchers have chosen to focus on the content of thought, they have distanced themselves from the ideas of Piaget. For example, Emler and Dickinson drew on Moscovici's (1984) notion of 'social representations', arguing that: 'Cognitive-developmental principles can tell us something about the sequence in which children acquire knowledge, but not everything about the particular knowledge they will acquire. This also depends on its currency and availability in their various social milieux' (1985, p.197). But this study was criticised by Berti and Bombi (1988), who argued that the problem is not to discover which information children assimilate, but to identify 'the processes through which children assimilate the information which is dominant widespread and important within their community' (1988, p.22).

Stages, and the definition of an adult level of understanding

The identification of stages of development is one of the most influential aspects of Piaget's theory; at each stage the structure of children's thinking is distinctive, and transition to a new stage marks a fundamental reorganisation of structures of thinking.

Piagetian studies of children's economic understanding have followed Piaget in identifying stages. Researchers have generally categorised children's responses to questions asked in interview; these categories of response are then seen as levels of development within that particular concept. Thus, in discussing the example below, Burris argued that the distribution of responses 'suggests a possible developmental sequence from the first type of explanation to the second to the third' (1976, p.194).

Children's explanations of why some people get paid more money than others for their jobs:

Type of response	% giving response	
	2nd grade	5th grade
Work more or harder	84.6	63.4
More important, functional or helpful work	15.4	36.7
More training or education required	0.0	16.7
TOTAL	N=26	N=30

* Excludes 'don't know' responses. Column totals exceed 100 per cent because of multiple responses.

(Burris, 1976, p.192)

Some writers have then attempted a synthesis of the levels identified within the various economic concepts to produce generalised levels, which have in some cases been equated to Piagetian stages of development (e.g. Berti and Bombi, 1988).

The stages are said to represent qualitative changes in thinking; however, it is not always easy to see what is meant by this claim, and theorists are rarely explicit on this point. For example, Furth saw qualitative difference as something which is recognisable, but need not be systematically analysed, saying: 'there is as little point to expect an experimental proof on this score, as, say, on the difference between the music of Bach and Chopin' (1980, p.76).

One difficulty with the stage model is that it involves an assumption that development proceeds evenly in all concepts; Meadows points out that in studies of children's economic understanding 'data about the uniformity of 'stage' across different concepts or the separation of 'stage' are not usually conclusive, and are often simply not presented' (1993, p.141). Lea *et al.* suggested that Harris and Heelas's

(1979) theory of 'local constructivism' may be useful in this context; this envisages the child 'working simultaneously in a number of relatively autonomous cognitive valleys' (Lea *et al.*, 1987, p.219). Progress within each of these, Harris and Heelas argue, has a stage-like character, but there is little communication between valleys. The domain-specific approach, adopted by Berti (in this volume), has similar characteristics.

A further problem with the identification of stages of economic understanding is that in every study these have been arrived at through a cross-sectional approach; there is no evidence that every child will pass through each stage in turn as s/he develops towards a mature understanding (which is the basis of Piaget's stages).

Progression through Piagetian stages involves development towards the achievement of mature, rational thought (Wood, 1988). This idea has been contested: young children have been shown to be more logical thinkers than Piaget suggested, and adults to be less logical (e.g. by Donaldson, 1978). Meadows suggests that: 'perhaps here Piaget was using himself as a prototype and forgetting that the rest of us are, probably, sloppier thinkers, content with localised under-standing, not pushing its limits outwards, and quite capable of be-lieving contradictory things?' (1993, p.201). Just as Piaget envisaged formal operations as the highest, and adult, stage of thought, Piagetian theorists investigating children's economic and social understanding assume progression through stages to reach a level of understanding which is variously described in terms of classical economics (e.g. Linton, 1990), or the ideas of non-specialist adults (e.g. Berti and Bombi, 1988).

The use of classical economics has the advantage that it incorporates the notion of rationality, and thus is clearly related to other goals of development. However, the economic behaviour of individual adults does not generally conform to the economists' model. Rational Economic Man would behave in such a way as to maximise individual income (Lea *et al.*, 1987), but in reality people do not do this: they may compartmentalise their finances (Lewis *et al.*, 1995), or may be motivated by moral values (Etzioni, 1988). Webley (1983) questioned this use of the economists' view as a 'correct' one when considering children's ideas, and Blyth pointed out that the classical model of perfect competition which it embodies is that of 'the pure case of any subject' (1992, p.194), whereas in reality we meet only impure cases; the real world does not function in the same way as the economists' model. This is why comparison of children's responses with those suggested by classical economics has resulted in some bizarre interpretations. For example, Linton asked children: 'If I wanted to buy a suede coat more cheaply, would I be better to buy it in the winter or summer?' (1990, p.89). This was designed to test understanding of supply and demand; the 'correct' answer was that suede coats would be cheaper in summer because the demand would be less and therefore the price would fall. However, in reality prices of winter clothing are reduced in the January sales to dispose of stock.

Berti and Bombi explicitly rejected the notion of using classical economics as the adult stage, saying that they would instead take 'the common sense of adults rather than scientific economics as our reference point' (1988, p.25). However, they did not indicate what these ideas are or say how they identified them. It is questionable whether most adults do in fact have a reasonably comprehensive and thorough economic understanding (Furnham and Lewis, 1986)

Furth attempted to be more explicit about his notion of an adult level of thinking. He suggested that adults have an 'adequate framework' (1980, p.4) for making sense of societal events, and listed twelve statements which he says seem true to any adult in this society; for example:

Acquiring a societal role, such as an occupation, implies a constellation of various societal and personal prerequisites.

Not all societal customs are law, nor are personal morality and societal law synonymous.

Two principal ways of acquiring money are paid work and buying and selling. (1980, pp.4–5)

He explained:

42

> Naturally these statements are not known to adults in an explicit manner, nor is it likely that they would be listed even after some effort and reflection. But what is important for consideration is that the adult's acting, thinking and talking on everyday societal issues is in accordance with these statements. (p.5)

He asserted that five- to six-year-old children do not hold any of the conceptions he listed, believing instead, for example, that societal roles are achieved through the personal wish of the individual; that events happen according to known rules; and that money is freely available. 'Development' occurs when childish conceptions give way to an understanding of the adult statements.

All these theorists appear to see children as proceeding up a single ladder of understanding to an 'adult' level. However, it is at least possible that adults do not all arrive at the same understandings of the social and economic world, since experience is so varied. This is the point on which Dahlberg *et al.* (1987) depart from the mainstream developmental view. While they accepted some themes of the developmental approach (that there is development in children's capacity for making abstractions from the immediate concrete setting, and for handling more and increasingly complex information), they rejected the idea that there is a 'correct' adult view of social relations. Thus they did not accept the notion of a single course of development in which some children or groups have less developed understanding than others.

Emphasis on norms and normality

Developmental psychology tends to emphasise what Ingleby called 'spurious norms of development' (1986, p.299), including 'the child' and 'the family'. Burman (1994) shows how this emphasis is used to pathologise all those who do not fit the 'correct' patterns, that is, single-parent families, working mothers, minority cultural groups, and so on. Psychology has tended to take the behaviour of the white middle-class man as a measure of 'normality'; the poor, women and non-Europeans are seen as deviant and abnormal (Venn, 1984). Thus, as Rose argued, Normality is not an observation but a valuation. It contains not only a judgement about what is desirable, but an injunction as to a goal to be achieved. (1989, p.131). Venn pointed out that while 'psychological explanation attempts to account for deviations, it does not address the normality of the norm' (1984, p.131). The normal course of economic understanding is seen as being reflected in the responses given by the majority of children in research studies. However, this conceals the way in which the norm has been very carefully constructed through the topics investigated, samples selected, questions asked, and analysis of data.

For example, in studies of children's understanding of work, this has generally involved an emphasis on 'normal' work arrangements. Some theorists begin by identifying the characteristics of work; Burris (1976) assessed children's ideas about work against the characteristics of labour in a modern capitalist society, identified as follows:

- labour is organised and directed under hierarchical relations of authority;
- labour is complexly divided into specialised tasks which are stratified in terms of their relative value and status;
- work roles are unlikely to express the personal needs or interests of the worker;
- work is (at least partially) motivated by something extrinsic to itself, the payment of a wage;
- work involves a greater degree of external coercion and a lesser degree of individual autonomy than leisure activities;
- work is isolated from and opposed to other spheres of every-day life in which the worker feels more fully himself (leisure, family, private life).

(p.162–4)

Moreover, Burris argued that:

these characteristics of work are simply taken for granted by most adults as elementary 'facts of life'. Common sense dictates that one must have money to survive, that money is obtained by getting a job (i.e. by selling one's labour) and that jobs are by definition, at least minimally unpleasant and confining. (Burris, 1976, p.164)

Thus unemployment, housework, voluntary work, and, by his emphasis on wage labour, all forms of self-employment, are eliminated from consideration. This emphasis on full-time paid employment is reflected in many studies: it is only among adolescents that understanding of unemployment has been investigated (e.g. by Webley and Wrigley, 1983; Furnham, 1984; Giron, 2001).

A second way in which the norm has been constructed is in the choice of sample: children whose family economic arrangements do not conform to an expected norm have often been explicitly omitted. For example, Dahlberg *et al.* (1987) excluded children from one-parent families and those who were not indigenous English speakers. Berti and Bombi (1988), in their investigation of ideas about payment for work, used a middle-class sample attending private school; Berti, Bombi and Lis (1982), investigating production, used a working-class sample who all had fathers working at the Fiat factory and mothers who were housewives. If samples are selected to reflect 'normal' work arrangements, it is hardly surprising that the researchers find that these children develop an understanding of such arrangements. Moreover, in Britain, many children who are economically active, and might therefore have developed a more 'advanced' economic understanding, have self-employed parents and work in family businesses; such children have often been ruled out by the criteria for sample selection.

The wording of some of the questions asked implies that society is organised in certain ways. For example, Goldstein and Oldham (1979) asked 'how do people get jobs?'. The presupposition here is that adults are in paid employment. However, this will not accord with the experience of some children, for whom work may not involve getting a job, but rather, setting up a business, or cultivating land owned by the family. Similarly, the way the data has been analysed in many research projects privileges 'normal' responses; in Berti and Bombi's study of children's ideas about the source of money the highest level identified was 'money comes only from working' (1988, p.64), yet for many children money is not related to jobs, but rather to collecting benefits from an office. Such children would be considered to have deficient understanding (as would those whose families have inherited wealth). While this picture of society in which paid employment is the norm may have been more accurate in the nineteen fifties, it has considerable limitations in a post-industrial society, ignoring both unemployment and the increasing variety of work arrangements including self-provisioning and self-employment (Pahl, 1984).

These various ways in which 'normality' has been emphasised all tend to militate against any consideration of the variety of experiences that children may have. The next section will review the ways in which this has resulted in pathologising of groups who do not match the norm.

Variations in understanding among different groups

Piaget's concern was to describe the universal course of development of what he termed the 'epistemic' subject. 'For Piaget, the individual subject is an exemplar, the typical representation of the species' (Venn and Walkerdine, 1978, p.79). Thus he did not investigate differences between individuals or groups that might be seen to result from differences in experience. Nevertheless, his writings show that he believed that 'primitive' peoples were less cognitively developed:

> If we begin to lose faith in humanity, in the possibilities of progress of which mankind is capable, there is nothing that will so reassure us as to look back at the past and compare society today with those so-called primitive peoples .... We will realise in fact that the primitive is intellectually and morally even more the slave of self-centredness and social coercion than we are liable to be. (Piaget, 1933, p.21, quoted in Burman, 1994, p.160)

Many subsequent researchers have compared levels of development of different socio-economic and cultural groups. The 'lag' in concept development of children from lower socio-economic classes has been widely reported in Piagetian studies (Dasen, 1972). Cross-cultural investigations have been designed to see whether the sequence and rhythm of development of economic understanding are affected by different cultural experience, or whether they are universal. Such studies have generally found that the level of development of logico-mathematical thinking among people in traditional societies lags behind that of those in modern industrialised societies (see Dasen, 1972; Dasen and Heron, 1981).

In this section I will consider findings from investigations of children's social and economic understanding. A number of researchers have analysed their results by social class, and have generally found some differences between the pattern of responses of middle-class and working-class children. Typical of these is Burris:

> Children from middle-class backgrounds tended to be somewhat more 'advanced' in their development of economic concepts than children from working-class backgrounds. That is, at any particular grade level they tended to give responses which were either more accurate or representative of a higher developmental stage than those given by working-class children. (1976, p.227)

Similarly Berti and Bombi, commenting on Emler and Dickinson's research, argued that the working-class children's ideas (supporting egalitarianism in payment for work) were those that are found in younger children, and the data should therefore be seen as showing 'the effect of class as a retarding influence' (1988, p.22) rather than Emler and Dickinson's explanation, the effect of different experiences. Berti and Bombi did not indicate *how* class membership retards development; the developmental superiority of the middle classes was seen as a fact of nature.

Some researchers have put forward explanations for their findings that working-class children show lower levels of social and economic understanding. Burris found that some of the differences he had found were strongly related to differences in general intelligence. However, it is important to remember here that just as levels of social and economic understanding are constructed, so too are intelligence scales; intelligence is defined as that which is measured in IQ tests, and normal intelligence is the mean score in such tests.

Burris suggested that other differences between working-class and middle-class responses were more related to 'different patterns of economic socialisation for children of ... different class backgrounds' (p.247); referring specifically to social-class patterns of parental discipline and moral education. This explanation blames working-class parents for their children's relatively limited understanding. Similarly Jahoda (1981) argued that certain forms of social knowledge are heavily information dependent, and that middle-class children have a more sophisticated understanding because they inhabit a society which is richer in the relevant information. Again, working-class parents are seen as failing to provide what their children need, in this case information.

Other researchers have argued that working-class and middle-class children develop different ideas because each group assimilates ideas that are current in their communities. For example, Dahlberg *et al.* (1987) found that middle-class eight-year-olds had a stronger classification between manual and non-manual work than working-class children of the same age, and that they valued non-manual work more highly whereas the working-class children placed a greater value on manual work. Dahlberg *et al.* suggested that this contributed to the social reproduction of class relations 'in that working-class children by valuing manual labour become socialised into accepting their place within it' (p.91). They commented that the middle-class children's views related more closely to those of the dominant groups in society (which seems hardly surprising); however, they avoided suggesting that this is therefore a more 'advanced' understanding.

Similar investigations have reported similar patterns of responses. For example, Emler and Dickinson (1985) asked children aged seven to twelve years to estimate the income of people in different occupations, and to comment on the fairness of the predicted income differentials. They found very few differences relating to age, but considerable differences by class, with middle-class children making greater income differentials and being more likely to argue that these were fair. Emler and Dickinson pointed to Tajfel's (1972) intergroup theory, which predicts that members of high status groups will emphasise their distinctiveness in comparison to low status groups. However, like Jahoda, their main explanation was the uneven social distribution of knowledge. They argued that middle-class children have more detailed and extensive knowledge about work available to them in the context in which they live. Thus while attempting to distance themselves from developmentalism, Emler and Dickinson characterised the understanding of working-class children as less detailed, extensive and salient than that of middle-class children. Like Dahlberg *et al.*, they suggested that the working-class children's limited knowledge may contribute to the reproduction of class distinctions in that they see little difference between the economic rewards received for manual and non-manual work, and thus do not have sufficient knowledge on which to base vital educational decisions which will restrict their later choices. Simmons and Rosenberg, in their investigation of children's perceptions of the stratification system in the USA, made a similar point:

> It is apparent that those children who are penalised by the stratification order today and whose prospects are least good are less conscious of its nature than those who at present benefit most from the system and whose prospects are brighter. (1971, p.246)

A similar conclusion is made in a recent study of children's representations of wealth and poverty by Bombi (forthcoming); she demonstrates that children from wealthy families depict considerable differences between rich and poor people, while those from disadvantaged backgrounds minimised the differences. Bombi concludes that this perception tends to make those who are disadvantaged less discontent than a more realistic appraisal of contrasts in wealth would have done. These studies demonstrate the difficulty of maintaining a position that characterises working-class experience as 'different but equally valid' (Walkerdine and Lucey, 1989, p.37).

Occasionally, working-class children have been found to have a better understanding of economic issues than middle-class children. It is interesting to see how this has been dealt with by researchers.

Tizard and Hughes (1984), analysing transcripts of four-year-old girls talking with their mothers at home, pointed out that the middle-class children were more often confused about the relationship between work, money and goods. They referred to a conversation between a middle-class girl and her mother in which the girl is puzzled by her mother's reference to paying the window cleaner, and another conversation in which a working-class girl very clearly understands the relationship between her father's work, payment, and ability to purchase goods. They suggested that this difference resulted from experience:

> Perhaps because their fathers' work was more clearly related to money, rather than the interest of his job, or because with a more limited income the arrival of the weekly pay packet was a more important event, the relationship between money and work was more often discussed in working-class families. (p.123)

Walkerdine and Lucey (1989), discussing the same transcripts, commented that Tizard and Hughes did not suggest that the working-class child who understood the relationship between work and money had reached a higher developmental level; her understanding of waged labour was simply part of her concrete everyday reality and did not involve advanced abstract thought. In contrast, the middle-class child's questioning is interpreted as demonstrating 'intellectual search' or 'the power of the puzzling mind' (p.123); that is, it demonstrates that four-year-olds have more advanced powers of thinking than Piaget had credited children of this age with. It is assumed that thought develops from concrete to abstract, and the middle-class child's 'puzzling mind' is an attempt to deal with ideas which for her are abstracted from her everyday reality, and is therefore construed as advanced thinking. This example demonstrates the contradictions between two different pinnacles of development: abstract rational thought and an adult level of economic understanding, and shows how those children who apparently have greater economic understanding can be categorised as less developed.

The implication of all these studies is that the socialisation provided by working-class parents is unlikely to offer their children the opportunity to better their position. Thus research into children's social and economic understanding repeats the pattern of pathologising the working class for their lower developmental level. However, in cross-cultural studies a rather different pattern is found, in some cases demonstrating a more advanced understanding in the less 'developed' country. These results have been interpreted as indicating that experience in a particular aspect of economics may lead to a far earlier understanding of concepts in that area. For example, Jahoda (1983) investigated children's understanding of profit in Scotland and Zimbabwe, and found that whereas the sample of children in Scotland understood profit by about age eleven, the sample in Zimbabwe grasped this concept at about age nine; he characterised this as a European 'lag' in development. Those children in Zimbabwe who had personal experience of trading had the most advanced understanding, but even if they are discounted, the rest of the sample still had understanding significantly in advance of that of the Scottish children. Jahoda suggested that the earlier understanding of profit could result from peer communication and from living in a society where trading was widespread and important. Similarly Hong Kwang and Stacey (1981) found that Chinese children in Malaysia achieved understanding of the concept of profit a little earlier than Western children, and also understood gambling from a young age; they related this to differences in child-rearing and the popularity of gambling in that society. Understanding of the bank has been another focus for cross-cultural studies. Ng (1983) showed that children in Hong Kong had a more advanced knowledge of banks than Jahoda's Scottish sample; and Wong (1989) found that children in Hong Kong were more advanced than those in the United States. Both Ng and Wong attributed this to the business ethos characteristic of Hong Kong society, and Wong offered a detailed analysis of this ethos and of the educational system to explain the advanced understanding of the Hong Kong sample. In all these studies the suggestion has been that variations in experience in contrasting cultural and economic contexts will affect the speed of progress through the different stages.

However, Berti and Bombi (1988) expressed reservations about the claims made in cross-cultural studies. They pointed out that the samples used are small, and it is not possible to generalise from them, as Jahoda did, to speak of European 'lag' in relation to Africa. These comments seem somewhat perverse, as Berti and Bombi themselves had labelled differences found by Emler and Dickinson as social class retardation, yet samples were of a similar size in both studies. However, their views concur with those of most developmental theorists: working-class and 'primitive' peoples are not seen as reaching such a high level of understanding as the middle classes in the west.

Other studies have emphasised the differences in response by children in various countries: for example, Dahlberg et al. (1987) found that the meritocratic ideology was strongest among English children, whereas the Swedish children put more emphasis on equality. They interpreted this as different understandings rather than different levels of development, in accord with their rejection of the idea of a single adult stage.

Approaches that focus on children's experience

So far, this chapter has identified a number of problems with the way the developmental framework has been used in studies of children's social and economic understanding. These include conceptual limitations, such as very limited attention given to social interaction, the ways in which structure and function of thought have been distinguished, and the definition of an adult level of economic understanding. There are also problems of a moral/political nature: the assumption of a single course of development through stages with 'the vectorial quality of being 'stages towards adult mastery'" (Harré, 1974, p.245), and the emphasis on norms and normality. These have led to pathologising of those groups and individuals whose understandings do not match this model: in particular the working class. To label differences as developmental 'lag' or 'retardation' seems to be, in colloquial terms, a 'cop out', since no further explanation need be sought for the differences found; or in the words of Morss: 'the appeal to development as an explanation causes other potential accounts to remain unconsidered' (1996, p.50).

This results in part from developmental psychology's emphasis on the individual rather than on society: 'psychology tended to treat only the properties of the individual as variables; the culture became in effect, a constant. Social inequalities tended to be explained in terms of psychological ones ('blaming the victim')' (Ingleby, 1986, p.299). Henriques *et al.* (1984) argued that one effect of this has been that responsibility for problems such as unemployment has been located in the individual, characterised as 'unemployable'; psychologists have not viewed this as an economic or political problem to do with power and exploitation.

Even when experience has been considered as an explanation for differences in understanding, researchers have not generally investigated children's experience, but rather, have made assumptions about the typical experience of children of different social classes and cultures. There have been repeated calls for more attention to be paid to variations in experience. For example, Furnham and Thomas (1984) argued that studies of children's economic understanding have failed to explain the large variations in the development of understanding; they suggested that to explain such variations will involve investigating experience and identifying factors which contribute to understanding. Webley (1983) expressed regret that no attempts had been made to produce a characterisation of the environment which would allow for variations in the development of thought other than those resulting from social class distinctions. The focus on the structure of thought has been questioned by Lea *et al.*: 'by looking at economic cognition as another instance of a general process of cognitive development, we may be paying inadequate attention to the variations in thought that are brought about by content' (1987, p.376). They also emphasised the need to pay more attention to differences between individuals, commenting that 'individual differences may be important; it is through the creative leaps of individuals that collective representations are modified' (p.378).

Ingleby (1986) pointed out that, in the nineteen sixties and seventies, the realisation that cognitive psychology did not pay enough attention to the varieties of development and to individual differences led to a new interest in the role of culture and experience, and that this tended to result in a return to social learning ideas in which environmental factors were given primacy. But while McGurk (1978) posed the concept of socialisation as an alternative to developmental theories, there are certain similarities between the two. Just as developmentalism assumes a 'normal' course of development, so socialisation tends to assume that there is one 'normal' course of socialisation. If the product of socialisation turns out to be undesirable, responsibility is seen to lie with the socialising agents (Schaffer and Crook, 1978), and groups and individuals who do not conform to norms may be pathologised. In this way the concept of socialisation can be seen as sharing the moral/political problems of developmentalism. Moreover, while socialisation is ostensibly concerned with the child's experience, Prout and James (1990) pointed out that most theorists also draw on psychological models of development, for example by assuming a process of maturational development in the child. This sets limits to socialisation by preventing it from succeeding if it is attempted before the child has reached an appropriate stage (e.g. Berger and Berger, 1972). Indeed, Roland-Levy (forthcoming), drawing on Youniss (1978) argues that developmentalism describes the framework, and socialisation the content, of understanding, and that the two theoretical stances are not incompatible. Thus, while socialisation emphasises the child's experience, it also shares many of the same problems as developmentalism, including biological limits to socialisation, identification of norms, and pathologising of those who fail to provide a 'successful' socialisation.

Several strands of research into children's social and economic understanding have accorded greater importance to experience. One approach is to focus on children's social and economic behaviour. This approach follows from the assertion that 'children's social relationships and cultures are worthy of study in their own right' (James and Prout, 1990, p.4). Observing how children act is one way of finding out what they understand. From this perspective, Lea *et al.* (1987) called for studies that examine the economic world that children construct for themselves, including playground swapping and bartering. This has remained an under-researched area, partly because of the difficulties of observational studies. Dunn's (1988) study of young children and their families, *The Beginnings of Social Understanding*, is an important exception here.

A number of researchers have focused on children's accounts of their behaviour. For example, researchers in Sweden have gathered children's accounts of their pocket money, saving, spending, earning etc. (Elvstrand; Justegård; Näsman and von Gerber – all forthcoming).

Another way of focusing on experience is the evaluation of curriculum interventions. The last decades have seen attempts in some countries to design curricula that teach children about economic understanding. While some have resulted in comments on the positive outcomes in terms of pupils' enjoyment and interaction, others have been implemented as part of well-planned and thorough research projects – most notably the interventions carried out by researchers in Italy. The earliest of these, reported in Ajello *et al.* (1986, 1987), involved the design of a teaching programme for children from eight to eleven years that would make pertinent information available to them in a way that could stimulate their thinking and result in earlier acquisition of particular economic concepts. More recent intervention studies have been led by Berti (e.g. Berti and Monaci (1998) and Berti and Ugolini (1998)). What is notable in these studies is that Berti has made a considerable shift in her thinking from a Piagetian framework to a domain-specific approach, drawing on the ideas of Carey (1985) and Chi (1988). Her current thinking is set out in detail in her chapter in this volume. She claims that the intervention studies show that changes in children's conceptions within a particular domain can be brought about by quite short interventions, and that these appear to result from accretional transformations rather than radical restructuring. However, Berti's recent work has focused on teaching aspects of societal understanding that are remote from children's experience (law, the judicial system, the bank) and it is thus possible that the children did not have firm conceptions (or misconceptions) at the outset. The domain-specific approach, while distinct from Piaget's stage theory, still assumes cognitive development: Berti talks about interventions to bring about 'the acceleration of one developmental sequence'.

It is difficult to move beyond developmentalism because, as Walkerdine argues:

> The very idea of development is not natural and universal, but extremely specific, and in its specificity occludes other marginalised stories, subsumed as they are within the bigger story. The big story is a European patriarchal story, a story from the centre which describes the periphery in terms of the abnormal, difference as deficiency. (1993, p.455)

The most worrying feature of developmentalism is precisely that it 'occludes other marginalised stories'; Morss argues that it is hegemonic, and 'must be seen as violently suppressing alternative ways of thinking and being' (1996, p.51). For this reason he maintains that 'it is not enough to be non-developmental' (p.48); this approach fails to take seriously the problems with developmentalism. For even in ostensibly non-developmental approaches, developmentalism tends to recur. What is needed is an anti-developmental approach. This involves a critical scrutiny of developmentalism and the search for systematic alternatives to developmental explanation.

Social constructionism: an anti-developmental perspective?

I therefore turn to a more recent perspective: social constructionism. This clearly has considerable potential for a critique of development, drawing on the notions of discourse and narrative. The focus on interaction rather than on the properties of the mind is also helpful in getting away from developmental assumptions. Similarly the emphasis on social, historical and cultural specificity is useful in that it militates against asserting a single course of development and defining norms.

The common feature of all the various schools of thought that can be identified as social constructionist, according to Ingleby (1986), is an approach that breaks down the individual/society dichotomy by asserting that mind is a social phenomenon, and that as the science of the mind, psychology should be concerned not with individuals, but with 'what goes on in the space between them' (1986, p.305). This emphasis is in sharp contrast to cognitive developmentalism, which is concerned with the development of structures in the mind, and socialisation with its emphasis on the internalisation of society by the individual. Shotter, in an epilogue to Conversational Realities, takes a similar view:

> Common to all versions of social constructionism is the central assumption that – instead of the inner dynamics of the individual psyche ... or the already determined characteristics of the external world ... it is the contingent really vague (that is, lacking any completely determinate character) flow of continuous communicative activity between human beings that we must study. (1993, p.179)

There are various approaches with this common thread of interest in what happens between people, and not all theorists using such an approach identify themselves as social constructionists (Ingleby, 1986; Burr, 1995). I will draw on a range of writers who take a broadly social constructionist approach.

An essential feature of social constructionism is the notion that meaning is jointly constructed in talk with co-participants (Shotter, 1993). Talk is performative, and speakers construct their audiences in their talk. Interaction between people inevitably takes place in specific contexts; thus a second feature of social constructionism is a concern with the situated nature of all activity. This includes the specific setting, the participants and their purposes, as well as the culture, period of history and social and economic arrangements (Burr, 1995). Interaction has been investigated by some theorists entirely in terms of talk, but many also emphasise the role of action. Foucault (1972) emphasised that discourses and practices should be treated as if they were the same thing, since material practices (for example, the practices involved in a medical examination) are always invested with meaning and thus have the same status as spoken or written communications.

Through talk and action people are said to be *constructing* versions of the world. Potter and Wetherell considered that that the term 'construction' is apposite because:

First, it reminds us that accounts of events are built out of a variety of pre-existing linguistic resources, almost as a house is constructed from bricks, beams and so on. Second, construction implies active selection: some resources are selected, some omitted. Finally, the notion of construction emphasises the potent, consequential nature of accounts. Much of social interaction is based around dealings with events and people which are experienced *only* in terms of specific linguistic versions. In a profound sense, accounts 'construct' reality. (1987, pp.33–4)

The final point is particularly relevant in considering children's constructions of adult work, which may to a large extent draw on talk and other media because children are separated from many forms of work.

In this context my main concern is how far social constructionism can be seen as an anti-developmental perspective. Most social constructionists have not been concerned with children's learning, so the question of development has generally not been relevant and has not been discussed. An exception was Harré. He has repeatedly argued against developmentalism, pointing out (1983) that any hierarchical account of children's development can be turned on its side and a set of stages seen as a set of alternative ways of thinking which are not necessary sequential; thus he argued that Kohlberg's (1976) stages of moral development are alternative moral theories which all involve the same cognitive capacities. Similarly Harré challenged Piaget's account of stages which he considered to be 'a reflection of an ethnocentric view of the relative *worth* of different forms of higher mental functioning' (p.223). Nevertheless, his own account of childhood is still essentially developmental; he suggested that 'There is a cognitive capacity that does change. This is the ability to deal with more complex tasks and to handle greater masses of material' (1983, p.225).

In his search for an anti-developmental formulation, Morss (1996) rejects social constructionism as he concludes that it incorporates some elements of developmental thinking. However, he uses a rather narrow view of social constructionism, focusing only on the work of Harré, Shotter and Gergen, whom he describes as the 'Old Guard'.

He emphasises that they have all been writing over a long period, and that their views have changed. Shotter and Gergen have both taken on the move to postmodernism. Shotter (1992) argued that postmodern psychology should focus on local and personal narratives, concerned with social identity in practical daily social life. Gergen and Gergen (1986) suggested that such narratives might be evaluated by their rhetorical power, generative potential, and ideological, political and social implications. They chose to examine the dramatic impact of developmentalism, and argued that the Piagetian narrative carries rhetorical conviction in its clearly defined end point and elaborate account of the events leading up to this. Thus developmentalism is presented as one narrative among many others. Morss suggests two reasons why these writers have not been more active in writing against development; he points out that their interests in psychology are far wider than simply development, and concludes that they 'do not see development itself as enough of a problem' (1996, p.47).

A wide range of other writers can be identified as social construc-tionists; however some of these prefer to use other labels: discourse analysis (Potter and Wetherell, 1987); situated learning (Lave and Wenger, 1991); critical polytextualism (Stainton Rogers and Stainton Rogers, 1992). The writers I consider have not all been con-cerned with children or development, but their ideas may neverthe-less offer some way forward.

Many of those whose interest is situated learning start from develop-mental theory, often drawing specifically on the ideas of Piaget or Vygotsky (e.g. Rogoff, 1990; Mercer, 1992). They criticise develop-mentalism for its lack of concern with social context, and rather than introducing context as an extra variable, they attempt to modify the theory so as to put context into a central position. But they still assume that there is something that develops. However, others have offered a more forceful rejection of developmentalism. The group who have been concerned with situated activity among adults (e.g. Scribner, 1984; Lave, 1988; Lave and Wenger, 1991) to some extent side step issues of development by choosing to focus on adult problem solving in everyday contexts. This stance has been adopted by Lave as a result of her rejection of the normative view of the person as a rational scientist and problem solver, and of the distinction commonly drawn between everyday thinking (seen as primitive or non-rational) and scientific, rational thought. In particular she challenged psychology's context-free characterisation of cognition. In order to move away from these conceptions, she argued that persons, culture, social world and everyday must be treated as objects of analysis, in an attempt to develop a theory of practice. Her arguments can then be seen as anti-developmental.

I also include the post-structuralist work of Henriques *et al.* and Walkerdine in my broad category of social construction. Morss considers that Walkerdine's (1984) use of a Foucauldian viewpoint is 'one of the best examples yet available of an anti-developmental formulation' (1996, p.134). However he argues that when both Walkerdine (1984) and Urwin (1984) draw on Lacan they incorporate some developmental notions into their accounts.

Another perspective that strongly rejects developmentalism is the 'critical polytextualism' of Stainton Rogers and Stainton Rogers (1992) and Curt (1994). They accept the relativistic implications of post-structuralism, arguing that there are no absolute grounds for any particular moral stance. However, they consider that it matters what stories are told, and why. Developmental explanations are for them a cause for concern in that they suppress alternative accounts. 'We are not interested in trying to improve developmentalism by correcting its errors. What we are arguing ... is that the whole enterprise of developmentalism needs to be abandoned altogether!' (Stainton Rogers and Stainton Rogers, 1992, p.42).

I have argued that one of the problems with both developmentalism and with the concept of socialisation is that both lead to the identification of norms, and the consequent pathologising of certain groups. Morss points out that Bradley (forthcoming) considers that even social constructionist accounts which describe subjectivity as produced by discourse have this same tendency to create norms by appealing to 'universal and regular processes of transformation'

(1996, p.151). Similarly Lock (1994, p.2, quoted in Morss 1996, p.151) claims that social constructionism posits 'ordering principles to the temporal course of construction'.

The difficulty here is perhaps unavoidable. The nature of language is that we talk and think in categories or concepts rather than particular instances. All our concepts are based on the typical or normal instance – of a tree, cat, bus driver, factory or whatever. Other examples are recognisable, but unlike our notion of the typical instance. This is fine, so long as we do not then pathologise them, say, by identifying a black woman bus driver as a problem. In the context of research, the focus should perhaps be on diversity rather than the typical case. However, in examining diversity, it is difficult to avoid also constructing a norm. While I have attempted to take an anti-developmental stance in my research into children's constructions of work (Hutchings, 1997), I do not claim to have resolved these problems.

Implications for anti-developmental research

Finally I consider the implications for researchers of the various ideas discussed in this chapter. Firstly, in taking a social constructionist view, we should avoid the idea that there is something in the child's mind which can be accessed, and simply focus on what is said or done in a particular context.

In designing research, we need to recognise that all constructions are jointly made with other participants, rather than individual. We should be aware of our own contributions as both initiator and audience (which would apply even in solitary constructions such as individual pieces of writing). We also need to bear in mind that the context of construction cannot be neutral, and must affect the nature of the construction. It may be more useful to investigate children's constructions of specific social and economic contexts than to look for generalised understandings and abstractions, since this reflects more closely the ways in which we normally construct ideas. Constructions may be of past, present, future or unfamiliar social and economic contexts; construction involves a combination of fact, imagination and desire in each case. A possible approach might be to get the child to insert her/himself imaginatively in a particular context and to tell a story, rather than to attempt to check up on their factual knowledge. (This approach is very clearly different from the developmental one which rejects both imaginative elaborations and repetitions of what others have said: Furth, 1980.) The focus should not be the accuracy of children's constructions, but rather, how they are constructed, and what they draw on; it is of questionable value to compare children's constructions with some supposed view of reality such as the researcher's own constructions, or those of the average adult (Berti and Bombi, 1988).

In analysing children's constructions, we need to be aware of the various discursive practices in which they are positioned. They are children attending school and living in a society that generally positions children as powerless, innocent and in need of protection. This discursive positioning may produce particular fantasies and desires. However, this particular construction of childhood is culturally specific, and will not necessarily represent the discursive positioning of all children. We also need to be aware of the economic realities of life for the children and their families.

We should note that children may draw on discourses or interpretative repertoires, as well as on observations and memories. They may also draw on their own participation in social practice as a resource. It may also be interesting to note how children draw on resources that were acquired in specific circumstances and how they use them in new constructions. What links do they make between different social and economic contexts?

Finally, we must avoid the temptation to oversimplify in order to create a model; the world is messy and complex, and the complexities are an essential aspect of all thinking and interaction, not a superficial phenomenon.

4

Intergenerational differences and social transition: Teachers' and students' perception of competition in Hungary

Márta Fülöp[1]
Institute for Psychology, Hungarian Academy of Sciences, Budapest
Department of Psychology, University of Szeged, Szeged, Hungary

There are relatively few studies in the psychological literature that aim to reveal the similarities and differences of concepts, views, beliefs or attitudes between different generations. There are even fewer that connect these with the rapid societal changes from socialism to a democratic political regime and a market economy in the former socialist countries of Central and Eastern Europe.

Present day adolescents, who began their schooling after the political changes of the late 1980s, could be the ideal builders of the new democracies and we might expect them to have political, economical and social concepts that, as a consequence of living in and directly experiencing the changed structure, reflect the ruling ideology of the new political system rather than that of the previous regimes. However, these young people are being socialised by their parents and teachers, who were brought up during the previous social system and became adults and working people in a completely different ideological system. If this is so, it is a very important theoretical and practical question as to how the parents' and teachers' ways of thinking change, and how their ideas are reflected in the young people's ideas. In other words, how effective is the intergenerational transmission of values when compared to the influence of the changed ideology of the political arena and the social reality that young people perceive around them in their everyday life?

This chapter consists of five main parts. The first three parts are theoretical introductions: the first reviews the literature on intergenerational transmission of values and conceptions of social, political and economical questions; the second the literature on social transition and social change and how they effect different generations; and the third examines these two topics in the context of societal changes in Central and Eastern Europe. The fourth and fifth parts are based on an empirical study carried out among Hungarian secondary school teachers and secondary school students. As competition is a key element of contemporary social change, the fourth part compares how teachers and students perceive the role of competition in present day Hungary. The fifth part discusses teachers' ideas about the role of the school in preparing students for future competition and the possible ways teachers and school can do that.

Intergenerational transmission of values and beliefs related to social and political processes

The transmission of a culture means spreading mental representations from one person to the next. Transmission takes place through communication, in which social orientations and norms are 'transported'. The common means of transmission of values and beliefs are by socialisation and enculturation (Schönpflug, 2001). Socialisation consists of concrete practices by educators, while enculturation may consist of explicit, deliberate learning, but may also take place in the form of implicit, unintentional learning. The process of cultural transmission does not lead to a constant replication of culture in successive generations: rather, it falls somewhere between an exact transmission (with hardly any difference between the generations) and the complete failure of transmission (with hardly any similarities). The culture of the future generation may also be somewhat like the reflection in a curved mirror: some things are smaller, some are bigger, and some parts may even be upside down.

From an ecological perspective of development and socialisation (Bronfenbrenner, 1979), the settings and environments in which people live and grow can be viewed as systems, which exist simultaneously at various levels. The microsystem is composed of the network of ties between people and their immediate settings, such as family, school and friends. The mesosystem consists of the ties among major settings in the person's life, for example the ties between family and school. The macrosystem is composed of broad, institutional patterns in the culture such as political, social, educational, and economic systems. In addition to these three there are critical exosystems like the media. According to Bronfenbrenner, adolescent development takes place within the immediate social contexts of everyday life: the family, the peer group, the school. These are embedded in the multilevel environmental strata and convey the transmission process.

There are three major areas where we can find studies in relation to cultural transmission processes between generations, mainly between parent and offspring. One area of research concentrates primarily on the transfer of emotional reactions, e.g. aggression or anxiety, from one generation to the other (e.g. Doumas *et al.* 1994). The most characteristic examples of this line of research are found in the the Holocaust literature in psychology, where it is increasingly common to study how the trauma of Holocaust is transmitted from grandparents to the second and even the third generation of Holocaust survivors (e.g. Virág, 2000). Another major area is the study of the process of acculturation among immigrants, for example second and third generation Mexican-Americans to the USA (Knight and Kagan, 1977), Pakistani and Indian immigrants to greater London (Furnham and Shiekh, 1993), and Soviet immigrants to Israel (Knafo and Schwartz, 2001). The third area is the transmission of values, political attitudes and ideologies between generations. Most of the studies within this research area were conducted until the 1990s in the USA, a country that, in spite of many changes such as the great depression, different waves of immigration, and the feminist movement, has not gone through profound political-ideological structural changes in the twentieth century.

In terms of intergenerational transmission of ideologies, beliefs and values there are several theoretical assumptions. One is the socialisation theory (Erikson, 1950; Kohn, 1983) in psychology, the other is the social status theory (Acock, 1984) in sociology. Similarity in attitudes between generations, according to the traditional socialisation theory, is the consequence of successful parental socialisation, in which children learn their parents' values, beliefs and attitudes through both direct teaching and indirect observation. Childhood socialisation is seen to be so intense, prolonged, and psychodynamically important that the attitudes and values formed by the family context will persist well into adulthood. Schönpflug (2001) speaks about the role of models for a young person to copy in terms of attitudes, morals, social values, and political beliefs, and suggests that it is clear that mothers and fathers (vertical – parent–offspring transmission), teachers (oblique transmission) and peers (horizontal transmission) differ in the importance of the role they play in this process.

The social status theory in sociology assumes that parent–child attitude similarities are not only the result of socialisation, but also have more to do with successful intergenerational transmission of class and other prominent social statuses that structure life experience and mould social attitudes (Acock, 1984; Slomczynski *et al.*, 1999). What parents transmit may be social statuses, more than attitudes or values. In this way, similarities in social structural position may create attitudinal similarities between parents and adult children through a common-cause association, that is, that parents and children have undergone similar attitude-shaping experiences (Glass and Bengston, 1986).

Research on the intergenerational transmission of attitudes has shown that the older generation seems to be highly effective in passing on its attitudes, and that parents' attitudes – especially mothers' attitudes – are significant positive predictors of children's attitudes in adulthood. In other words, this similarity is not confined to the period in which children are young and living with their parents (Glass and Bengston, 1986; Dalhouse and Frideres, 1996). The results are however, contradictory in the case of political ideology, religious beliefs, value orientations, and general points of view concerning social reality. Some researchers indicate that these are only moderately transmitted from adults to their children (Jennings and Niemi, 1982; Kohn, 1983), while others like Glass and Bengstron (1986) found that there is a significant impact of parental attitudes on adult children's attitudes, and that this does persist across religious and political ideology scales. The extent of similarities and differences can be influenced by the age and developmental phase of the different generations and by the cultural background in which they are embedded.

The younger generations' beliefs and orientations are partly dependent on those of the older generation as well as everyday life experiences Adolescence is often a period in which the influence of the environment on the integrated processes of cognitive, social and emotional development is particularly apparent. In adolescence, people begin to develop abstract conceptualisations about their society and an understanding of the political concepts that are central to the ideologies of their time (Erikson, 1987). It is often a time when young people develop dispositions to participate actively in, or to withdraw from, social and political engagement in their communities and nation (e.g. Jennings and Niemi, 1982).

At the same time, adolescents may share few of the adult statuses that their parents hold, and may be facing developmental tasks of independence and differentiation from their parents (Erikson, 1950). They are trying to establish their own identity: so, relying on developmental theory, we should expect that their views will be different from those of their parents. Developmental theories emphasise the rebellious nature of youth, as young people attempt to separate and establish independence from their parents. But as they move into adult roles and establish this independence, their need to differentiate themselves from their parents decreases. Studies of intergenerational transmission might therefore show different results between adolescents and young adults with respect to parents.

The cultural context can also significantly influence what is trans-mitted, and to what extent, between generations. According to White (1993) in the United States, the use of the word 'teenager' refers not simply to a specific period of life, but also to a certain kind of behaviour that is to be expected during those years, and particularly the problems and conflicts between generations that are apparent during this period. Western psychologists like Erikson, for example, focus on creating a mature self, but in accord with individualism; this prioritises separation and autonomy and a result of this is that intergenerational opposition is understood to be an essential element of adolescent lives (White, 1993). However, this is not the case in Japan, where there is a cultural preference for continuity rather than a conflict between generations. Japanese teenagers do not seek separation from their parents and they do not want to see the world in a different perspective in order to mark their autonomous and separated individualised adult self (Simmons, 1996). While in the United States, Western Europe and Scandinavia a young person is expected to leave home after finishing secondary education, and to start a relatively independent life, this is not the case in Japan, Southern Europe and in the former socialist countries in Central Europe such as Poland and Hungary. The culturally prescribed strength of the relationship between generations can have different consequences on the perception young people have of society in these countries.

This 'normal' process of intergenerational transmission can be altered when social values and political beliefs have to change in *both* generations, because of rapid and dramatic socio-political-ideological transitions in the society: an example of this would be the societal transformation that took place from socialism to a demo-cratic political regime and a market economy.

Social transition in Central-Eastern Europe and its effects on different generations

During the late 1980s and early 1990s great socio-political and economic changes occurred in Central and Eastern Europe. The citizens of these countries and the western democratic states assumed that these transitions would be rapid, and that the transition to a more western-style democracy and a healthy and wealthier market economy would be completed within a few years. However, it soon became clear that these changes would be complex in nature and that the process would take longer than had been anticipated. For several segments of the population, the changes made general life circumstances worse and disillusionment followed. Bruszt and Simon (1991) carried out a series of public opinion polls before and after the first free parliamentary and local elections in Hungary. Within a year, public opinion about political and economic issues changed substantially. Prior to the 1990 parliamentary elections the majority of respondents were generally optimistic but follow-up surveys showed vastly different results: 71 per cent replied that they and their families were either somewhat worse off, or much worse off economically, than they had been the previous year. In 1993, 77 per cent of the Hungarian population thought that their financial situation had deteriorated when compared to five years earlier. Only 7 per cent reported improvements (Andorka, R. *et al.*, 1994). East Germans were highly in favour of the market economy, but then decreased their acceptance continuously, from 77 per cent in 1990 to about 33 per cent in 1995 (Pollack, 1997).

A number of recent empirical studies on Central and Eastern Europe have been devoted to the psychological reaction of people to the societal transformation from a socialist planned economy to a market economy and from a communist society to a capitalist one (for example, Bruszt and Simon, 1991; Rose and Mishler, 1994). These studies were based on an assumption that history is driven by 'hard' economic and 'soft' mental-spiritual factors, that are directly or indirectly interrelated, and that transformation is not only a question of marketisation and privatisation (that is, not only economic process) but a set of delicate and complex socio-political and

69

psychological changes, a switch of values and 'public spirit' (Berend, 1993). In other words, structural changes and people's mentality and way of thinking (Gumpel, 1993) are intertwined and mutually influence each other. The effects of social change do not apply uniformly to an entire population. Rather, the effects vary as a function of history and the individual's age, life course or developmental status at the time of the social transformation (Crockett and Silbereisen, 2000). Baltes and Baltes (1990) and Trommsdorff (1999) emphasise that starting from a lifespan perspective of development, different ages and cohorts have different socialisation experiences, life transitions and developmental tasks, even if they live in the same historical time. Adolescents' attitudes and beliefs are for instance more labile than those of adults (Elder, 1974). This must be taken into consideration when studying the effects of drastic socio-political change on individual thinking.

The main socialising agents of present day young people are their parents and their teachers, and they were socialised during the period of socialism, and were young or middle-aged adults during the political changes. In contrast to this, their children – the so called omega-alpha generation of the transitions, meaning that they are the last children of the old system and the first adults of the new one (Van Hoorn et al., 2000) – only started their schooling at that time, so for them 'change' is not a salient event but is taken for granted. Paradoxically, this means the society they are growing up in has stable characteristics. Thus adaptation to change means very different tasks for these two groups of people.

Social change implies both risks and stresses and new options and opportunities for development. A person can experience changes in the social environment such that the previously successful attainment of goals is blocked, or that previously unattainable goals can now be realised. The balance between these two sides is not the same for those in different phases of their life, or for individuals who held different social positions before the changes. Studies of the effects of unification in East Germany demonstrate that, for some age groups, the transformation was a high risk factor, whereas for others it was advantageous. For example, East German males born around 1940 had a lower belief in internal control directly after unification than any other male group in East or West Germany. But for one particular cohort (males of around 50 years of age) the turmoil after the reunification turned out to be a high risk, because of decreased chances for employment at this age (Trommsdorff, 2000).

Adolescents' perceptions of and reactions to periods of transition may differ in significant ways from the perceptions of adults. Younger people can probably adapt more easily, but among adults there is a greater chance of failure for those who are unable to adapt to the new demands or take advantage of new opportunities. Adolescents are not yet fully integrated into adult society and are therefore freer to search and to define their relationship with the social order (Erikson, 1968). But this is less possible in middle age, as later in life there is a decreasing probability that an individual can switch to a different pathway. The younger person is *expected* to change more. For instance, in a study by Reitzle and Silbereisen (1997) on collectivist values, those who were already adolescents at the time of the unification of East and West Germany showed fewer changes in attitude than those who were younger at the time of unification. The fact that values change in different ways in different age groups is also demonstrated by the children of Russian immigrants to Israel, who tend to adopt the prevailing values in the new country not only faster but also to a greater extent than do their parents (Knafo and Schwartz, 2001).

How do adults adopt new concepts and ways of thinking after the collapse of the former socialist system, in order to meet the new institutional requirements? There are many changes. For example, people who expected to work all their life may now have to face life-long unemployment, or may have to invest resources and achieve new competences in order to cope with these unexpected changes (Trommsdorff, 1999). These significant changes in a middle-aged people's lives require them to articulate the evolving political constructs and to redefine important aspects of their social and personal identities – and to do so at a phase in their lives when significant changes in these areas are normally not expected. In a stable society it is the adolescents who have the task of developing elaborate social, political and economical concepts such as democracy, the free market economy and citizenship: but in the rapidly changing societies of East and Central Europe it is the adult population who have also to develop the same concepts. Adults and adolescents both struggle: either to establish (adolescents) or to redefine (adults) their identity, and in this process adolescents seem to concentrate more on personal development rather then on social-political development. Van Hoorn *et al.*'s study (2000) showed that both Hungarian and Polish adolescents are not very involved in politics and that they do not perceive that the social changes will influence their life tremendously: instead, they concentrate on establishing peer and family relationships and do not see themselves as affected by social changes in the country. This is certainly very different for those in their parents' generation. For example, according to national opinion polls, Hungarian adults had significant concerns about the economy (Van Hoorn, *et al*, 2000), and this contrasted with secondary-school students who had generally low level of concerns about this.

This is related to young people's social status as dependants, as well as their limited time perspective when compared to adults. Van Hoorn *et al.* found that Hungarian and Polish adolescents centred on the present, and discussed the transitions within an extremely limited historical framework, giving only limited consideration to the near past or the near future. Their inability to situate the transitions within a broader time frame meant that they had less complex views of the socio-political changes and greatly limited their socio-historical analysis of the transitions. It may be that the adult population is generally more pessimistic and negative about the changes than adolescents (Bruszt and Simon, 1991; Trommsdorff, 2000; Van Hoorn *et al.*, 2000). High rates of depression – approximately 15 per cent of the adult population of Hungary – are also attributed to the fact that many are unable to cope with the social trauma of political changes (Harmatta, J., head of the National Psychotherapy Council, personal communication, 10 August 2001).

Intergenerational transmission in the time of rapid social change in Central and Eastern Europe

Boehnke (2001) points out that in the current scientific discourse on values, two important topics have been discussed at length but have hardly ever been addressed together: value transmission and value change. Value change studies do not take value transmission processes into consideration, while value transmission studies – even when they take social context into consideration – disregard societal change processes. Boehnke's statement is true about political ideas and concepts concerning social phenomena.

Social change operates at multiple levels, and macro-level changes are moderated or mediated by the main actors in a young person's life at the micro level, very often their parents. Glass and Bengston (1986) suggest that social theorists have for many years stated that families maintain continuity in social ideologies over time. Because of this, the family was considered conservative (slowing the pace of social change) and monolithic (influencing individual beliefs in a forceful and consistent manner). Generational ties were considered to hinder rapid social change. But such processes presuppose a relatively stable social context around the family. What happens if the society in which parents grew up differs dramatically from the society in which the children grow up? The beliefs and attitudes that seemed to work for the parents are no longer necessarily useful for their children. How, and to what extent, do adults change their social ideologies? how do different generations within the same family adapt to profound changes? and what kind of influence does each generation have on the other? For example, young people may look increasingly to non-parental sources of information and support – or they may rely even more on their family's values.

In the last decade there have been a growing number of studies carried out in former East Germany (for example, Schönpflug and Silbereisen, 1992, Schönpflug, 2001), in Poland (Slomczynski *et al.* 1999; Van Hoorn *et al.* 2000) and in Hungary (Van Hoorn *et al.* 2000) that address this theoretical question. Their results point in the same direction, namely that the family and parents have a decisive role in the way that young people view the political changes and social transitions. According to Silbereisen (2000), political discussions with adolescents in the family start earlier in life in the former East Germany than they do in West Germany, suggesting that these young people get many views about political change from their parents.

Van Hoorn *et al.* studied the development of Hungarian and Polish adolescents' socio-political identity and explored their views of their changing society and of the role that family, peers and the media play in the formation of their views. They found there was a divergence between the changes in the macrosystem and the microsystem, and that the most important influence on the formation of the young people's views was – overwhelmingly – the family. This might be the result of several factors. First, the great majority of Hungarian and Polish adolescents viewed themselves as members of a close and well-functioning family. Secondly, in contrast to adolescents growing up in Western Europe or in the United States, they did not view this stage in their lives as a time of presumed intergenerational conflict, nor did they think that the more independent their views were from their parents' the better. They repeated commonly heard phrases, and sometimes referred to specific expressions of their parents. Their emotional reactions to the changes were highly dependent upon the ways that their parents conveyed their feelings about the changes. This was true even among those who talked about some disagreements and arguments with their parents

Slomczynski *et al.*'s study in Poland confirmed the basic premise of this socialisation theory, namely that the family plays a pivotal role in shaping the value system of the new generation. They found a correlation between parental and offspring's values, for instance towards authoritarianism and conservatism. However, their results also pointed to the role of social status in defining attitudes towards the major socio-political changes in Poland: those who occupied higher positions in the stratification system of society and who were financially more successful are more open-minded and less distressed about the systemic changes than are others, and this is also so for their children.

Studies also show that, while historical transitions influence adolescents' psychosocial development, it is the family who screen what reaches the adolescents: the family functions as a kind of buffer (Van Hoorn *et al.*, 2000). Trommsdorff and Chakkarath (1996) found that a strong, emotionally based family which was child oriented, increased the resilience of East German children and adolescents during the dramatic transformation in the economic, political and social system following unification.

Interestingly, there are no studies that examine the role of teachers and their views in preparing adolescents for social change (see Trommsdorff, 2000) or the formation of their socio-political and economical views in the former socialist countries. Although nobody questions that teachers are part of the socialisation process (according to Bronfenbrenner they belong to the microsystem), they are still not considered to be significant adults in the research tradition of psychologists (rather than the research tradition of educationalists). There are studies that discuss the role of the family in defending adolescents from social change, such as Elder (1974) or Conger *et al.* (2000), and these discuss how economic hardship or pressure influences the adults in the family and the consequence of this for adolescent-age children. Transmission studies concentrate on interfamily transmission: for instance Van Hoorn's study carefully examined the roles of parents, peers and the media in the formation of socio-political attitudes of adolescents, but did not ask about teachers or school. There is a lack of studies, in spite of the common view that teachers, just like parents, can be role models and act as mediators or moderators of social change. Crockett and Silbereisen (2000) suggest that this may be because, under the socialist regime, schools were supposed to be responsible for socialising children to be 'good citizens', and were required to instil values reflecting a 'socialist personality'. After the political changes, however, personality development became the almost exclusive province of the family, and the role of schools was rather limited to teaching cognitive skills. Therefore schools are afraid to 'impose' their own views on students, as this is not considered to be democratic (Davies, *et al.*, 2001). Teachers are also somewhat reluctant to convey and teach concepts related to politics and economics, because they do not feel prepared to teach students about the changing political-economic system that they are also living through. Another explanation might be that the traditional socialising institutions of society, such as schools, are by definition not accustomed to dealing with systemic change. Structural changes did not reach the educational system quickly or deeply enough, and this left the educational system unable to take the lead in socialising students to the rules of the 'new world', and left this role for the family. This has caused a serious fall in the (relative) value attributed to educators, teachers and the entire system of education, which has been further pushed down the slope by decreases in funding because of the very high costs of transition. Teachers, once highly prestigious members of the socialist society, have become unable to prepare the students for the new rules, since they themselves were not prepared for them.

For teachers, the political changes did not bring new opportunities: instead, their social status and financial situation have worsened. They experienced a great deal of stress in their professional lives. Teachers' salaries suddenly became relatively much less than other highly educated people (in Poland, about 50 per cent of the government workers are teachers). These changes undoubtedly affect teachers' perception of the political changes, because an individual's location within the social structure exercises an impact on their psychological functioning, and affects what and how they will think and feel about society. Slomczynski *et al.* found that it was largely the personal-level economic success that determined the degree of support given to systemic change: thus teachers, who consider themselves as the economically most unsuccessful amongst the highly educated, are in a difficult situation.

Students' and teachers' perception of the role of competition in present day Hungary

To study perceptions of competition can be relevant for several reasons. Firstly, competition is an interdisciplinary concept, that can be conceived as a psychological, social, economical and also a political phenomenon. In the last decade, competition, previously an ideologically denied and banned phenomenon in Hungary, became highly required and praised at all levels of society, from politics to everyday individual life, in the former socialist countries (Fülöp, 1995). The very rapid transition at every level of Hungarian society required citizens to change their perception and understanding of competition, and also to alter their attitudes and values in connection with it.

Competition has been seen by many western experts to be not only the key for individual advancement but also necessary for national survival (Rich and DeVitis, 1992). The way that young people perceive and conceive competition is a meaningful topic of study, because their ideas represent the past, the present and also the future of competition in that society. The past is represented in what they carry on with themselves from their parents' and grandparents' views – generations undergoing major social-political changes – and from their society's historical characteristics. As adolescents and young adults are in a developmental phase when they are fast absorbing the 'world' around them, their ideas also reflect the present. The way young people construct the meaning of competition might also represent the future. Those who are now between 16 and 18 years old will actively form their own society. How they handle competition at the individual, interpersonal and group level, in the economy and in politics will influence not only their personal but their society's future too.

Ongoing political changes in the former socialist countries – the appearance of the market economy, unemployment and competition in the job market, the growing number of enterprises that require a competitive spirit, and so on, presents us a unique possibility of studying in what way and how ideological concepts change, appear and disappear in a society.

In the new, harshly competitive environment, characterised by scarce resources, there is a new and highly positive ideological attitude towards competition, but it seems that there is also total confusion about the personal and interpersonal and moral requirements and consequences that accompany it (Fülöp, 1995). This is partly because there have been no explicit and well-structured principles or rules to govern competition, and people have not been prepared for the emotional consequences of open competition. The transformation to market economies in former European socialist countries shifted the nature of the personal and social skills necessary for success. Being able to compete, to stand up after losing, and to withstand the stresses of competition are now essential in societies in transition. Young people need to realise that, in a society governed by the principle of competition, they can gain more and they can lose more, and that they have a greater individual responsibility for the result. The way in which they learn to cope with the new requirements of competition is of central importance.

There are relatively few studies in the psychological literature that aim to examine similarities and differences between the different concepts, views, beliefs or attitudes of students and teachers. Although competition and competitiveness have been studied excessively, in social psychology, educational psychology and personality psychology there have been no studies of how young people (the alpha-omega generation) and teachers (adults in middle age) in postsocialist societies construct the meaning of competition, of how they relate to competition, of how their ideas are related to their experiences with competition or of how these ideas are formed by the cultural-political socialisation process.

Perception of a social phenomenon is determined by several factors, such as the person's own experiences, the significance of that phenomenon in the person's life, personal interest, the perception of significant others, and information gained about it primarily from the media.

The following study is taken as an example of how different generations, teachers and their students view the same social phenomenon. It is part of a more comprehensive investigation of adolescents' and teachers' views on competition. It was conducted in 2000–2001 among Hungarian secondary school teachers and secondary school students.

Subjects participating in the research were secondary school students, aged 16 to 18, and secondary school teachers (mean age: 40.1). The two samples comprised 266 students and 150 teachers from different secondary schools in Hungary.

A questionnaire with open-ended questions was distributed among the students and the teachers asking partly overlapping questions about different aspects of competition:

- What do you think about competition in general?

- Do you like to compete? Please explain your answer

- What do you think about being competitive and being successful in Hungary?

Students and teachers gave free descriptions of their ideas, and content analysis of the answers revealed the dimensions that the students applied when thinking about a certain aspect of competition. In the following we give a general summary of the qualitative and quantitative analysis of answers given to the question: What kind of role does competition play in present day Hungary?

The respondents perceived the role competition plays in Hungarian society along five different dimensions:

1. the area of competition

2. the intensity of competition

3. the emotional evaluation of competition

4. its positive consequences

5. its negative consequences.

Several different categories were identified within these dimensions, and the students' and the teachers' response frequency was compared.

Area of competition

When describing the role of competition in their current societies, both students and teachers wrote about the areas where they saw competition as most prevalent. They mention altogether 14 different principal areas of competition, thus encompassing a wide variety of possible competitive processes. Teachers mention more areas than students, and the most frequently mentioned area is competition in the economy (business, industry, stock market, quality and price of goods). For students, it is competition for money that takes the first place. However this is also the second area for teachers. Both groups agree that '*Money is the most powerful incentive and the final goal in Hungarian society*'. This high rating of competition for money reflects the economic conditions of the country. Inglehart (1990) argues that if there is increased economic prosperity in the formative years of the individual (the years up to late adolescence), this leads to a higher fulfilment of basic needs which in turn leads to less materialist values in the younger generation. This argument thus suggests that rich families can be assumed to raise fewer materialistic young people than poorer families (Boehnke, 2001). The results of my study show that, in a society where the middle class is very narrow and the majority of the population have experienced a major worsening of their economic situation, competition for money remains an important area and is significantly more often mentioned than it is by students and teachers in much wealthier societies, such as Japan and America, where I have conducted comparative investigations (Fülöp, 1999).

In the previous political system a secure, full-time job was virtually guaranteed for everybody, so unemployment and competition for jobs was an unfamiliar scenario. Ten years after the political changes, students and teachers take the existence of the job market for granted, and accept that getting and keeping a job is not self-evident. This type of competition, for employment, is mentioned significantly more frequently by students than by teachers (students' third most frequent mention). Although the financial situation of teachers dramatically worsened after the political changes, teachers are rarely threatened by unemployment: competition for jobs is something they observe rather than experience themselves. However, competition for promotion, high status and leadership is mentioned significantly more frequently by teachers, as these are part of the everyday reality of their adult lives.

80

Competition in politics is also a new phenomenon, and a necessary part of democratic society. Both groups consider this an important and necessary form of competition, though they are rather disgusted by the manner and style of political parties' competition against each other.

Hungary's international role and position is significantly more important for students. They emphasise that Hungary must compete with the other big European countries to achieve a better position, and that if Hungary wants to join the European Union it must increase its achievement and perform better than the other former socialist countries.

Both students and teachers mention competition for sheer survival (for food, and shelter, for example) referring to the shocking increase in the rates of homelessness, and families living below the poverty line.

Education as an area of competition (over school grades, for college admittance, and so on) was only the seventh most frequently mentioned area by teachers and students. Competition in this area was seen as much more important in Japan and the United States when examined in a comparative study (Fülöp, 1999, 2001). The explanation of this is twofold. During the socialist period, education was one of those rare areas in society where there was already competition, as the school system was extremely selective and only 10 per cent of a given cohort could continue into higher education. Now almost 30 per cent of an age cohort enter higher education, and there are plenty of places for those who − although they cannot meet the expectations of the entrance exam − have the financial resources to pay for their studies. Thus exceptional achievement is no longer the prerequisite for getting a certificate in Hungary. The second explanation is that in the United States and Japan the educational system teaches the students 'the name of the game' in society: however, in Hungary schools and colleges do not do this, and accordingly education loses its importance as an area of competition.

Competition in sports, science, technology, the entertainment industry, and looks (beauty, clothing) are also mentioned, though very rarely.

The intensity or the prevalence of competition

Students and teachers refer to this dimension in five characteristic ways: very intensive, too intensive, growing in intensity, not intensive enough, losing its intensity. The students refer to the intensity of competition more frequently than do teachers, but the majority in both groups see competition in Hungary as generally very intensive, and say that competition plays an enormous role in society. Everybody is seen to compete with everybody in everything, and the competitive spirit permeates everything. Among the students there are more who explicitly say that the level of competition is still not enough and that it should be more intensive, while among the teachers there are more who reluctantly say that competition is still growing in intensity. Approximately the same proportion in both groups think that competition is too intensive and should be controlled.

Evaluation

Competition is a very important characteristic of socio-political change in Hungary, and one cannot be indifferent to how the future generation and their teachers evaluate its present social role. Competition can offer both risks and challenges. The results of competition are striking. Among the teachers, only 1 per cent considers the role competition plays in society as purely positive, and among the students only 16 per cent accept this. In contrast, more than half of the teachers and more than one-third of the students evaluate competition in purely negative terms. This suggests that competition is not highly appreciated among these groups, although the younger generation has a significantly less negative viewpoint than the adults. The biggest group among the students took a neutral, descriptive, and taken-for-granted approach to competition. The number of positive answers given by students was low, but still relatively higher than the response given by teachers. Almost a quarter of teachers combined both positive and negative opinions about competition, reflecting a more complex view, but this position was rather rare among the students.

Positive consequences of competition

The few respondents who consider competition to be positive, or to be both positive and negative, name eight different positive consequences.

1. Competition develops the country in general.
2. Competition aids the economy.
3. It helps innovation and technology.
4. Competition develops culture and civilisation.
5. Competition facilitates intellectual development.
6. It improves the self.
7. Competition develops motivation.
8. Competition serves the selection and survival of the fittest.

A paradoxical result is that while teachers generally had much more negative views of competition than students, those among them who had both positive and negative or purely positive opinions were much more specific about this, and mentioned more positive consequences than students.

Negative consequences of competition

Both groups elaborated at greater length on the negative consequences of competition than they had done on positive consequences. Those with negative views wrote more, and mentioned more negative aspects: both teachers and students appeared to be more aware of the negative aspects, teachers more so than students.

Respondents who rated competition negatively listed seven negative consequences. Most frequently mentioned by both teachers and students were the association between competition and:

- immorality
- aggression and interpersonal conflict
- pragmatic and money-oriented people.

Other aspects were increased stress, self-centredness (extreme individualism), discrimination (inequality, big gap between poor and rich, losers and winners), and the destruction of the country, though these four items were rated in a different order in each of the groups.

Immorality as a consequence of competition was most frequently mentioned by both groups: they wrote about corruption, bribery, fraud, theft, cheating, lying, misleading and misinforming others as a result of competition in both the political and the economic sphere. They saw this as leading to mistrust in politicians and businessmen, and explained that many people in Hungary had still not acquired the culture of competition. Society presently lacked well-functioning mechanisms or rules able to control uncontrolled competition.

There is evidence of social cynicism in the answers: some said that being honest and working hard do not lead to a better life and success in present day Hungary. Secondly, both groups mention aggression. Competition is considered to be cut-throat, a life and death question in which people don't hesitate to use aggressive means in order to win or achieve their goals. A picture of a very violent society evolves from the analysis of the answers. In terms of a free market economy. it is seen as something regulated only by jungle law, using the Darwinian metaphor. Thirdly, both students and teachers think that the result of the economic changes and free market economy is that people's central value has become money, and that most people are narrowly focused on earning enough or more of it, and are ready to use whatever means to gain bigger and bigger fortunes.

Summary

The free market economy is a fundamental condition of capitalism, and a pluralistic political system and free elections are core elements in the concept of democracy. Because of this, competition has become a key concept in those societies where these structural changes towards the free market and democracy have taken place. However, meaning is constructed within a given social and life context. The meaning of competition for Hungarian teachers and students, a decade after the political changes, is controversial; moreover, the socio-political changes have been experienced in different ways in the two generations. The teachers – essentially middle aged – see competition in society in a more detailed and complex way than their adolescent students. They mention more areas of competition, and have a deeper process of analysis of the positive and negative consequences of competition. Students have a generally more surface approach, referring to the areas and to the intensity of competition, but much less frequently to the social consequences of the competitive processes. This would require a more differentiated picture of the potential impacts of the competitive processes. Teachers appear to have better structured ideas about competition, and they evaluate it much more negatively. There does seem to be a generation gap in this area: the students have a more vague understanding, are more accepting and allow competition as a necessary requirement of society. But even the students, when compared to their Japanese and American counterparts who were born in a society with long-term market economy and democratic traditions, are alarmingly negative about the competition characteristic of the new capitalist society.

Despite these differences, there is also significant similarity between students' and teachers' answers: they construct the meaning of competition in present day Hungary in the same way. This similarity might be the result of socialisation/transmission/enculturation processes or of independent experiences in the same cultural-historical context and media representation.

Teachers' ideas on the role of the school in preparing students for future competition

There are two broad conceptions of the teacher's role, as 'the educator' and as 'the instructor'. Under socialism, the teachers' role was 'the educator of the socialist personality' – their role was to produce a certain type of person or citizen, while in the west the teacher's role was rather 'the instructor' (Trommsdorff, 1999). Teachers who previously had the task of socialising students and transmitting certain values to them might now hesitate to transmit their own perceptions, so that teachers might now, to a certain extent, be seen as non-adaptive to the new context.

With this consideration in mind, we asked the 150 Hungarian secondary school teachers (Fülöp, 2001) if they though that it was a task for the school to prepare children for forthcoming competition in life. This question was intended to reveal whether teachers saw their role as being a socialising agent, linked to the particular social-political-economical phenomenon of the systemic changes.

The overwhelming majority of teachers (92 per cent) thought that school should play an important and significant role in preparing students for competition in life. But most of them also saw this as a constraint that was connected to political changes. Reluctantly, they feel that a responsible teacher cannot do anything except help students adapt to a society in which competition is part of everyday reality. In contrast to this, a much smaller group see it as a good and important task to bring up competitively-minded people, and that this will lead to the improvement of society. Both groups emphasise that students should learn about constructive and ethical competition, so that they are able to withstand or overcome the immoral, aggressive and self-centred competition that presently characterises Hungarian society. To do this, students should learn to compete in a way that leads to their self-development and the recognition of their own strengths and weaknesses and of their comparative advantage, instead of the destruction of their rival. In other words, they should learn to work hard for their own aims and rely on their own achievements instead of blocking others who strive for the same aim. They also should learn the rules of fair play and keep to them. They should learn to cope with winning and losing. As winners they should feel sympathy with the losers and as losers they should be able to acknowledge and respect those who were more talented and skilful than themselves, and instead of giving up, should stand up and continue working hard to win next time. As competition frequently causes stress, students should also acquire a kind of routine and inner capacity to cope with stress.

However, when it comes to actual practice in schools, teachers do not think that current Hungarian schools prepare 'good' competitors for society, partly because teachers themselves were not socialised for an openly competitive world. They are also sceptical about whether the 'idealistic' values about competition in its protective environment that school *could* teach students about are resistant to the everyday immoral competition prevaling in Hungarian society. Those who do not adapt to the rules of cut-throat competition, yet still survive and succeed, belong to a rare and privileged minority. A dilemma emerges from the teachers' answers. If their axiom is that school should prepare students for reality, then short-term survival requires that students should be aggressive, immoral and tough in terms of competition in Hungary; but these are not characteristics a school can strive for. However, teaching to be moral and competing in a constructive way, relying on one's own hard work instead of illegal means – which are surely necessary in the long run – might be totally naive and idealistic in the present context. Teachers do not get any kind of professional training or support in this area: they have only a vague and rather confused idea about the ways that a school might fulfil its task in connection with competition.

Chapter summary

The decline of the socialist governments in Central and Eastern Europe, and the resulting political and economic reorganisations of the 1990s, provided a dramatic illustration of the far-reaching effects of social change (Crockett, Silbereisen, 2000). How this affects young people has important implications for our future in a global community, because the youth of today become the adults of to-morrow. The transition to a democratic society requires that so-called omega-alpha generation (Van Hoorn *et al.*, 2000) grow into adults who trust in democratic processes and who work to create trustworthy governments – and do not grow into socially cynical and disappointed young people, full of mistrust towards social institutions and processes. This is particularly important, because the initial excitement about transitions has been replaced by cynicism: democracy and the market economy were not instant successes.

Parents and teachers play a significant role in shaping the way of thinking of the present day young people who are also experiencing significant changes in their life. In other words, if these young people are to grow up to enable their societies to become more democratic, then their families and teachers are likewise challenged to develop a democratic identity. It seems that schools and teachers in their present status are not adequately prepared to help the younger generation to meet the requirements of the new social system, for instance how to compete for better social status. Therefore the family will have to take up this role, and this will cause a strong social reproduction: parents who know how to do it and who are successful in the new system will have children who are also successful, while parents who have difficulties in adapting to the new system will have children who also don't have a chance to learn how to adapt in their education.

Note

1   The studies reported in this chapter have been supported by grants received from the Johann Jacobs Foundation and the Hungarian National Research Fund (No. T 029876). Special thanks go to Mihály Berkics for the statistical analysis of the data.

5

Children's understanding of society: psychological studies and their educational implications

Anna Emilia Berti

*Department of Developmental Psychology and Socialisation,
University of Padua, Italy*

A n understanding of society has been recognised as a major component of adults' general knowledge (Carey, 1985; Wellman, 1990), and a major target of schooling in democratic societies (Ahier and Ross, 1995). However, the study of its antecedents in childhood and the processes promoting its improvement has never been a major concern for developmental and educational psychologists, who have mainly focused on children's conceptions of the physical and natural world, people and interpersonal relations, and spatial and arithmetic knowledge. Studies concerning children's understanding of society are therefore at the fringe of mainstream research on cognitive and social development, and education.

In this chapter I present first the main approaches within which studies on children's understanding of society have been carried out. Then the developmental course of children's understanding of society will be outlined by summarising data collected mainly (but not exclusively) in western societies within those approaches. I will focus on political notions, only touching on economic notions about which thorough reviews are already available (Berti and Bombi, 1988; Lunt and Furnham 1996). After highlighting how these data can be interpreted differently according to different theoretical frameworks, I will discuss the theoretical and practical significance of some intervention studies on teaching economic and political notions.

Different approaches to children's views of society
Studies on 'political socialisation'
Interest in children's views of society was first stimulated among American political scientists, rather than psychologists. It was political scientists who, from the late fifties to the early seventies, promoted studies on 'political socialisation', on the assumption that values and attitudes underlying adults' political behaviour develop during childhood and remain reasonably stable through life (Dennis, 1985). However, due to their focus on attitudes rather than on knowledge, these studies have provided a fairly modest contribution to our understanding of children's notions of society. Further, in keeping with a behaviourist view, these studies were aimed at testing the extent to which children had internalised the values necessary for the stability of the political system, rather than at examining their conceptions (Haste and Torney-Purta, 1992). The view of a passive and receptive child, gradually moulded by various socialisation agencies, such as family, school, peers, and television, suggested examining (seldom with univocal results) the correspondence between parents' and children's party choice, teachers' and students' attitudes, and the assessment of the influence of different socio-cultural variables, such as ethnic group, socio-economic status, and sex (Gallatin, 1980). Due to the large number of participants required to control these variables, the method most often used was a large survey with written questionnaires, which prevented both a thorough examination of children's understanding and the involvement of children younger than eight to nine years.

Although based on different assumptions, European studies conducted within the framework of the social representation approach have also stressed the importance of socio-cultural variables, thus sharing the same focus as the mainstream political socialisation approach (see Emler and Dickinson, 1985; Emler, Ohana and Moscovici, 1987).

Cognitive-developmental studies

From the 1970s to 1980s, some cognitive-developmental studies on children's understanding of society were also published (for example Adelson and O'Neil 1966; Berti and Bombi, 1988; Connell, 1971; Furth, 1980; Jahoda, 1979, 1981; Moore, *et al.*, 1985; Stevens, 1982). The cognitive-developmental approach, inspired by Piagetian theory, posits that children develop through a stage-wise sequence, where each stage (sensory-motor, pre-operational, concrete operational, formal operational) is characterised by general, across-the-board, logical structures, which affect children's thinking and performance in different domains, such as their interaction with peers and adults, and their construction of physical, social and psychological phenomena. Followers of this approach therefore aimed to identify stages of economic and political understanding based on, and secondary to, Piagetian stages.

Piaget himself paved the way for investigating children's societal understanding in the 1920s with a pioneering exploration of the concept of nation (Piaget, 1924), and three decades later with a more systematic investigation of the notions of motherland and foreigner (Piaget and Weil 1951) involving children from five to twelve years. However, while studies on economic understanding (reviewed in Berti and Bombi, 1988) consider a wide age range, those on political understanding, apart from few exceptions (Connell, 1971; Jahoda, 1964; Berti, 1988; Amann-Gainotti, 1984), have focussed on adolescence (Gallatin, 1980). This is coherent with Piaget's view that only during adolescence do children start becoming involved in adult society and interested in understanding institutions and ideologies. This is seen as a consequence of the fact that they now consider themselves as similar to adults, and their mastering of formal operational thinking which, according to Piaget, is a necessary prerequisite for dealing with the complexities of social institutions and ideals (Piaget and Inhelder, 1969).

The domain-specific approach to cognitive development and education

Apart from studies by myself and my colleagues, reviewed below, very few studies have been carried out within the most recent approach to cognitive development, the domain-specific approach, which nowadays has a leading role in educational and developmental research (for instance, Leiser, 1983; Siegler and Thompson, 1998; Torney-Purta, 1994). Whereas in Piaget's theory children develop a limited number of across-the-board logical abilities, which set the ground for understanding specific notions, in the domain-specific approach children develop a number of largely independent theory-like conceptual structures (see Wellman and Gelman,1998). As with the social representation and political socialisation approaches, the domain-specific approach gives a pivotal role to relevant information, thus *allowing childrens' conceptions not to be constrained* to one developmental sequence: different paths might emerge, according to different motivations, experiences and opportunities to acquire relevant and understandable information. But unlike them, it also stresses that children's concepts are interconnected, showing how the interpretation, of new information is constrained by conceptions already possessed, and how changes in some concepts affect other related concepts (for example: Vosniadou 1991; Duit 1999).

Studies based on the domain-specific approach have largely concentrated on few conceptual domains, such as naive psychology, biology, physics and arithmetic, thus showing how this approach relies on the Piagetian legacy. Developmental psychologists have mainly studied infants and pre-school children, wondering what domain-specific knowledge they possess and to what extent it is channelled by innate constraints (Wellman and Gelman, 1998). Educational psychologists have focused on the relations between students' conceptions and the scientific theories taught at school, examining how the former could hinder or help acquisition of the latter. These studies have shown that young children also possess coherent conceptions, and that at all ages students are resistant to abandoning their beliefs, even when utterly wrong. Often they never acquire or they misinterpret scientific notions taught in class, or revert to them after leaving school (Duit, 1999). These results have led some scholars (for example: Carey, 1985) to suggest that similar processes intervene in children's cognitive development and in the history of science. In both cases there are different degrees of change, from accretion or enrichment to the restructuring of a cognitive domain. Restructuring, involving a deep revision of previous conceptions, is parallel to a scientific revolution, and takes a long time (even years) to occur, or may not occur at all.

Children's understanding of society

Cross-sectional studies of children's understanding of society can be summarised in the four-step sequence set out below. As in most descriptions of level sequences, ages are used to represent rough averages, and substantial variations must be allowed for.

No understanding of societal institutions (pre-school years)

Before the age of about six there is no understanding of economic and political institutions. Lacking the prerequisite arithmetical knowledge, children do not understand the value of money and how money is used in buying and selling (Berti and Bombi, 1988). Further, they do not differentiate between activities related to occupational roles and the activities that people perform because they feel like it. For instance, according to children, the police catch criminals because they want to (Berti and Benesso, 1998, Study 1); bus-drivers drive buses so that people don't have to go on foot (Berti and Bombi, 1988); teachers can either chose to stay at home, or go to school because children have to learn, not because it is their job (Tallandini and Valentini, 1995). Although children are generally aware that their parents make money by working, they also think that money is lavishly distributed by banks or is obtained as the change given by shopkeepers. Lastly, children of this age do not yet distinguish politicians from other important people appearing on television, thus not showing the vaguest idea of a political world (Connell, 1971).

The beginning of economic understanding (six to eight years)

Understanding of societal institutions begins around the age of six to seven years, with a better comprehension of the value and function of money, and an awareness that people perform certain activities because these are their jobs, permitting them to earn a living. Children now also represent banks as places where people deposit their money to protect it from thieves, rather than as sources of money. At first children do not have the notion of an employee. They describe all, or most people, public servants included, as self-employed, that is as owning the means of production they use (for example, workers own the factory, bus drivers own the buses) and being paid by their customers (for example, teachers by their pupil's parents; bus drivers by passengers. Berti and Bombi, 1988; Tallandini and Valentini, 1995). In this way children appear not to differentiate public institutions from private ones. Further, they do not know what the law is, or do not distinguish laws from other kinds of social rules. However, they think that serious infringements, such as murder or theft are punished with imprisonment, the duration of which is decided by the police (Berti, Guarnaccia and Lattuada, 1997).

Further development of economic knowledge, without knowledge of the State (eight to ten years)

Around eight years of age, two notions fundamental to the understanding of both economic and political systems emerge: the notions of a boss/owner, who owns a factory or business, gives orders and makes payments, and of an employee. At first children mention several sources of the money owners use to pay their employees, such as getting it from their own job, or from banks, Local Council, Government or even from employees who must pay in order to be hired. Not until the age of ten to eleven years do children realise that bosses pay their employees with the money acquired from the sale of goods or services produced by their work, and that retail prices must be higher than wholesale prices for shopkeepers to make a living (Berti and Bombi, 1988; Furth, 1980; Jahoda, 1979).

Although sometimes mentioning political role and institutions, such as mayor, president, local council and government, at this age children do not yet distinguish bosses, who are politicians, from other kinds of bosses, such as the owners of factories and businesses, representing both as giving orders personally. They also believe, for instance, that both a factory-owner and the mayor or president have achieved their position thanks to their wealth or career (Berti and Bombi, 1988). Nor do they distinguish between different political roles, such as premier, mayor, or the queen (Connell, 1971).

Several converging data testify that from eight to ten years a naive politics, with the notion of the *state* as its kernel, has not yet emerged, although children already possess some notions necessary for its construction. At eight to ten years children define the state in terms of a territory and the people who inhabit it, without mentioning law or government. They construe borders only in geographical terms (for example as mountains, coastlines or rivers) or in physical terms (for example as walls, moats and palisades) and do not know what a country or capital city is (Berti and Benesso, 1998; Delval, 1994). They decode the words *union* and *separation* as found in political contexts (such as the union of ancient Egyptian villages into a kingdom; the separation of Croatia from Yugoslavia) in physical or social terms only; that is as the construction of a single big village, or all the people moving to a single village, in the first case, and the construction of walls or moats, or some of the inhabitants moving away, in the second (Berti, 1994).

Coherent with these views, from eight to ten years war is depicted as a battle similar to those in westerns or other films, and simulated in children's games, without any large-scale organisation. Younger children attribute all decisions regarding starting, developing and ending a war to individual fighters. Older children attribute some decisions to fighters and others to political authorities such as *president, government* or *state*. In both cases, the reasons for starting a war are not given, or they are identified in emotions such as hatred, envy, revenge. On the other hand, the reasons for ending a war (when given) consist of the fighters being tired or no longer willing to fight. Wars either have no consequence for the losers, or result in their being killed, made slaves, or having their territory taken away by the winner (Berti and Vanni, 2000).

After eight to nine years children, at least in Italy, have some knowledge about the law, but it does not yet involve the notion of the state. They define laws as rules, or things that one must do, and mainly mention traffic laws and the prohibition of killing or stealing as examples. This early view of the law is that it is restrictive, as children mainly attribute to it the function of preventing disorder and crime. Italian children believe that laws are made by the police, the local council or by parents, who then make them known through television, notices or verbal communication (Berti, Guarnaccia and Lattuada, 1997). However, in an American study, children of the same age said that laws are made by the president (Moore *et al.,* 1985). Children at this age also know something about judges, to whom they attribute the task of deciding on guilt and punishment. However, they do not yet conceive them as public servants, mentioning only other judges or the people involved in a trial as those who pay the judge (Berti and Ugolini, 1998).

The emergence of a conceptual political domain (around eleven to twelve years)

The full emergence of a naive politics, at about eleven years, is shown by how children define the term *state* and construe processes in which states are involved, and how they represent individual political institutions and the roles involved. At around eleven to twelve children explicitly mention government or laws in their definitions of the notion of state (Berti and Benesso, 1998). They decode unite and separate in political terms, respectively describing the foundation of a centralised government and an independent local one, (Berti, 1994). They represent war as a clash between nation states, attributing decisions about starting and ending to political authorities, and the battle itself to an organised army having heads who, according to most children, collaborate with, or are subordinate to, political authorities. They describe the causes and consequences of war in terms of economic or political domination (Berti and Vanni, 2000).

At about eleven years, children distinguish between different political roles (such as mayor and premier) by assigning them different degrees of power and connecting them (although incorrectly) in a command hierarchy (for example the premier gives orders to the mayor: Connell, 1971). This allows children to conceive a state as a territory where a central power makes laws and its decisions reach the whole country, thanks to local authorities. Police, army, judges and teachers are now described as public servants, paid by taxes (Berti and Benesso, 1998; Berti and Ugolini 1998). Laws are seen as prohibitions and orders created to prevent disorder, and infringement is followed by punishment such as imprisonment or fines. Children do not yet know that the law regulates the most important relations between people, the working of the state and its supply of services. Thus the idea of law is still seen solely as restrictive (Adelson and O'Neil, 1966).

Further refinements of economic and political understanding
Between the ages of twelve and sixteen years there is a refinement of both economic and political understanding. Children distinguish between the owner of the means of production and the 'boss' who directs the workers, and between a private owner and a public institution. They understand that the former pays employees with the money earned from selling the goods or services produced by the business, the latter through money raised through taxation (Berti and Bombi, 1988). Children also know about bank interest, although only a minority understand how a bank makes a profit through the difference between deposit and loan interest (Jahoda, 1981). In the political domain, children recognise different types of government, such as republic, monarchy and dictatorship (Agazzi and Berti, 1995); they begin to understand ideologies and their relation to social classes and parties (Connell, 1971). Their view of the law includes regulative as well as restrictive functions (Adelson and O'Neil, 1966; Tapp and Kohlberg, 1977), and they now know that judges are public servants and also assign them the task of settling civil claims (Berti, Mancaruso and Zanon, 1998).

97

Understanding particularly salient societal notions.

Few cross-cultural comparisons have been carried out on societal knowledge. In the economic field, Scottish children's understanding of banking (Jahoda 1981) has been compared with Dutch (Jahoda and Woerdernbagch, 1982) and Hong Kong children (Ng, 1983). Although the same sequence has been found in the three countries, children appeared to progress at a different rate, Dutch and Hong Kong children being more advanced than the Scots. This difference has been interpreted as due to the greater importance and availability of information about banking in the Netherlands and in the business ethos characteristic of Hong Kong, which also influences economic socialisation. A large-scale survey of children's economic understanding, carried out in European (Austria, Denmark, Finland, France, Norway, Poland, West Germany and Yugoslavia) and non-European (Algeria, Israel) countries, showed a clear age-related progression, while the differences between the countries were harder to interpret (Leiser *et al.*, 1990).

In the political field, to my knowledge, there are no cross-cultural comparisons of children's cognition, although the evidence available suggests that noticeable age-related differences occur even when historical conditions or specific events make certain political institutions or processes particularly salient or emotionally involving.

The Gulf War was a very important current issue for Italians, who were participating in a war for the first time since the end of World War II. However, although Italian children from first to eighth grades, interviewed a few months after its end, did know that a war had occurred, only fifth and eighth graders knew about Iraq's annexation of Kuwait (involving the latter being ruled by the former). Third graders said at most that Saddam Hussein had tried to take over oil deposits or territory (Berti 1994). Further, Italian children from the same grades appeared to know very little about the role of the public prosecutor, although interviewed in a period when magistrates had become very prominent as a consequence of the 'clean hands' investigation. Almost nobody knew what the term *public prosecutor* meant. In addition, although all children from the age of

98

eight years had heard about Antonio Di Pietro (a public prosecutor who was regarded as a national hero at the time), only from the age of 14 years did a majority of them attribute to him the task of making charges or conducting an investigation, while others misinterpreted his role (Berti and Ugolini, 1998).

Australian children from five or six to sixteen years, interviewed about the Vietnam War while their country was participating in it, had nearly all heard of it (many had relatives or neighbours who had been conscripted, been wounded in the war, or died). However, younger children represented the war as a conflict between 'goodies' and 'baddies', and only adolescents showed an understanding of ideologies (Connell, 1971). Many Northern Ireland children at the age of six did not acknowledge a conflict in their country and only a minority of them described the fighters as belonging to two different factions (Sani et al., 2000).

Interesting age-related differences were also observed in young Mexican children from an Amerindian community who had been fighting for years against the government, which was supporting a project (the construction of a golf club, several hotels and hundreds of luxury houses) which would have radically changed the economy and tradition of the area (Corona, 1999). The conflict between local and national political institutions was very salient, and children (from primary school on) participated in all resistance activities of the community (such as assemblies, marches, and demonstrations in front of the Senate). However, although at all ages children understood that the use of their land was at stake, they showed different conceptions of the actors involved, depending on age. For first graders, people from far away, such as the Italians and Chinese, wanted to take their water and fell their trees. From third grade on, children said that the government was involved, and described various ways to make the community's point of views heard, such as marches, sending letters, attending the Congress. However, third graders depicted the government as comprising rich and bad men, thus showing a simplified version of the view of the political structure as very corrupt, which was a widespread view among adult members of the community. From sixth to eighth grade, children focused on the representativity of the government and its relations with the electorate.

Where children's misunderstandings come from and how to prevent or direct them

Scholars who have investigated children's political understanding from a Piagetian perspective mainly related the conceptions found at a certain age to general stage-dependent characteristics, such as the ability to perform concrete or formal logical operations. For instance, according to Adelson and O'Neil:

> When we examine the interviews of eleven years-olds, we are immediately struck by the common, pervasive incapacity to speak from a coherent view of the political order. Looking more closely, we find that this failure has two clear sources: First, these children are, in Piaget's sense, egocentric, in that they cannot transcend a purely personal approach to matters which require a socio-centric perspective. Second, they treat political issues in a concrete fashion and cannot manage the requisite abstractness of attitude (1996, p.297).

From a domain specific view, children's conceptions are seen instead as the result of an interaction between the type and organisation of information generally available to children of a certain age in a society, thanks to television, school and adults' talk, and the 'naive theories' present at that age which constrain the interpretation of this information. Rather than reflecting across-the-board logical operations, misconceptions arise when children's theories cannot fill the gaps in their information, and they necessarily turn to inappropriate analogies and generalisations.

For instance, the idea that the owners of factories, banks, and buses get the money to pay employees from their own job, found in many eight- to ten-year-olds (Berti and Bombi, 1988), originates with an inference from a correct belief, developed at the age of about six or seven: people work to earn money. The idea that activities performed in the execution of professional duties are motivated by desire, taste, or other personal factors, widespread at four to five years, is likely to be the only available explanation of those activities for children who do not yet have the notion of an occupational role with formally defined obligations. When children do not have an idea of the hierarchical organisation of the state, they cannot differentiate between public servants, such as teachers and police, and other employees. If children are not explicitly taught that the law also has the function of organising and regulating, and the judge the task of enforcing it, they are bound to assign them the function most frequently popularised by news and films, that is defence against crime.

The prominence of societal events and institutions (as in the cases described above) is not sufficient, in the absence of the prerequisite knowledge, to promote children's understanding of the corresponding concepts. Societal institutions are made up of rules and of nested organisations involving complex sets of roles, of which neither the totality nor the significant parts are accessible to direct experience. They can only be described by a complex network of propositions: a type of discourse unlikely to occur unless somebody is intentionally instructing somebody else.

The Piagetian and domain-specific approaches are also in disagreement about the extent to which didactic intervention can promote children's conceptions. In the Piagetian approach, the acquisition of complex conceptual structures relies on developing underlying logical operations which cannot be accelerated through instruction (Inhelder *et al.*, 1974). In the domain-specific approach there are two views of cognitive development and learning. The first sees them as consisting of accretional transformations, such as the addition of concepts, rules and beliefs, and the links between them – and possibly deleting or forgetting those previously held – thus taking place gradually and in a piecemeal fashion (Chi, 1988). This view allows for great advances to be promoted through didactic interventions, if the target notions can be presented through a sequence of steps and the wrong beliefs are challenged. The second view sees cognitive development and learning as also involving radical restructuring, similar to scientific revolutions, and brought about by mental operations different from those involved in accretional-type cognitive changes (Carey, 1985). This view would predict that interventions aimed at producing large and deep changes would meet strong resistance.

Intervention studies on societal understanding

The few intervention studies in which children have been taught some political and economic notions, have shown that erroneous ideas can be successfully transformed through interventions lasting from one to several hours, depending on the age of the children, their possession of prerequisite knowledge or skills, and the quantity and complexity of the notions taught.

For instance, a single lesson of an hour on the notion of a shopkeeper's profit was differentially effective for third graders, depending on their ability to understand that if each commodity is sold for the same amount that has been paid for it, then the total expenses and revenue must also be equal (Berti, 1992). It took only a couple of hours to teach fifth graders the notion of bank interest and bank profit (Berti, 1999), while it took much longer to teach these notions to third graders: they believed that each person's deposits were kept separately, that money for loans came from different sources, and did not know about interest (Berti and Monaci, 1998). The curriculum for third graders also covered several other topics (such as cheques, automatic tellers, the difference between current and savings accounts), which is one of the reasons why it took much longer. Another reason was that, unlike the fifth graders, third graders needed considerable exercise in arithmetic to be able to understand the notion of interest, and several units had to be devoted to this task.

Other studies on the teaching of economic notions have also highlighted noticeable progress. They have shown that successful learning takes place when children's preconceptions are challenged and when all the necessary information is provided gradually in a supportive learning environment and through the promotion of active participation (Ajello et al., 1986, 1987; Kourilsky and Carlson, 1996). Correspondingly, failure in learning appears to be due to a poor fit between children's previous knowledge and the information made available to them at school (Berti, 1991).

In the political field, third graders were successfully taught several interconnected notions (law, state, the main Italian political offices, the working of the school system and the role of the judge). Before the intervention, children appeared on the one hand to have no conceptions (either correct or incorrect) of political organisation, and on the other to have misconceptions of those social institutions, such as school and police, of which they do have direct experience, while being unaware of the wider system in which the institutions are embedded (Berti and Andriolo, in press). At post- and delayed posttests, one and ten months after the intervention, children knew that a state is a territory where particular laws, made by parliament, apply, and that the enforcement of these is provided for by the government using money obtained through taxes to pay the employees involved, such as teachers, police and judges. On the whole, these children showed knowledge of the target topics similar to, or even higher than, those found in other studies of thirteen- to fourteen-year-old Italian children (Berti and Ugolini, 1998; Tallandini and Valentini, 1995).

Theoretical implications of intervention studies

The intervention studies on banking described above (Berti and Monaci, 1998) and political notions (Berti and Andriolo, in press) also included delayed post-tests, several months later. They showed very few changes in both the experimental group, whose progress was very stable, and the control group. Generally, changes in the control group were of a rather trivial accretional type, consisting of the addition of isolated information. In the case of banking, children became more knowledgeable about the fact that the source of money to pay cheques is from the deposit of the person who pays it, and that banks can lend money. In the case of political notions, more children knew the name of the capital of Italy, and the existence of Parliament, without understanding what a capital city is, or what the tasks of, and means of appointing Parliament are.

Cross-sectional studies of children's conception of both the natural and social worlds usually show a distance of years between the most mistaken conceptions and the more correct ones. This has led followers of the Piagetian view, and those who draw the parallel between cognitive development and scientific revolution, to assume that

- a long time is needed for children's conceptions to progress

- this length of time is evidence of the operation of intrinsic constraints on learning, due to the fact that the necessary logical structures have not yet emerged, or that a type of cognitive change, similar to scientific revolution, is involved.

However, the significant and stable progress made by the experimental groups in the above interventions, compared with the limited change found in the control groups, suggests that what cross-sectional studies of societal understanding highlight is the slow progress of children who have had little opportunity to obtain relevant information, or to be involved in significant experiences concerning the target notion, rather than the operation of intrinsic constraints on learning. Major changes in children's conceptions appear to involve neither the emergence of new logical structures, nor the activity of special mental operations, but to be the end result of a long series of the same type of mental operations underlying accretional-type cognitive changes.

Didactic implications of intervention studies

We have seen above that a good fit between children's previous knowledge and the information made available to them at school results in deep and long lasting advances. Unfortunately, in the field of economic and political education such a fit does not often occur.

An analysis of the economic notions presented in a sample of Italian textbooks for third, fourth, and fifth grades has shown that, with only one exception, their authors had taken for granted that children already possessed substantial economic knowledge, by presenting superordinate concepts (such as industry, trade, services) without introducing the most basic ones (such as buying and selling, different types of work, employment and how it is financed, and banking). In general, these books did not try to challenge misconceptions or to fill gaps that might have been expected at the different grades, according to the literature (Berti and Ferruta, 1999). A great discrepancy has also been found between political notions, taken for granted by the authors of text books on social studies (Beck *et al.*, 1989) and history (Berti, 1994), and the knowledge that children actually possess. This may be the origin of some of the misunderstandings described above. Great changes in children's societal knowledge should therefore be expected from innovative school syllabi, textbooks and teaching – changes consisting not only in the acceleration of one developmental sequence, but possibly in the emergence of diverse sequences.

The studies reviewed make some suggestions for innovations of this nature, but most issues need much more research and pedagogical reflection. For instance, there is no doubt that schools should teach societal notions that are not usually taught, and that such an approach should allow for active participation by the children, by interviewing holders of various societal roles, visiting business and institutions, and watching and discussing television programs and newspaper articles. What is much less clear is exactly when to teach particular notions.

For instance, at which grade should bank interest and profit be introduced? We have seen that at fifth grade this topic required only a couple of hours, while at third grade it needed a much longer intervention, part of which was devoted to arithmetic exercises. It may be questioned whether it is worth spending more time teaching a notion early, which could be taught more easily a few years later. On the other hand, teaching economic notions provides children with a meaningful context in which to practice arithmetic skills that would have to be practised in any case. Further, understanding a certain institution might facilitate understanding others, thus reducing the amount of time and effort required to learn about them. For instance, learning about banking in the fifth grade turned out to be related to children's understanding of payment of factory employees before the intervention (Berti, 1999).

A question related to this is when to teach children about the value of money and its use in buying and selling, which is a prerequisite for understanding the working of all modern economic exchanges. A curriculum on this topic was implemented in a first-grade class, with the twofold purpose of laying the ground for work on fundamental economic notions to be developed in the following years, and also of providing a meaningful context in which to practice arithmetic in the first-grade syllabus (Carbone, 2000). Although both aims were successfully fulfilled, the teaching required more time than had been anticipated (13 hours, spread over six weeks).

The dilemma, therefore, is whether to postpone the notions that depend on the mastery of arithmetic skills until those skills have been acquired, or to link social studies and arithmetic, using the former as a context that renders the latter richer and more meaning-ful. To resolve this dilemma, further intervention studies are necessary, aimed at assessing the effectiveness of the teaching of various economic notions at different grades, as well as its fallout on other notions, and its possible links with arithmetic and other disciplines.

This dilemma does not arise with political notions, which are inter-twined with history rather than with arithmetic. The curriculum on the notion of state mentioned above turned out to be very successful on the whole, although there were some shortcomings discussed in a paper in press (Berti and Andriolo). It appears well suited to third graders, and helped them cope with learning history, which in Italy currently introduces ancient history at this grade. Third-grade textbooks usually treat ancient history by mentioning different types of states (the Greek polis, Egyptian and Israeli kingdoms, the Assyrian empire, the Roman republic and empire) and use many terms to refer to political entities (such as state, kingdom and empire), offices (*government, king, pharaoh, senator,* and so on), and actions (*govern, conquer, subdue, form an alliance*) without any explicit explanations. Unrealistic assumptions about students' know-ledge of political institutions were also found in historical narratives presented in American social studies textbooks for the fifth grade by Beck and McKeown (1994), who documented the resulting mis-understandings.

106

This illustrates a general problem in the teaching of history. Unlike textbooks of nomothetic sciences (such as physics, chemistry, economics), in which key terms are introduced with explicit definitions and following a logical order that reproduces the hierarchical organisation of the conceptual framework of the discipline, history textbooks follow the chronological order of events and processes. The sociological, economic, and political concepts used are taken for granted and not treated explicitly. Learners therefore need to be taught about them in other contexts, which, as shown by Berti (1994) and Beck and McKeown (1994), has not always happened.

In conclusion, while arithmetic is a prerequisite for understanding several economic notions, economic and political notions lay the ground for understanding history. Planning and timing these subjects should be intertwined accordingly.

The knowledge of certain economic and political institutions and their workings, to which this chapter is devoted, although fundamental to understanding current political life and approaching the study of political history, is not sufficient for participation in the political system. Much more is involved, and must therefore be provided by the school: values such as tolerance and respect for human dignity; skills such as arguing, analysis of different sources of information, participatory decision making; and knowledge of the most important topics involved in political decisions (such as the economy and environmental issues). This is a vast task, that cannot be confined within a single subject. Although social studies can contribute to it, it requires the involvement of the whole school system.

6

Identity and pre-school education

Riitta Korhonen
University of Turku, Finland

Children participate in pre-school education at different ages in different countries in Europe. The legal age for starting pre-school can be from three to six years of age, depending on state legislation. So it is not possible to make simple statements about the pre-school child, because of this range of ages. For instance, in discussing children's readiness for various activities, or their level of thinking, the amount of time spent in the pre-school may vary considerably between children in different countries. There are also different cultural matters and behaviour found in different countries.

Erikson (1962) suggests that a child's personality develops in different stages and periods of time, and that environmental considerations are an important element in supporting this development. During the first year, a child needs security and care to build up their confidence. This is a critical and important stage for their future. At this point, a child has the possibilities of either trusting or not trusting other people. The next level, in the child's second year, is a growing independence. The child is both sure and unsure in his or her activities, and in her or his relationships to others. Erikson's next stage has the child showing initiative as well as feelings of guilt, at about three to five years of age. Finally is the activity stage, in which the child has experiences of both working hard and of failing: this period is from age six to twelve.

In all of this, developing values, ideas of their own identity and of internationalism, culture and tradition are important areas of education; children must learn both to know and accept themselves and also to understand others and the differences between people. How can they do this?

What is identity?

There are many synonyms or near synonyms for identity (oneself, I, the self, we, self-perception, self-image, self-representation or self-awareness, the ego, and so on). Identity is a central concept in social psychology: it probably could be considered as one of the main concepts of the field. Social and personal identities are different. The basis of the concepts of identities is that every individual is characterised by a series of social features, which demonstrate his or her membership of a particular group or category. Social identity is codified as that part of the self which concerns cognition that arises from social ecological positions (Deschamps and Devos, 1998, pp.1–2).

Identity also is about how each individual constructs or builds his or her personal self. Everybody has their own particular image of their self; there are general broad common characteristics, but variations in the individual details that make for differences and uniqueness. Individual identity is constructed from culture, language and in relationship to other people. It is not constructed from nothing, but is a social process. An identity is the essential element of what it is to be a human being. Sometimes it is difficult for a child to understand if he or she belongs to the girls' or boys' group and how he or she ought to behave or act and how they build their identity (Deschamps and Devos, 1998).

There are other concepts that are central to the notion of identity. Borba (1989 and 1993) and Aho (1996 and 2000) have both made models that described the various elements or parts of identity that contribute to self-esteem: these are security, selfhood, affiliation, mission and competency.

110

Self-esteem is described as being a part of the affective and evaluative self-image. Self-esteem and self-confidence have both affective and cognitive aspects. Borba and Aho's theory of self-esteem suggests that security is the basis for developing all the other areas. These others develop later, and there are similarities with Erikson's theory.

These theories of the development of identity all suggest that a child needs security, success and independence to develop and grow. As European societies have developed in the recent past, cultural differences in social identity have become more evident and pressing, and specialist approaches in cultural differences have developed. Teachers must now discover how children and their families from different cultural backgrounds and groups understand and appreciate particular characteristics, such as, for example, independence, self-motivation and what it means to be a good learner.

The changes in the societies of Europe in recent decades mean that there are now many differently expressed systems and regulations that constrain school and education systems and educational organisation and administration in different countries. The characteristics of different national identities bring more diverse views. It is not easy to say what is the right way to develop pre-school education. However, we can say that it is important to see the whole context of the child. The whole affects the all. One way to organise this whole-structure view is to examine what social environments there are around the child, and thus what are the key elements of the whole context in which he or she is living. There are many and various pressures to provide pre-school education. Despite all the varieties of different systems across different countries, there is a common or general idea that at least some group or social activities should be provided for children before the beginning of the official school years.

Pre-school curricula are very different, and every country has its own specific plans, regulations, laws and provision for these. But again, there are some universal elements: one of the most common parts is to provide possibilities to develop basic learning (Metais, 1999).

Contextualism and constructivism

When one compares the pre-school curricula of different countries, it is possible to note both consistencies and differences. The most common important features are that pre-school education should support and develop the mother tongue, should support thinking skills and encourage independent behaviour. In terms of learning practices, there is one very common feature now found in European pre-school education, which is often called child-centred education. This is generally understood as meaning that the child should be active and the subject of their own education, and that the role of the teacher should be to support and arrange the child's learning possibilities. In this situation teachers have an important responsibility. There is an alternative view of child-centred education, which is very different and not a professionally acceptable approach – that children can simply decide for themselves what they want to do or not, and how they do it. This is not real child-centred education: children cannot make choices alone or decide everything. In true child-centred education there are in practice many spoken 'half decisions', in which parents and teachers act as advisers, and offer suggestions, guidance and support to children (Hytönen, 1992).

The local circumstances of the child will bring their own constraints and possibilities to this. There are many situations where, for example, the child's physical condition and surroundings must create very different ways of centering the education on the child. If a child is living in the countryside, it may be impossible to walk alone to school because of the distance and the need for some protection along the way. Their ability and potential for independence is therefore different, though the child would have the necessary abilities and awareness. In city surroundings, a child will learn to do different tasks independently, and the reasons to act are different, and differently determined in view of the physical circumstances. Parents and institutional educators have to decide together what are their aims for the child. The child has the right to be cared for, and also the right to have the best possibilities to learn for their own personal needs. It is natural that the responsibilities for children are expressed in very different ways in different cultures.

We can compare how the enculturation of child-centred pre-school education is progressing in different countries. It is clear that it is in the society and community that a child learns, from what he or she sees and what kinds of experiences she or he has. Also of importance is that children can utilise the same fundamental origins to develop their social identity. The most important element for this is the family, a child's relatives, and the other immediate physical and social surroundings. With these, a child can build his or her owns understanding and ways of dealing with right and wrong, and can develop ethical and moral models. Those activities which it is expected or required that a child should do alone and independently are also expressed in different ways in different cultures.

One of the major theoretical disciplines that lie behind pre-school curricula, and on which they are based, is cognitive psychology; and the two significant models that are employed within this are contructivism and the contextual learning model.

Hujala *et al.* (1998, p.214) have described the learning process in pre-school education through a model of contextual learning that is shown diagrammatically in Figure 6.1.

Figure 6.1 shows the theoretical foundation of the learning process in childhood and pre-school education. The whole lived environment – home, pre-school and all the other social institutions around a child – is an important support in the learning process. The pedagogy of learning is integrated to this whole environment. Conceptualising learning and pedagogy in this way allows for the possibility for children to learn many different things and get and use experiences of the real social world in their development of their identity. This kind of model demonstrates the holistic nature of the child's learning and development. The most important thing, and the basis for all of a child's learning and life is that he or she has very good care and protection in his or her environment.

The successful provision of all these factors should guarantee a learning environment in which the child receives care, develops his or her self-confidence, and is allowed to develop her or his emotional life without disturbance. From the cultural point of view,

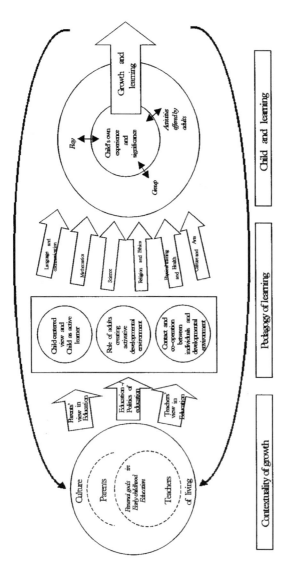

Figure 6. 1: The contextual view of learning process in the pre-school: the model created by Hujala *et al.* (1998, p.201).

creating this kind of learning environment gives the child the probability of coming to know his or her own culture, and of being able to identify with it. Educated with reference to their own culture, children can learn together the social rules, and create with each other their own play and social culture. The responsibility of teachers and parents is thus to arrange activities and provide good learning environments for the children. While child-centred education is good, teachers need to recognise that what must be achieved is good balance between child-centred and teacher-directed education. The plan for pre-school curriculum in Finland is based on the idea of integrated subjects, in which there are not different subjects but only learning and development areas. These are the educational goals of daycare and pre-school education, which lie behind everything. There is both caring and learning in the daycare system, and Hujala *et al.* (1998, p.4) call this combination 'educare'.

The curricula for pre-school education are integrated so, that all of the important factors and subjects are included within the curriculum. The underlying idea is that some topics are included which allow children to have the possibility of acquiring experiences and different kinds of learning activities. In planning this there should be present at least two very important elements. The first is that the theme must be used to adapt the contents; and the other is that all learning is seen as continuous, and that it goes from the concrete level to the abstract level. One of the most important areas must be social connections and social development (Hytönen, 1992).

The goals of early childhood education are in generally very similar in many countries, and they include due emphasis on physical, social, emotional, aesthetic, cognitive, ethical and religious education (Metais, 1999).

How should we develop the curriculum, to make it suitable particularly for children who are in pre-school education? We ought to be able to make it support and increase children's motivation for learning, and support their natural development in language, social skills, thinking, and so on.

Developing the child's identity in the pre-school group

School institutions are rather autonomic, and each has its own meaningful features, which are used only in the world of school. There are certain values and identities that are exclusively for schools, and these vary considerably. Institutions of this kind tend to be open and in contact with a large cultural, social and symbolic environment. The context is of a nation, laws, common opinions, professionals and so on: and on the bottom of these are built our own system for schools (Deschamps and Devos, 1998).

There are practical levels and rules found in every educational institution and schools and pupils must comply with them very careful if they are to achieve respect and establish their place in that community.

This applies just as much in the pre-school: they have their own unique practices for everyday activities, such as conventions, manners for eating, rules for taking part in outdoor activities, and so on. Children and their families must know about and accept these. We may ask if these rules and manners are necessary and essential for children's development, and especially if they contribute to children's development of identity. Certainly, the written curriculum, found in all countries, is the most important determining element. But this is not sufficient in itself: the way the teachers and the other staff implement the curriculum and carry out the daily running of the class is also very important. The climate that is established in the pre-school, both for the individual and for the whole group, is of key importance. Some of these rules might not be in the children's best interests; perhaps, for example, they might be made to wait too long for their turn to do something, or they might be required to keep silent for too long – both these situations could be in opposition to the culture of the child's own home life. In situations such as these, children will not be able to feel that they are successful. These practical considerations of organisation might be determined by a shortage of space or of staff. These aspects must be looked at critically, and teachers need to be aware of the consequences of them. Shortages of staff or of toys, for example, can give rise to damaging competition, or other negative outcomes, and these in turn can construct a poor self-image in the child, and mean that the child can develop an oppositional view of social rules. Teachers can and must control these organisational aspects. (Holt, 1996; Hujala *et al.*, 1998).

In good examples of pre-school environments, the children's social arrangements become the place where they learn social behaviour and co-operation with their peers. They can find their place and develop roles for themselves in a positive way, and this is an important part of the way each of them builds their own identity: through getting feedback from others, one develops a realistic idea about oneself. Pre-school children may be together physically for many hours a day, and during the pre-school year they will spend a long time together, so the influence of other children and of the teachers is comparatively large. The learning environment in the pre-school time can be good for all children, and to use this well, cooperation with homes, parents and the future primary school teachers will be necessary.

The successful achievement of all this demands considering a range of views, and then reflecting on and making positive evaluations around the following five aspects:

- the children's abilities and awareness of group activities, and their level of social development

- the culture of the families, and all the other factors that are 'behind the child' – the understanding and utilisation of this is part of the agreement that is achieved between the pre-school and the child's parents

- the teacher's abilities and readiness to see and act with the child's culture, and to create – with this in mind – a good learning environment for the child

- good planning and the development of appropriate methods in teaching and learning

- the use of critical argument and thought in developing new activities.

Young children do have not strategies for protecting themselves from developing unfavourable aspects of their identity. A young child does not get to choose the important partners who will influence his or her identity, such as parents, family or teachers. These partners' attitudes and thoughts will influence the child's own attitudes and their definition of their identity. A child will thus learn to feel and behave in the same way as those others that they learn with, and learn to act in the same way towards those from different nations, ethnic or cultural groups. If a child's nationality or background is different from that of his or her teacher, and from that of the other children in the class, then there are two possibilities – one very good, and one the opposite. A child can tell if he or she is accepted and loved or not. If a child, through such rejection, becomes ashamed in some way for a part of his or her own culture and identity, if he or she feels that the society of which he or she is part does not accept them, then they will try to abandon that identity very soon and to change it. This conflict in the child's mind leads to stress and identity confusion. (Deschamps and Devos, 1998; Harrison, 2001; Hujala et al., 1998.)

It is usual that there are children from minorities who would like to be integrated into the majority culture, but this is a question more of merging than of integration. There are important questions to ask about what are the child's rights to build his or her identity in peace. In these situations it is necessary that teachers talk with the parents and make compromises.

The role of the pre-school group and the company of other children of the same age are critical in children's social development. This kind of learning environment gives children the opportunity to play and talk together, and be together in many ways – learning co-operatively, working together in different groups on different activities.

There is a wide range of developmental areas in which it is good for children to be learning together; this way they become altruistic, and help and share with each other. These qualities, and many other important features, must be learned during the early years. Only during these early years do children have the possibility of learning them in natural ways, through everyday unstructured activities. Teachers must recognise that this is important, and they must arrange activities for children that provide such a learning environment.

Many researchers suggest that the single most important factor in daycare and pre-school development are the educators and the teachers. The success or failure of teaching or daycare education is dependent on their personality and their relationships to the children and their education. The second most important factor or resource is the social relationship between the children: the peer group itself is an agent of socialisation. Pre-school settings offer the company of other children and thus each child has the opportunity to learn to live together, and to learn and develop the social talents which define human social behaviour. Trying to teach social behaviour in large groups becomes self-defeating. Research shows that children can become overburdened if they have to deal with too great a number of social relationships. It is also very difficult for the educators to try to keep up with oversized groups. The peer group of a toddler is very important in the development of his or her own identity.

Play is also fundamental. Children learn about social life and become acquainted with the world through playing. Children find their own place in the community, and can test their abilities in relations with other children through play. This is one of the basic activities of pre-school pedagogy, and staff who are well trained in managing play can help children realise their potential identity and develop their social skills through play activities.

Conclusion

Teachers' tasks are changing though the basic activities and responsibilities are the same as before. Change always demands flexibility, awareness and development to meet new demands. Nowadays it is commonplace to remark that schools must change because society is in a state of continuous change. The development of new technology and of new learning environments opens up new possibilities. Changes in the content of knowledge also now affect the processes of learning. A teacher needs to interact with the new environment to find the appropriate and best methods and strategies (Harrison, 2001) The discussion is now focused on how far teaching should follow the new technology and its demands, and the extent to which tradition and old values must be preserved. These are key and important questions for education. For what kind of world must children be ready in the future? What must they know and be able to do? How can we support children's development of identity and self-confidence in early years and in pre-school with such new futures?

Teachers and parents need to develop this sort of idea, and they have to think through what is best for children, and from this they will have control over the learning situation. Questions arise, such as: what are children's basic needs for feeling safe and secure in their identity nowadays? It is essential that teachers and other adults understand the situation of the child, and are able to arrange a good environment, with the possibilities for growth and development – in homes, kindergartens, daycare centres and pre-schools, all before official schooling starts. It is before school starts that children learn about their emotions and build their identity, in the society of their equals – other children of the same age. This period is essential for the development of identity in so many way.

All those involved in creating and maintaining the learning environment need to guarantee that each child will get the care that will allow his or her confidence and emotional life to develop without disturbance. Children from each and every cultural group must be given the opportunity of knowing about their own culture and of creating their own appropriate identity. In their own culture, children can learn together social rules and be together to create their own new cultural forms. The responsibility of both teachers and parents is to arrange activities for children which create a good learning environment. While child-centred education is important and good, teachers need also to recognise the necessary balance between child-centred and teacher-directed education.

Institutions have an identity of their own: for example, as a daycare system or a school. What kind of identity can a child hold in a pre-school setting? Are there some forms of specialisms which children want to get? What influences do institutional identities have on a child's personal development and individual identity?

One task of the pre-school is to prepare for starting school. What is it to become a school pupil and make the transition from pre-school? What kinds of identifications are there to be seen? Those children who have siblings often know more than those children who are in their first children group.

Identity is not only the individual's self image: it is much more – which language, which culture and which society the child chooses to offer to the world. It is also changing over time.

One of the most important tasks in pre-school education is to provide confirmation of the child's natural learning, enabling him or her to enjoy his or her childhood, to build their own self-esteem and identity in peace and at their own pace.

7

Children's national identity and attitudes toward other nationalities in a monocultural society: the Polish example

Beata Krzywosz-Rynkiewicz
University of Warmia and Mazury in Olsztyn, Poland

Introduction

Poland is one of the most monocultural countries in Europe. 96.1 per cent of the population have Polish nationality and 90.7 per cent of them belong to the Catholic church (*Encyklopedia PWN*, 1999).

There are three reasons why an analysis of the sense of national unity among the Poles and of their attitude towards widely understood 'differences' (national, religious, social) is of particularly interest. Firstly, Poland belongs to a group of countries that were isolated from many other countries in Europe for many years. The lack of free contact, information and cultural exchange has probably affected both the feeling of national identity and the perception of others. Secondly, it is important to look at the sense that Poles have of supranational ties, or their willingness to develop these, shortly before Poland's planned integration with the European Union. And thirdly, an analysis of Polish children's attitudes towards members of other nationalities may help – at least partially – to answer the question asked by many researchers: can psychological phenomena or social processes such as discrimination and prejudice be explained by national differences and a lack of everyday contacts with other cultures? Poland, being a monocultural country, may act as a control in this kind of study.

This chapter addresses some of those questions, though not examining the whole of Polish society. This analysis is limited to the attitudes of primary school pupils aged between seven and twelve years. This group is of particular interest as a research subject. While on the one hand such children (like other Poles) are members of a monocultural society and do not live next door to representatives of other races, nations or religions, on the other hand (and in contrast to their parents and elder sisters and brothers) they have never experienced life isolated behind the iron curtain, with access to only selected information. Having had the opportunity to read books and newspapers, to watch television, to learn foreign languages, and to establish personal contacts, they have been able to get to know people from different cultures, and have been able to travel to different countries. It may therefore be easier for them to develop relations with members of other groups.

This chapter focuses on the question of whether it is possible that people who grow up in a monocultural country, in which citizens have had very little direct experience of dealing with representatives of other nationalities, can remain open to other cultures, and if such an experience is conducive to the development of a spirit of community with other Europeans.

The chapter is divided into five sections. Firstly there is a short theoretical introduction to the phenomena that will be examined: national identity and the perception of other cultures. The second section analyses the sense of national identity found in Polish children, and particular cognitive and social categories associated with this. It also examines the local ties of young Poles. Section three explores issues of tolerance toward others; it presents research on children's prejudices and stereotypes through their perception of representatives of other nations. It also discusses an investigation into Polish children's knowledge, acceptance and experience of national and religious differences. Section four is concerned with the role of school in modifying children's attitudes. Are teachers willing to introduce knowledge about other cultures into the school curriculum? Finally, the fifth section examines the correlation between a sense of national ties and European identity.

This analysis is illustrated by the findings of six studies of pupils and their teachers. Four of these were conducted by myself or my colleagues. Each is numbered following the order in which it appears in the chapter:

(a) I – national/local identity and tolerance for others, conducted in 1999 on a group of 30 children aged seven to twelve;

(b) II – the sense of national identity among older primary school pupils in a mono- and multicultural environment, undertaken in 2001 on two groups, each consisting of 40 children aged ten to twelve;

(c) V – teachers' perception of multicultural education, conducted in 1999 on a group of 30 primary school teachers;

(d) VI – European identity, undertaken in December 2000 on a group of 45 children aged seven to twelve.

Some of the results of these studies have been presented in part elsewhere (I and V: Krzywosz-Rynkiewicz *et al.,* 1999); they appear here in their full form. Studies II and VI are original and appear for the first time.

There are numerous references in the Polish professional literature to the national identity and tolerance of adult Poles, both living in the country and abroad (Jarymowicz, 1992; Malewska-Peyre, 1992; Boski, 1992; Kofta and Sedek, 1999). Others deal with the national identity of young people (Lukaszewski, 1998, 1999; Nikitorowicz, 2000). However, none of these provides a systematic description of young children's sense of national identity or their attitudes towards others. I therefore will use some interesting classic results from Barbara Weigl's investigations in 1993 to complement studies I, II, V and VI above:

(e) III – stereotypes and prejudice against members of other nationalities, conducted on a group of 58 children aged seven to ten;

(f) IV – stereotypes and prejudice against members of other nationalities, conducted on a group of 181 children aged eleven to twelve.

All these investigations were made in specific regions of Poland. The studies I have undertaken with my colleagues gathered results from the north-eastern part of Poland, adjoining Russia, Lithuania and Belorus. Barbara Weigl gathered her material (III and IV) from the south-western part of Poland, bordering on Germany and the Czech Republic. However, regardless of the region, the most visible foreign nationalities in Poland are Gypsies and Romanians. They are therefore frequently referred to in the research presented in this chapter, along with the citizens of neighbouring countries.

National identity and children's perceptions of social relationships

We need to consider two key theoretical questions: the concept of national identity and the psychological phenomena that are associated with this, and the rules that govern children's perception of social relationships.

National identity as a crucial element of social development

Identity is a fundamental characteristic of every human individual. It is connected with our feeling of uniqueness, integrity and individuality. An important element in the development of our identity is our environment. Identity allows us to develop both our sense of self and our sense of belonging to a group (Schlenker, 1985). Parents, friends and schoolmates and teachers all convey messages to us that contain evaluations and opinions about what we are like. We observe their behaviour and rituals, and identify ourselves with them, in this way internalising social objectives and values. Some of these then become in time our personal objectives and values. It follows that the ties we establish with a group are a specific kind of social identity. Malrieu (1980, quoted in Bikont, 1988), who perceived identity in a developmental way, claimed that 'the child develops part of his/her identity by participation in social life. The child is his/her name, class at school, nationality, sports team... this is his/her external identity.' According to Turner (1981), social identity is connected not only with membership of a given group, but also with an awareness of this membership.

National identity is a special case of social identity. Firstly, it is built on a stable criterion of a non-transferable nature, which is mutually exclusive of other criteria (Jarymowicz, 1994). Secondly, it concerns joint participation within the confines of a large social community. Thirdly, it is an identity which is shared by many people, and fourthly, it refers to a common code, which is accepted *a priori* (Greenberg *et al.,* 1992; Reykowski, 1995). It follows from this that we can define national identity as the feeling of distinctness and uniqueness of one's own nation, and the perception of oneself as a rightful member of that nation.

There are two problems concerning the relationship between research and the nature of national identity. The first of these is the activation level of the phenomenon of national identity. It is well known that the form of identity that is manifested, and its intensity, depend on the situation in which a given person is placed. The sense of national identity is activated by a particular context, such as a threat from others, or being compared with others. This is different from latent identity (Lukaszewski, 1999), which is a dormant element of our consciousness. The investigations presented in this chapter were not designed to provoke clear situations or contexts that would activate feelings of national identity. However, it seems that the level of latency has rather different dimensions in situations where children come from mononational, rather than multinational environments. Living alongside members of other nations probably evokes a state of permanent confrontation or valuation. The section below that considers evidence from study II examines the effect of processes such as these on national ties.

Secondly, it should also be noted that national identity (as with any other kind of social identity) may be either descriptive or evaluative

(Wojciszke, 1991). The former is connected with a depiction of those characteristics that enable one to distinguish a particular identity category. The latter concerns the process of valuation, and is usually observed when the sense of national identity is activated by some situational, personal or mental contact with another identity category (in this case, some other nationality). Most of the studies in this chapter present descriptive aspects of national identity. The evaluative aspect appears only in the children's evaluation of selected other European nations below.

Children's perception of social relations

Because this chapter describes not only the phenomenon of national identity, but also children's perception of other nations, some discussion of children's comprehension of social relationships is needed.

Piaget's classic studies stress younger children's egocentric perception of the world, when their processes of thinking are of a pre-operational character (Piaget, 1926). During the first years of life, to the age of about six or seven, children's conceptions of social relationships are rather limited and are permeated by evaluative opinions. Livesley and Bromley (1973) stress that over time the characteristics of others that are created by children become more diversified and detailed, and that assessments are gradually replaced by descriptive categories. By the age of twelve, children are more willing to describe people's inner states rather than their physical features. The ability to conduct formal operations, which develops with age, makes it possible for some twelve-year-old children to integrate information so that they can describe things at an abstract level and formulate generalised opinions.

Because the research presented in this chapter concerns children aged between seven and twelve, we can expect them to describe people with complex characteristics. However, some children may still concentrate on physical aspects such as appearance or behaviour. Egocentrism – observed mainly in younger pupils – means that we should also anticipate some contradictory judgements and stereotyped generalisations.

National identity of children

This section presents two studies (I and II). The first is concerned with the national and local identity of younger primary school pupils, the second compares the national identity of young Poles living in a monocultural environment with the national identity of a group living in a frontier region characterised by its multinational population. Together, these studies allow us to identify some of the characteristics of national ties of children living in a homogenous society.

National and local identity in a monocultural environment – study I

A randomly selected sample of 30 younger primary school pupils (seven to twelve years old) (Krzywosz-Rynkiewicz *et al.*, 1999) were questioned individually. These semi-structured interviews allowed us to encourage even very shy respondents to participate, and to formulate questions in different ways if they were not at first fully understood. The respondents were asked three questions, each of which could be asked in different forms, depending on the child's comprehension.

1. *Who are you? / Which country do you live in?*

2. *Are you Polish?*

3. *What does it mean for you to be Polish?/How can you recognise a Pole?/How can you tell that someone is Polish?*

From the answers given by the children, we established categories of descriptions of national identity: the frequency with which these occurred is shown in Figure 7.1. Irrespective of their age, the children most often employed use of the Polish language and living in Poland as the characteristics of being a Pole. Older pupils were able to give more complex answers, while younger ones at first paid attention to visible features, such as language or skin colour. The younger children's understanding was based on external criteria, and may be connected with thinking at the level of concrete images. Older children, aged ten to twelve, referred much more to categories that derived from an individual's roots. They emphasised the role of family in defining nationality, stressed the importance of not just the place of residence, but also the place of birth, and the parents' nationality. For this older group, national identity is based on abstract criteria, of a stable rather than a situational character. Some descriptions, used much less frequently (though by all age groups), were responses that related to volitional categories such as feeling a Pole, or devotion and attachment to Polish culture and tradition. Children also talked at times about national identity at the emotional level, in terms such as love for the mother country.

The fact that even younger children were able to define precisely their sense of national identity led us to ask them about their conceptions of local identity: we wanted to discover if this was equally clear to them. We expected their ties to the particular region in which they lived to be rather weak, because of the historical circumstances of the area. The study was conducted in north-eastern Poland, in the Warmia and Mazury district. Before World War II this was part of East Prussia (Germany), inhabited mainly by a German-speaking population. In 1945 it became part of Poland, and most of its native inhabitants (known as autochthons) migrated to Germany over the next 20 years. Those Poles who, before the war, had been living in what is now Lithuania, Belorus and the Ukraine were displaced after 1945 to occupy the Warmia and Mazury district. Today only a small percentage of the population of the region are indigenous: the great majority are people who originated from different parts of Poland. But almost all of the children examined in the study – and even their parents – were born in the district, which is for them their homeland. To uncover their ties with this locality, we asked the following questions.

1. *What is the name of the region you live in?*

2. *Are people living here distinguishable?*

3. *If so, what distinguishes them?*

The great majority (77 per cent) of children mentioned the geographical-historical region (Warmia and Mazury district) as their place of residence, while 13 per cent of them mentioned the administrative area (the Warmia and Mazury province). From this it

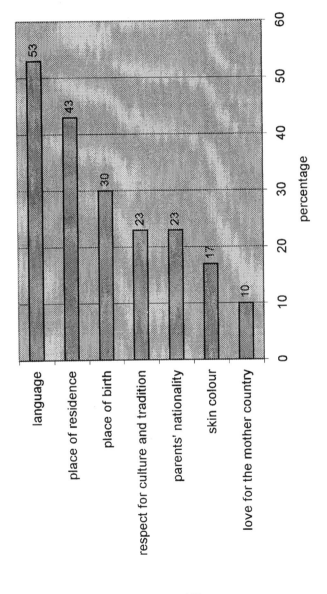

Figure 7.1: Categories connected with the national identity of younger primary school pupils

may appear that their feeling of local identity is equally as strong as their national identity. However, when they were asked what distinguishes the people living in this region, our respondents were not able to be specific. Some of them mentioned folk costumes and dances, and local dishes, but when asked for more detail, they could not name these dishes or describe the costumes. Other children suggested typical Polish customs – such as celebrating Christmas or Easter – as being local characteristics. It therefore appears that their sense of local identity is limited to knowledge of the region's name rather than of its specific characteristics. We can even hypothesise that many of them do not identify themselves with the district at all: some children mentioned very general patterns of behaviour, such as eating with a knife and fork, or fishing, as characteristic of the inhabitants of Warmia and Mazury. Only a few pupils mentioned local legends.

National identity in a mono- and multinational environment – study II

To explore and extend the conclusions drawn from study I, we conducted a second study of a larger group of pupils. We also wanted to compare the views of national identity held by children coming from a homogenous society with the identity categories of young Poles who lived in areas where they would have direct contact with people of other nationalities. Under the direction of the author, a student of social pedagogy at the University of Warmia and Mazury carried out a comparative study with Polish children in a mononational area (from Olsztyn – the capital of the Warmia and Mazury district) and children in a multinational region (from Bielsko-Biala, at the border between Poland and Belorus). There were 40 children in each group. For technical reasons we had to limit the groups to the older age category of ten to twelve years. These pupils do not have difficulties in writing, so the study was conducted with written open questions and answers, organised on a group basis. All the children were of Polish nationality, so they were asked, as in study I, 'What does it mean for you to be Polish?' Figures 7.2 and 7.3 show the descriptive categories they employed and the frequency with which they were used.

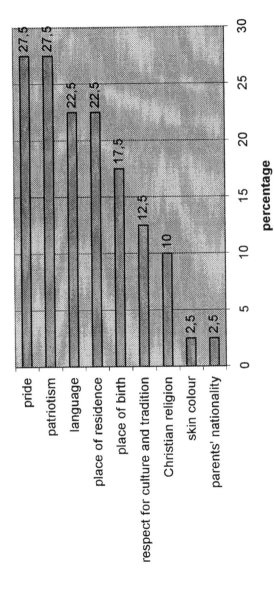

Figure 7.2: Categories connected with the national identity of older primary school pupils from a multicultural region

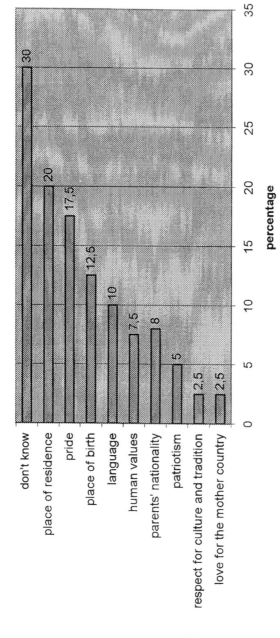

Figure 7.3: Categories connected with the national identity of older primary school pupils from a monocultural region

There are significant differences in the responses concerning national identity between the two groups analysed. Firstly, the children from the homogenous region found it more difficult to define their national ties. This tendency had not been observed in the previous study, which had been conducted at the individual level. This lack of direct contact with each pupil may have meant that they were not sufficiently motivated to respond. But between the two groups in this study, in which the research conditions were identical, there was a considerable difference. Children from the multinational region used emotional arguments much more frequently, in phrases such as 'to be proud', 'to love, to fight, to defend', and 'to prevent disrespect for the mother country'.

To conclude this section on national identity, we may suggest from these studies that:

- young Poles have a fairly clear conception of their national identity, which in the case of younger children tends to be based on external categories (such as language and appearance), and in the case of older children to be based on more permanent categories, such as the place of birth and the parents' nationality

- the feeling of national identity is dominant over any feelings or ties with the local region in which they live

- those children living in a homogenous social environment often have greater problems in defining national identity than do children from more mixed areas

- national identity in these multinational environments is of a slightly different nature, and more based on emotional categories.

Children's attitudes towards other nationalities

In this section I will analyse children's attitudes towards other nationalities about which they have some knowledge. Are young Poles open and tolerant, or do they display elements of prejudice and stereotypes towards people from other nations? We will firstly examine their attitudes towards others at the descriptive level, and in the section that follows this, attitudes towards other nationalities at the evaluative level.

Children's tolerance for other nationalities (continuation of study I)

In analysing the nature of tolerance, our study concentrated on three elements: children's experiences of those from other nationalities, their factual knowledge of these nationalities, and the level of acceptance and tolerance that they showed towards them

Experiences with other nationalities

Our first objective was to discover the extent of children's experience in meeting people of other nationalities, and to note the degree of closeness of these contacts. We asked children three questions to ascertain the degree of distance in their experiences (the number in brackets is the percentage of children who answered affirmatively):

1. *Have you ever **met** people of other nationalities? (93 per cent)*

2. *Have you ever **got to know** people of other nationalities? (80 per cent)*

3. *Have you ever **played** with them? (63 per cent)*

As can be seen, almost all of the children said that they had met people from other nationalities, and the majority of them said that they had had close contacts with those people. It was only the younger pupils who were more likely to declare that they have never met or played with people from other countries.

We also wanted to determine from where children derived their knowledge about other nationalities. They said that they had learnt about different cultures from the

mass media (70 per cent)
family members (40 per cent)
school (37 per cent)
schoolmates/friends (10 per cent)
the Church (3 per cent)

It was noted earlier that these pupils in contemporary society are in a new and different situation than their parents had been in: for example they are able to travel abroad without hindrance. But when we asked how many of our respondents had been abroad, only 33 per cent of the children we questioned had visited other countries

Knowledge about other nationalities
Our initial questions were designed to establish the categories that were used by children to describe other nationalities. We wanted to find if these categories were similar to those used in describing their own nationality. In response to the question 'What does it mean to be of different nationality?', the pupils responded:

to speak a different language (43 per cent)
to live in another country (23 per cent)
to be born somewhere else (23 per cent)
to have parents of different nationality (17 per cent)
to have a different skin colour (13 per cent).

Comparing these answers with those shown in Figure 7.1, it can be seen that there are similarities: the concept of nationality is rather general. On the other hand, the significance of one's own nation is of a personal nature, connected with categories such as culture, tradition and love of mother country.

Children of all ages in the sample were able to enumerate many nationalities they know, living both in Europe and in more distant continents (the Australians, the Nigerians). We asked them which nationalities they felt that they knew best. The results (which we found rather surprising) are shown in Figure 7.4: in this, the states neighbouring Poland are listed first, and the next three most often mentioned follow.

The best known nationalities were the Germans, the English, the French and the Americans. The other six of Poland's seven neighbours are less well known than these nationalities. In these cases geographical proximity does not lead to psychological feelings of closeness.

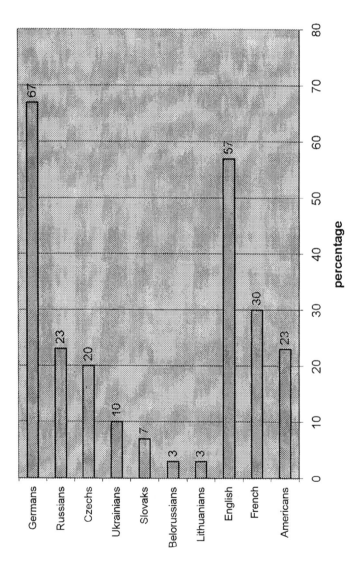

Figure 7.4: The nationalities the children know best

When we asked if they thought that people of other nationalities were living in Poland, 90 per cent of pupils replied in the affirmative. Despite the homogeneity of Poland, children were aware of the presence of national minorities.

We then considered which minorities were the best known. We also wanted to see if there was a correlation between the actual numbers of a minority living in Poland and the perception of the children about which were best known. We found that children generally believe that there are more of the better known nationalities living in Poland. According to the pupils, Poland is also inhabited by Germans, English, French and Americans. They also mentioned Gypsies, who do constitute a relatively large group in Poland, but other national minorities in Poland, such as Ukrainians and Jews, were named on as few occasions as were the culturally and geographically distant Vietnamese and Japanese.

Most children said that they would like to acquire more knowledge about other nationalities. They are first of all interested in the language, which may be linked to the fact that as many as 90 per cent of them learn some foreign language. Older pupils say that they also find the customs and culture of other nationalities interesting. This suggests that children seem open to contacts with other nationalities. Their basic motivation to learn foreign languages is the ability to communicate, willingness to gain knowledge and experience.

Acceptance for other nationalities

In this part of our study we wanted to find out if Polish children were accepting of people from other nationalities. We asked them:

1. *Are people who come from other countries similar to you?*

2. *Are they exactly the same as you?*

80 per cent of the pupils replied in the affirmative to the first question, 37 per cent to the second. We have shown that children's knowledge and personal experience of people from other nationalities increases with age, and generally becomes more positive: this was confirmed in this study. Of the seven-to-eight-year old children, 20

per cent believed that people of other nationalities were exactly the same as themselves. Children aged nine to ten said this in 30 per cent of cases, and children of eleven to twelve in 60 per cent of cases. Most of the children said that people of other nationalities would do the same kinds of thing as they do themselves: work, learn, practise sports, and so on. Only a few of them suggested that they would beg and steal.

We asked our respondents if there was anything they particularly liked about people from other countries. We gathered positive responses from 70 per cent of the children: they listed material goods and living conditions (13 per cent), culture (13 per cent), appearance (10 per cent), personality (7 per cent) and language (7 per cent). The other 30 per cent associated negative characteristics: they said that they did not like their moral behaviour ('they cheat, they accost') (13 per cent), skin colour (7 per cent) and language (7 per cent). These results seem optimistic and indicate that young Poles are rather tolerant, but we must set these findings against the information about which nationalities they feel that they know best (Figure 7.4).

All these results are also less clear-cut when we look at the level of children's acceptance of other nationalities from the perspective of social distance, expressed as the children's stated willingness to:

live in a close neighbourhood (63 per cent)
attend the same school (73 per cent)
play together (83 per cent)
share one desk at school (53 per cent).

As can be seen, as the degree of closeness increases (from neighbourhood, to school, to play) children show more acceptance for people from other countries. However, this tendency has its limits. While many children would be willing to attend the same school as foreigners, this category does allow them to control the precise distance ('I can, but do not have to, come into contact with them.') But the number of children ready to share a desk at school is a fifth lower, as this becomes closeness of a more compulsory nature, as is the neighbourhood example: both have an element of stability ('You are my neighbour, and this situation is going to last.') It is possible that this is the reason why 20 per cent fewer children say that they would be willing to live in a close neighbourhood than would be willing to play with friends from other countries, as this latter activity is situational and free from commitment or obligation.

Evaluation of other nationalities

The previous section suggested that Polish children are open to meeting people from other nationalities. We now wish to discuss how children evaluate them. Our earlier studies were based on open-ended questions, and did not seek opinions about members of individual nations. This section describes two investigations by Barbara Weigl, a psychologist at the Institute of Psychology, Polish Academy of Sciences. Those investigations also concerned younger pupils, but in contrast to our research described above, they were carried out in south-western Poland (close to Germany and the Czech Republic). Weigl's aim was to determine the correlation between children's own sense of national identity and their attitude to people from others nations at an evaluative level. Both studies focus on children's attitudes towards those nationalities whose members they are most likely to meet in that particular region. The first study was conducted on pupils aged seven to ten years, and the second on those aged eleven to twelve.

Perception of other nationalities by younger primary school pupils – study III

This study of 58 children was conducted in 1993. Its aim was to analyse their attitude towards their neighbours – Czechs and Germans – and to the significant national minorities – Gypsies, Romanians, and Jews. The study did not refer directly to children's opinions, but was based on five measures. Space does not allow a full description of the techniques: here I only present the findings which are most useful for the present chapter.

The children taking part in the study were asked to evaluate representatives of different nationalities at the following levels:

141

(a) Determination of qualities in particular nationalities. The pupils were told: 'We would like you to think about people of various nationalities. There are two envelopes on the table. One of them contains white sheets of paper, the other black sheets of paper. White sheets represent people's good qualities, black ones people's bad qualities. First think of yourself and take as many white/black sheets as you have virtues/faults (...). Now think of (for example) the Jews. Take as many white/black sheets as they have merits/shortcomings in your opinion.' The results are presented in Figure 7.5.

(b) Determination of social distance, measured employing the 'clock method'. Children were given a picture showing the face of a clock, with 12 places corresponding to the 12 hours. They were told: 'Imagine you are in camp. We have 12 tents. One of them (e.g. at the position of 12 o'clock) is occupied by (for example) a Gypsy. Which tent would you take? Mark it in the picture.' The distance selected is shown in Figure 7.6.

Perception of other nationalities by older primary school pupils –
study VI
This study sought to analyse the attitude of 150 older primary school children towards representatives of some of the countries adjoining Poland (Czechs, Lithuanians, Germans, Ukrainians) and to Romanians, who are a visible national minority. Their attitude towards members of individual nations was assessed using two techniques: the measurement of their preferences and territorial division.

(a) Preference measurement. Children were given a sheet of paper with five photographs of boys or girls (matching the sex of the child being questioned). Names and nationalities were written next to the photographs. Each child was told to imagine that that they were a participant at an International Youth Convention. They were asked to choose the person they would like to share a room with. The results shown in Figure 7.7 reflect the sum of the children's ranking of the nationalities: the most desirable room mate received five points, and the others fewer points, with one point for least wanted person.

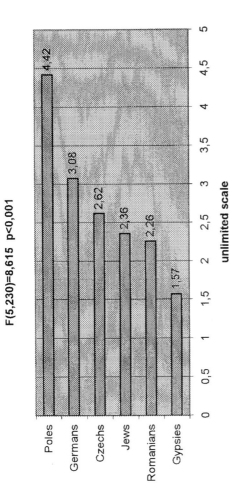

Figure 7.5: Qualities attributed to representatives of selected nationalities

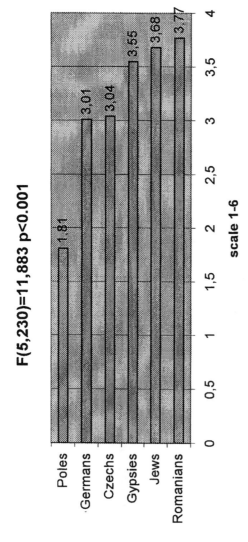

Figure 7.6: Average distance towards representatives of selected nationalities

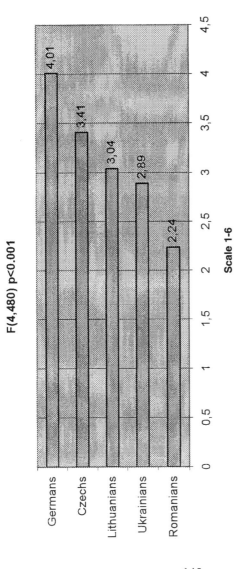

Figure 7.7: Preference for representatives of selected nationalities

(b) Territorial division. The children were given a sheet of paper showing a camp fire surrounded by 100 tents. They were told: 'All participants of the convention will stay at a camp site. The organisers wonder how many tents they should reserve for each group. Mark in the picture the area to be occupied by each group.' The results are presented in Figure 7.8.

To conclude this section on attitudes towards other nationalities, based on our own and on Weigl's studies, we can suggest the following:

- the level of acceptance declared by young Poles towards other nationalities is relatively high

- the degree of tolerance increases in the case of experiences of a situational character, particularly those over which they can exercise some control

- children demonstrate a decided preference for the nations of the west, and a corresponding disapprobation for eastern nationalities and poor minorities

- their opinions are governed by certain stereotypes

- children perceive their own national group extremely positively.

School as an environment moulding the opinions about and attitudes towards other nationalities

This section deals with attitudes towards other nationalities from the perspective of the school. According to children, school (together with the family and mass media) is the main source of their information about different nationalities. The section presents an analysis of teachers' views on the role of school syllabuses in multicultural education, and discusses the promotion of tolerance in schools.

Multicultural education according to teachers – study V
In earlier investigations (Krzywosz-Rynkiewicz *et al.,* 1999) we asked teachers about the role of multicultural education at school. We wanted to find out how much time they gave to promoting knowledge about:

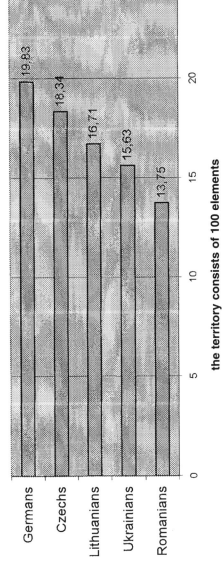

Figure 7.8: Results of territorial division among representatives of selected nationalities

their own nation,
other nationalities.

Their responses are shown in Figure 7.9.

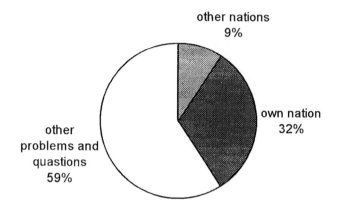

other nations
9%

own nation
32%

other
problems and
quastions
59%

Figure 7.9: Percentage of time devoted by teachers to
multicultural education

Teachers' willingness to extend multicultual teaching was apparent
and should be emphasised. When asked if the amount of time spent
on education about other cultures was sufficient, the majority of
them replied that it was not. It can therefore be anticipated that they
will accept the introduction of more multicultural elements into their
classes.

*Promoting the attitude of tolerance at school – an example of an
experimental module and its application*
The Polish educational system has been going through a radical
transformation, in which teachers have been given more autonomy
in drawing up syllabuses than they used to have. In view of teachers'
opinions on this, we may expect a growing demand for class
modules that will widely extend multicultural education. To help
meet this demand, I developed a module for a 15-hour workshop for
seven-to-twelve-year old primary school pupils. Extracts from this
are presented below: there are two parts to the module.

Part I: My nation and me. What is national identity?
(a 3-hour workshop)
Part II: Others and me. Perception of different cultures.

1. What does it mean to be different? (understanding) (3 hours)

2. What do I know about others? (knowledge) (3 hours)

3. Others and me – living together. (acceptance) (3 hours)

4. Others and me (experience) (3 hours)

One of the workshops (Part II, Session 1) is presented in detail.

Part II. Others and me. Perception of different cultures.
What does it mean to be different? (a 3-hour workshop)

1. *A group discussion led by the teacher.*

   The teacher and pupils discuss

   (a) 'What does it mean to be different?' The aim is to activate children's personal knowledge and experience about different characteristics. By exchanging ideas and experiences, children stimulate each other to think about the problem.

   Other discussion topics are:

   (b) How do you recognise a different person? Does he/she have any special features?

   (c) Have you ever met a different person? Why was he/she different?

   (d) Have you ever felt different from others? How would you describe your feelings?

   (e) Imagine that two boys come to your class. One is German – he lives not far from the border with Poland. The other is African and comes from Ethiopia. Is one of them more different than the other? If so, what makes him different?

   (f) If you wanted to learn something new, which boy could teach you more – the German or the Ethiopian? Why?

(g) Who would the effects of this learning/teaching process depend on – you or this boy?

2. *The teacher reads a story by Andersen,* The Ugly Duckling.

3. *Individual work.*

The teacher asks the children to prepare a conversation with a pre-school child (four years old) about the story. How would they explain to him or her why the duckling was unhappy? When the task is completed, children read and compare their texts. The teacher draws out different aspects of the duckling's situation.

4. *Group discussion*

The teacher and children discuss the duckling's situation using topics such as:

(a) Why was the duckling different?

(b) Would it be possible for the duckling to become similar to other ducks?

(c) Would it be possible for the duckling to be happy among the ducks, despite the differences?

(d) Could the ducks help the duckling to feel happier? How?

(e) Do people like those who are different? Why/why not?

(f) Have you heard about cases of discrimination in the world?

5. *Children work in small groups*

The teacher divides pupils into small groups (four to five children in each). The teacher tells each group 'Three boys come to your class: an African, an American and a Russian. Work out a game you can play together.' When the task is completed, children present their games.

6. *Children play together*

The children choose one of the games, and try to play it. Three children pretend to be foreigners, the others are Polish. When the game is over, children exchange their impressions.

7. *Discussion*

The teacher leads a discussion about similarities between people, using the topics:

(a) Why are you able to play together?

(b) How can you understand the rules of the game despite language differences?

This programme will be used in two ways, to develop the teaching of tolerance. It will provide the basis for classes for pedagogy students about the development of social, national and European identity in children. In this, considerable time will be devoted to promoting children's tolerance for other nationalities. The module will also constitute part of a postgraduate course for teachers, called 'Primary school teachers as educators'.

The module was tested for effectiveness by a social pedagogy student from the University of Warmia and Mazury. Conclusions from this section on the environment of the school are as follows:

• school plays an important role in moulding children's opinions about different cultures

• Polish teachers feel that too little time is devoted to multicultural education

• there is a demand for model class modules that could be used by teachers in their work with children

• such class modules need to be popularised among both pedagogy students and teachers.

European identity of Polish primary school pupils – study VI

In this section I focus on how the lack of everyday contact with other cultures affects Polish children's sense of unity with European countries. Can we expect openness to others, or does the monocultural nature of Poland result in children rejecting the different, and lead to the creation of a strong belief that the Polish nation, culture and tradition are unique?

Study VI was carried out in early 2001 with 45 children (18 girls, 27 boys) aged seven to twelve. Its aim was to establish:

1. *What is 'Europeanness' for children? What does it mean to be European?*

2. *Do they feel European themselves? What does it mean to be an European?*

Children were questioned individually. Some pupils were able to write down their answers, while those who could not dictated them to the researcher.

The concept of 'Europeanness' according to children
To find this out we asked the children to perform several tasks.

Firstly, they were given a list of 18 nationalities, and asked to mark on the list those nationalities which they felt were the most European (5 points), very European (4 points), rather European (3 points), a little European (2 points), almost not European (1 point), not European at all (0 points). A list of all European countries would have been too long, and the children might not have been able to concentrate sufficiently, and they might have guessed instead of analysing. We arrived at our final list of nationalities by including:

(a) the Poles (to see if the children associate their own national identity with 'Europeanness' or not);

(b) the Germans, the Czechs, the Ukrainians, the Russians, the Belorussians, the Lithuanians, the Slovaks, the English, the French and the Gypsies (representing the nationalities that are the best known to children. including Poland's neighbours, and the minorities characteristic of the region as in Figure 7.4);

(c) the Americans, the Vietnamese and the Japanese (well-known nationalities from outside Europe, constituting a kind of a 'control group' in determining the extent to which the concept of 'Europeanness' is connected with the geographical continent or cultural similarities and differences);

(d) the Portuguese, the Greeks, the Turks and the Norwegians (representing countries situated at the edge periphery of Europe, and not very well known to children: to find out if lack of contacts with these nationalities, having little knowledge about them, and their 'peripheral' location would influence children's perception concerning their 'Europeanness'.)

The results of this are presented in Figure 7.10.

Asked to justify their choices, the children gave a variety of reasons that can be grouped as follows. For more than 40 per cent, the degree of 'Europeanness' depended on popularity – 'they know all the new things, other countries follow them, you can hear about them on TV, they are active, and I know them'. About a fifth of pupils used *Poland-oriented* arguments – 'they are close to Poland, they are Polish'. A fifth also took into account the geographical criterion – 'they live in Europe/Central Europe'.

The children were often unable to justify their decisions when they said that a nationality had a low degree of 'Europeanness'. They usually mentioned the criterion of knowledge ('I do not know them, they are little talked about'), different culture ('their customs are different') and financial conditions ('they are poor'). Sixty-seven per cent of the respondents did not describe as European the representatives of those countries which they said were not situated in Europe: this was for most children the Japanese and the Vietnamese, sometimes the Americans. Many children also believed that such countries as Norway, Portugal or Greece do not lie in Europe. Probably insufficient knowledge of geography, combined with low levels of media attention about these nations helps explain this.

It is of particular interest that the pupils taking part in this study have contact with Gypsies, but did not include this group among the European nationalities. It seems that neither knowledge of the group nor its presence in Europe were sufficient for them to be seen as European.

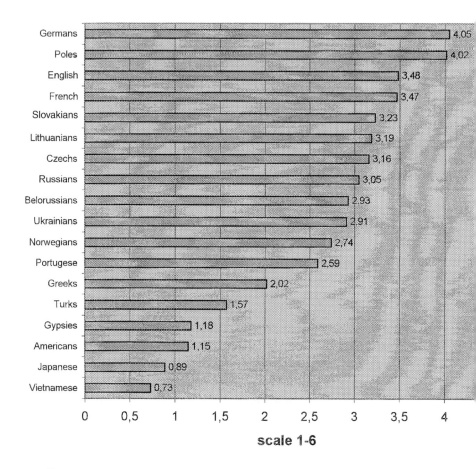

Figure 7.10: The most European nationalities according to the children

Europeans as perceived by children

The next stage of the investigation was to answer the question who, according to the children, are the Europeans? Do they feel European themselves?.

The vast majority (75 per cent) of children declared that to be a European means to live in Europe. They also mentioned the fact of being born here (9 per cent) and having European ancestors (7 per cent). Twenty-four per cent of them associated 'Europeanness' with certain attitudes and systems of values – 'contacts with the world, knowledge, helping the poor, the same culture and tradition'. Almost all of the children (91 per cent) said that they felt European because, as well as the fact that this continent is their place of residence and birth, they 'speak foreign languages, maintain contact with European nations, cherish similar traditions and follow a similar lifestyle'.

To conclude this section, we may suggest that:

- the criteria applied by the children to determine 'Europeanness' are, in order: popularity, Poland-oriented arguments and geographical position

- some children are aware of the significance of European tradition and culture, and treat them as an additional determinant of 'Europeanness'

- there is a clear tendency to perceive the south-western neighbours of Poland as very European, and to ignore the countries situated in the east

- the children demonstrate a marked preference for their own nation, treated as typically European, which may be connected with a strong sense of national identity and an egocentric perspective in the perception of the world

- Polish children feel European

- the criteria they applied to determine the degree of their own 'Europeanness' were similar to those used for describing national identity.

Conclusion

This chapter has concentrated on whether growing up in a mono-cultural country allows children to remain positive and open towards other cultures and whether it is conducive to the development of supranational unity. The studies described were conducted with relatively small groups, and the results should not be seen as leading to clear-cut conclusions. The issues discussed here should be treated as remaining open, and may provide the basis for further investigation.

My preliminary observations led me to expect that the lack of everyday contact with other nationalities might make it impossible to accept people from other nationalities, and produce very strong national ties. The problem seems to be more complex. On the one hand, the research results indicate that Polish children have well-developed ties with own nation, which dominate over their feelings of local identity. Depending on age, these ties are based on more fluid categories (language, place of residence) or more stable ones (place of birth, parents' nationality). Volitional arguments (devotion or attachment to Polish tradition) or emotional arguments (love for the mother country) are more sporadic. Some children found it difficult to say what it means for them to be Polish. But children from border regions have less difficulty defining their nationality: their descriptions are characterised by pride and responsibility for the homeland. It may be suggested as a conclusion that while the homogenous character of the area of residence does not affect the strength of ties with the children's own nation, it does influence a) the availability of descriptive categories for defining nationality ('I know very well what the ties with my country mean for me' as opposed to 'I have never thought about what the ties with my country mean for me'); and b) the kind of descriptive categories used ('visual ties' versus 'emotional ties'). It can be argued that, in the case of children from monocultural regions, the sense of national identity is clearly of a dormant nature..

Is such a latent national identity more conducive towards being open towards others? The answer is equivocal. At the level of making declarations, Polish children seem to be tolerant towards other nationalities, which suggests that they may potentially show acceptance for those from other nationalities. However, this openness is limited: it includes a distinct preference for their own nation and for the western countries. Eastern nationalities, and those from poor minorities, are clearly perceived as less important. The contacts Polish children have with people from different cultures are limited, and their evaluations are naturally based on stereotypes. Although almost all the children have met *some* people from other countries, only just over half of them had experienced any closer relations (such as playing together) with such people. It is not surprising that, in a country where national minorities constitute only three per cent of society, personal contacts with members of these minorities are rather rare. The mass media, family and school may all have a significant and positive effect on modifying children's attitude towards others.

Teachers have the potential to develop tolerance, even among the smallest children. At present, schools give multicultural education about a quarter of the time they allocate to teaching about Poland. Teachers are in agreement that this is too little. They appear open to change, and it is suggested that the demand for specialised class modules in this area will grow in the near future, especially given that the reform of the educational system in Poland now grants teachers more freedom in selecting both teaching methods and syllabus contents. The creation of such modules, both for pedagogy students and teachers, supports these attitudes of openness and understanding. It may also help teachers to take a new look at the educational materials that have been known for years: some of these (for example, the story by Andersen, *The Ugly Duckling*) can be used for multicultural education.

So, is growing up in a monocultural country conducive to the development of supranational ties? This question is of prime importance to Poland now, shortly before the country joins the structures of the European Union. Almost all Polish children *feel* European. However, they find the geographical criterion the most compelling explanation – for them, living in Europe is equivalent to *being* a European. Some pupils are also aware of European unity in the sphere of culture and tradition. Their strong sense of 'Europeanness' has another dimension: an egocentric perspective in their perception of the world. They claim that Poles are a typically European nationality, and they also see many similarities between their own country and Western European countries. West European nations are for them an exemplification of 'Europeanness', mainly because of their popularity, wealth and geographical position.

It seems that the open attitudes that are declared by Polish children are limited and considerably affected by various factors. Polish children have insufficient knowledge about national minorities living in their country, and often do not even realise that they are present. They ignore the countries situated in the east. The basis of their European identity is a focus on Western Europe, and a decided preference for their own nation. But their sense of identity is still developing: therefore the role of school in promoting acceptance for all cultures, not just the most favoured cultures, is significant.

8

When Students from Arles and Sparta meet: social representations and identifications

Aigli Zafeirakou

Faculty of Education, Democritus University of Thrace, Greece

This chapter describes an empirical study on the social representations of two groups of twelve-year-old students who participated in a school exchange between Arles, in France, and Sparta, in Greece. The two groups visited each other's towns during a week in the spring of 1994. The students used drawings and texts to express their perceptions of their own town and that of the town they were visiting.

The study was inspired by theoretical insights about social representations and identifications and uses qualitative and ethnographic methods. This chapter elaborates on two questions: firstly, what role does (and can) school education play in the way young students construct an image of their own town? secondly, how does the way a group represents its own town influence the way in which it tries to understand another town? The chapter also hints at some larger questions. Among what layers of representation does mutual understanding among students from different cultures work? How does understanding of the local and the distant relate? How do cultural interchanges across cultural borders affect mutual understanding, and how do they affect the educational project?

The educational and cultural exchange program involved pupils of the sixth grade of the First Primary school of Sparta (aged eleven to twelve) and pupils of the first grade of the Frederic Mistral College of Arles (also aged eleven to twelve). Each group visited the host town during a week in the spring of 1994 and tried to make sense of the urban and architectural environment of the town they were visiting. Students used drawings and texts to express their perceptions of their own town and that of the town they were visiting. These materials were used to understand better how these young students from two European countries conceive their own and others' urban cultural heritage. Cultural heritage refers here to both the historical and archaeological elements of the urban setting, as well as its contemporary aspects.

The two towns that participated in the exchange program were chosen for their similarities in historical importance and age, as well as for similarities in their demography and ecological environment. The Greek students came from the small town of Sparta, which has some 20,000 inhabitants. Set between the Taygetos and Parnon mountains in a valley filled with olive and orange trees, Sparta is still a *polis*, a town community very much determined by face-to-face relations. Its historical significance is widely recognised, not least by the local population. Although Arles is bigger (with 60,000 inhabitants), its own substantial history, archaeological importance, and ecological setting – in Provence on the banks of the river Rhône – made it a good match for Sparta. These similarities were judged to be an important factor in facilitating the interaction between the French and the Greek students in the context of this exchange programme.

The sections that follow consider various aspects of the programme: theoretical concepts; the choice of match between Sparta and Arles; the methods used in the exchange programme and related research; the social representations made by the students; and some theoretical and pedagogical implications of this kind of exchange programme.

Theoretical concepts

Several writers have shown that the way in which young students perceive historical, archaeological and the everyday aspects of their own town is subject to a variety of different influences, such as their family and school, the media, and their everyday experiences of the town in which they live. Scholars such as Frangoudaki and Dragonas (1997) for Greece, and Citron (1989) for France, have tried to understand typical national prejudices, and the way in which these are reproduced by teachers in their students, in particular through the use of school textbooks. Two observations can be made in this respect. Firstly, in both France and Greece, history is taught from an ethnocentric perspective which tends to underline particular elements of national, historical and cultural uniqueness. Whatever are the particularities of this approach in Greek and French textbooks, students from both countries will have been prepared to perceive another cultural environment – in this case another city – influenced by perceptions and prejudices that are inherent to their own culture. Secondly, what children learn in schools about history, and in particular about the history of their own town, is not a simple reflection of textbooks and teaching, but is also mediated by factors such as family and the media. Children construct their own layers of meaning in interaction with all of these and with other elements present in their environment. I will not elaborate here on the relative weight of each of these sources.

The design of the exchange programme – to which I contributed actively – was inspired by two ideas. First, the idea that encouraging students to adopt a comparative approach between the two towns would help us to understand better how the historical and archaeological elements, the ecological environment, and the everyday aspects of the home town, influence the way in which these young students represent their own town and other towns they visit. It was a conscious decision to bring together two more or less *equal* groups, at least in terms of their position inside their own society. The relations between the two groups cannot be conceived in terms of a majority and a minority group, or in terms of other obvious socio-economic or cultural differences. Secondly, the theme chosen for the exchange programme had to be explicitly cultural. It was decided that two towns, comparable in historical and archaeological riches, would offer an excellent *in situ* laboratory to study exactly how students create urban representations, by observing how they made use (or did not make use) of the variety of elements of the urban cultural heritage. Comparing the cultural heritage of the two towns would permit these young people to confront different values, logics and ways of thinking and representation in the comparison of each other's towns and cultures. The design would thus help to answer questions of both theoretical and pedagogical interest: what are the elements taken into account in such representations? Among what layers of representation does mutual understanding among students from different cultures take place? How do understandings of the local and of the distant relate? How do cultural interchanges across cultural borders affect mutual understanding?

The theoretical and pedagogical interest of this exchange pro-gramme between Arles and Sparta can thus said to be threefold.

1. From social psychology research into the social representation of urban settings, an analysis of the exchange programme can contribute to exploring the way in which young people, from different national backgrounds, represent their own town and an unknown town, through an international cultural and educa-tional exchange. The related research hypothesis is that, through analysis of the emergence of the different representations made by the two groups, we can better understand certain aspects of the way these youngsters conceive their own cultural heritage and that of others. Analysis of the exchange programme can address two questions: firstly, what role does (and can) school education play in the way young students construct an image of their own town? secondly, how does the way a group represents its own town influence the way in which it tries to understand another town?

2. From a pedagogical point of view, an analysis of this experiment helps to understand better the perceptions and representations of the students (and members of the teaching community) about their social, cultural and urban environment.

3. Finally, the results can contribute to good practice in the design and implementation of cross-cultural educational programmes.

Arles and Sparta

As has been explained, the decision to bring together students from the two specific towns of Arles and Sparta was not random. Both are small Mediterranean towns, situated a few dozen kilometres from the coast. Both are built on the banks of historic rivers (albeit of quite different size), the Rhone and the Evrotas. They are also both towns with a rich historical past.

The urban structure of Arles goes back to its foundation by Julius Caesar in 46BC. From its Roman origins, the spatial transformation of the town continued through the Middle Ages, the Renaissance and modern times with remarkable continuity. Its morphology gives it a strong organic aspect, and one that seems to be little disturbed by modern construction, at least in its old centre. The history of Sparta, and its topography, is far more fractured. From Mycenaean times till the Roman period, ancient Sparta showed continuous habitation in the areas bordering the river Evrotas. An obscure period followed, between the fourth to the seventh centuries. The town reappeared during the Frankish and Byzantine period, in the form of the city of Mystras, at the foot of Mount Taygetos, ten kilometres from the abandoned site of ancient Sparta. During the Ottoman occupation, Mystras too was abandoned and fell gradually into ruin, with the local population retreating into mountain villages. After Greek independence, Sparta was re-founded in 1834 on the site of ancient Sparta, on and between the ancient ruins. Greece had only just been created as an autonomous nation state and was in need of some strong symbols: new Sparta was intended to be one of these. Significant parts of nineteenth century Sparta have survived, most notably the essential elements of the urban plan as it was laid out in 1834. However, typical three-floor concrete apartment buildings (*polycaticia*), now dominate the view of the town: these are also in part to meet the demands for prevention of damage from earthquakes. Some material traces of its more ancient past, from before the nineteenth century, exist in isolated spots – under the streets, in some archaeological sites within and outside the city, and in Mystra.

While Sparta and Arles have equal wealth of cultural heritage, the history of their spatial forms was thus regulated in very different ways. In the case of Arles there has been a continuous readaptation of its construction, without any historical interruption or displacement of its settlement from the time of its founding to the present day. Buildings and other architectural elements of all ages coexist and rub shoulders with each another. Sparta, as a consequence of historical processes of construction and disappearance, rupture and substitution, covers an area that includes not only the present town of Sparta, but also Mystras and other parts outside the perimeter of the present town.

Research methodology

The educational and cultural exchange programme involved pupils from the First Primary School of Sparta and the Frederic Mistral College of Arles (in both cases, eleven to twelve-year-olds). The groups met on two occasions, each of a week: in Sparta in March 1994, and in Arles in May 1994.

I had already been directly involved in the organisation of other experimental cultural and educational exchange programmes. On this occasion, I wanted also to follow closely the way in which students perceived aspects of the largely unknown cultural environment they were visiting, and how these perceptions might change over the course of the week of the student exchange. To do this, I decided to make use of a variety of instruments, and in particular students' drawings and letters, as well as interviewing them. These instruments were deliberately introduced into the exchange program, in consultation with both groups of teachers, with the intention of enriching both our own and the children's understanding of the experience. The historical evolution of the two towns was chosen as the main dimension of the exchange programme. The teachers of both classes collaborated with their local archaeologists, architects, historians, and other professionals, as well as with local artists, on the design and implementation of the programme.

The research project both contributed to, and benefited from, these pedagogical conditions. Three activities were purposely introduced into the exchange programme for the students to help achieve the research objectives. These were:

- writing letters to students in the other town, in which the students described their own town, prior to the visit being made

- drawings of the town being visited, made both at the beginning and at the end of each visit, and each time by both groups of students

- short, informal (but recorded) interviews by the author with the visiting students, both in Arles and in Sparta, to capture their impressions of the host town in comparison with their home town.

These three instruments – letters, drawings and interviews – produced a rich set of materials. Thematic content analysis was employed to categorise the themes that were presented in the materials. The letters, for example, could be analysed on four thematic dimensions:

- contextual and historical dimensions of the home town

- ecological aspects of the town

- everyday aspects of the town

4• feelings and private information.

The drawings and the interviews were analysed in similar ways.

While it may be difficult to generalise findings of such a qualitative and ethnographic approach, thematic content analysis can contribute to our understanding of how social representations are formed in the course of this kind of educational experience, and the approach can also contribute both to the good design of exchange programmes and to the related training of teachers.

Thematic analysis of the letters

The letters written by both groups of students, preceding the visits, in which they described their own town, were analysed thematically. The analysis follows the four thematic categories already identified.

1. Contextual elements and the historical dimension of the town

The Greek students usually began their letters with a description of the geographical location of their town. They often present their town, and Greece, in a glorious style. For example, they might include sentences such as 'Sparta is only a small town in Greece, but it is the greatest in history' or 'My town is one of the best in Greece'. The Greek students also had a strong tendency to situate Sparta in a larger environmental setting, which they then often describe using superlatives: 'The mountains are very green', 'The river has a lot of water', and so on. Often these descriptions lack internal organisation (for example, not evolving from the general to the specific, or from regional to local, or vice versa). Precise geographical details are often missing.

The French students were generally more systematic. They were usually very precise in describing the geographical location of Arles, introducing sentences such as 'Arles is 100 kilometres from the mountains and 60 kilometres from the sea'. They may describe the Rhône delta, the Camargue, or Provence, although they rarely put Arles into a general context within France, whether geographical, political or historical. They hardly ever used superlatives to describe Arles, its surrounding region, or France.

Most of the students from Sparta mentioned aspects of Greek history in their texts, but these historical references were often of a very general nature. Typical sentences would be 'Sparta has a glorious history', 'Sparta has a lot of monuments', or 'Sparta's history is very famous', but they usually did not provide any further explanation of these statements. Five Greek students did give more background and historical information: they included elements that did not refer to the history of Sparta itself, but to the history of Greece in general. In the same way, students wrote that Sparta's Archaeological Museum is 'very interesting' or 'very rich', but again without giving any further explanation. Two students wrote that they felt 'proud' about the history of Sparta and of Mystras, the site of Byzantine Sparta, some ten kilometres from the current location of Sparta.

When the students from Arles presented the historical dimension of their town, they did so in a very different way to the students from Sparta: there were no superlatives, nor were there allusions to some kind of past glory of Arles. Only one student wrote 'Arles is a town rich in history'. When they described archaeological sites, they only listed one or two – usually the Arenas and the Thermals of Constantine. They generally gave only short descriptions of their town, and when they listed items such as monuments, they did not use qualitative adjectives to describe them. They wrote more neutral sentences, such as 'Roman people left a lot of monuments'. The students, with the one exception, introduced relatively few historical references.

2. Ecological aspects of the town

Many of the students from Sparta mentioned in their letters elements such as 'green trees', 'beautiful flowers', 'a very clean atmosphere', and 'very green parks' in describing their home town. We generally find the same stylistic elements as when they referred to the history of Sparta: idealisation and use of superlatives. But their descriptions are also influenced by the fact that the town – where the few parks and playgrounds are rather badly maintained – is set in a valley dominated by orange, lemon and olive trees and surrounded by high mountains. Some Greek students stressed the importance of taking measures to protect Sparta's ecology and environment. They wrote that they wanted to 'maintain for the future the greenery and maintain the nice smelling orange trees'. One student even described a school activity that was intended to help keep the town clean and to stimulate recycling. Others noted that there is 'not yet' a problem of atmospheric pollution in Sparta. This refers in part to the main avenue of the town being planted with palm trees, and to the way that people often cultivate gardens or maintain an abundance of plants on their balconies.

Only about half of the French students introduced ecological details into their letters. These students mostly referred to the delta of the Rhone and to the Camargue, mentioning horses, bulls, wild birds and other fauna and flora. They wrote sentences such as '[Arles is located] in a big plain with wetlands and roses', or 'There are a lot of herbs – thyme and laurel'. Surprisingly, not one of the French students mentioned the greenery in the city of Arles, not even the plane trees that are an outstanding characteristic of both the old and the new parts of the town. Their descriptions were rather matter of fact, and the French students did not give the impression that they wished to promote their town. Nor were there any references to any potential future ecological risks.

3. Everyday aspects of the town

Many of the Greek students gave a very positive image of the physical and everyday human characteristics of their town. Many described Sparta's town plan as one of the best in Greece, reflecting widespread local conviction cultivated both at home and in schools.

With regard to religious references, about a quarter of the Greek students wrote something in their letters about their local parishes. None of the French students did so in their description of Arles. Analysis of the students' drawings, however, gave the opposite impression: in their drawings, the Greeks represent fewer churches than the French, and in this respect the students gave less attention to religious elements of town.

The Greek students often referred to the people who live in Sparta, and to the type of work they do, and the amusements they participate in. They typically wrote that people from Sparta are 'very friendly', 'very united', and 'very hospitable'. Sometimes they mentioned aspects of their family life.

The French students made fewer or hardly any references to more intimate aspects of local life. The French students mainly described the actual town scene in a conscious, rather matter of fact way, mentioning squares and public buildings.

4. Feelings and personal information

About a quarter of the Greeks students wrote explicitly that they 'love' their town, and that they feel very happy living there: 'I love my town so much! (...) I will love it for ever and I will never forget it, even if I am far away!'; 'I love Sparta very much, and I hope that you will feel the same.' Others are more moderate in their feelings, but quite a few write that they are '(very) proud' to live in Sparta. The French students did not explicitly express sentiments of this kind, and did not get emotional or personal about their relationship to their town.

On the other hand, very few Greek students mentioned their private life. All of the French students start their letters by presenting themselves; their name, their age, their school. About half of the French students report on their sports and their hobbies. This kind of information is clearly an important part of the French students' letters, particularly since these are in general shorter than those of the Greeks.

Half of the Greek students included personal messages to their future visitors, in order to establish initial communication. One letter from a student was written completely in a personal style, communicating as to a friend. Just a quarter of the French students introduced more personal messages, for example expressing hopes for a good exchange experience.

The drawings and the interviews lead to the same kind of conclusions. For example, an analysis of their drawings shows that the Greek students systematically gave more attention than the French students did to archaeological and religious elements in their drawings of Arles. The French students, on the other hand, gave more attention to the everyday aspects of the town of Sparta. The French pupils also introduced more elements with a political or administrative reference in their drawings, for example depicting the town hall in their drawings of both Arles and Sparta. While some of the Greek students integrated words in the Roman alphabet into their drawings (such as publicity on shops and hotels), none of the French students introduced words in Greek.

Tentative observations on representation

From the viewpoint of the social psychology of urban representations, this kind of research contributes to the exploration of how young people, from different national backgrounds, represent their own town and an unknown town visited during an international educational exchange centred on a cultural theme. Through the emergence of the differences in the representations made by each of the two groups, differences in the way they conceive their cultural heritage are made clear.

This thematic analysis shows that differences in both the morphology and the content of the letters between the two groups are significant. The same is true for the drawings and the interviews. We know, from other research, that a variety of factors may intervene in how these differences arise, such as the different roles of teachers, the types of textbook, family, peers and media, as well as issues of local, regional and national culture and history. How social representations are being formed within the context of an educational exchange is subject to complex interactions that every child develops between these factors and their perception of the town in which they live (Chombart de Lauwe, 1987).

The Greek students described their town using superlatives and idealised descriptions. Perhaps this kind of idealisation operates particularly in relation to 'strangers'. Would they use the same words and descriptions if they were asked to describe their city for their parents, or for students living in another Greek town? Can such idealised descriptions be the consequence of a feeling of economic and political inferiority in relation to other European countries, and in particular to France, with all the connotations that country may have amongst Greek students? Or are these forms of 'idealisation' the consequence of ethnocentric instruction about Greek history?

The analysis of the drawings shows that the way in which students from both groups represent the town of the other is clearly influenced by the way in which they represent their own town. For instance, in their drawing of the urban plan of Sparta, French students clearly introduce some central elements and ways of organisation from their own town. The same is true for the drawings of Arles by Greek pupils. In terms of social representation, this practice refers to a logic of *transposition*.

The representations and identifications made by both Greek and French students incorporate elements from both the past and from current everyday life. The historical dimension seems to be integrated in a particular dynamic and functional way to give value to the present. The historical dimension also seems to play an integrative role, in the way that different aspects are used together to create representations of both the home town and the foreign town. Our analysis of how links between these different aspects are constructed helps us to understand the dynamic and complex manner in which social representations of urban settings are established. Of particular theoretical interest is the question of the degree to which strong personal feelings about the (home) town – positive or negative – play a part, as well as the role of feelings about family, friends and school.

Qualitative and ethnographic analysis of these kinds of student exchange programmes clearly produces very rich empirical material. But there are evident shortcomings in this approach. As observed earlier, it is difficult to generalise from analytical results, and this is nearly always the case with this kind of qualitative research. Even small differences in the teachers' instructions to students on how to write a letter about their town may inevitably lead to considerable differences in the content and structure of these letters. It is likely that many of these differences spring at least in part from differences in the instructions given to the students by their respective teachers, since the design of the exchange program did not call for strict identical forms of teacher instruction. This makes it difficult to conclude that the differences in apparent perception between the Greek and the French students are any more than subjective factors, rather that indicating rational versus more emotional ways of observing things.

This research confirms the appropriateness of using a variety of different instruments to collect evidence – such as letters, drawings and interviews – in order to contribute to a more complex reconstruction of how specific groups produce social representations.

Some pedagogical implications

Understanding better how twelve-year-old children construct social representations of their social, cultural and urban environment has direct educational implications. This knowledge can contribute to the improved design and implementation of intercultural education exchanges, particularly regarding pedagogic processes (including teaching and learning procedures) and the enrichment of curricula. It also contributes to improving the design, organisation and implementation of educational exchange programs *per se*. I will briefly refer to each of these.

Intercultural education

Intercultural education refers here to what pupils should learn in school about cultural diversity (Sierens, 2000). Understanding how twelve-year-old pupils think and conceive of reality, as analysed in this research, can play an important role in facilitating intercultural educational processes. Incorporating intercultural objectives, including international exchange programmes, into the school curriculum, means not only learning new content but also rethinking principles, strategies and methodologies used in day-to-day teaching.

The pedagogical processes

Teachers need to be provided with basic elements about the way young people think and construct their representations of reality. Understanding the dynamics of concepts such as social representation, identity and identification, will give teachers building blocks with which to construct effective intercultural projects. Exploring how twelve-year-olds represent their own town and another town, in the context of an exchange programme, is one way to offer teachers very rich material for a more personalised and active pedagogical approach. Understanding better how youngsters think and how they construct social representations will help teachers to better plan pedagogical processes, and in particular the intercultural dimension.

Enrichment of curricula

By approaching largely unknown aspects and interpretations of their own town and another, pupils from Sparta and Arles became young ethnographers. This has proved to be a particularly innovative experience in situations where the curriculum is mainly focused on national history, and less (or not at all) on local history, which is to an extent the case in both France and Greece. The exchange programme itself provided an innovative thematic enrichment of the curriculum.

Orientation and materials for teachers training in intercultural education

The Arles-Sparta educational project can serve as an example of good practice for a student exchange programme with a focus on intercultural education. Lessons learned from this can be used for orientation, and as materials for teachers who are training in intercultural education. These kinds of materials can be used to educate teachers in:

• a better understanding of the way young people think: social representation and the creation of identities are part of these thinking processes

• a better understanding of how students from different groups negotiate values and promote common values

• a better understanding of stereotyping and prejudices, and how these can play a part in young people's perceptions of diversity

• the design of content and pedagogical methodology of curricula for intercultural education

* the design, organisation and implementation of international educational exchange programmes.

9

Youth and European identity

Emilio Lastrucci

University of Roma La Sapienza

This chapter is concerned with the development of a *European identity* in young people, conceived of as a special form of *social identity*, and with the relationship between European identity and *national identity*[1]. This problem is analysed in two ways. The underlying analysis is based on a critical and comparative presentation of recent and relevant theories and models about the process of socialisation during adolescence, relating these to the construction of *social identity* and, more particularly, to the relationship between the development of historical consciousness and the process of political socialisation. This is set within a consideration of the findings of recent empirical research on socialisation, the formation of social identity and the development of historical consciousness (using especially the wide-ranging survey 'Youth and History', but also other more circumscribed inquiries in this area).

The 'Youth and History' project

The research project *Youth and History: the comparative European project on historical consciousness among teenagers* started in 1991 and ended, at international level, in 1998. Since then the researchers from the participating countries involved have disseminated the project findings and promoted less wide-ranging, more specific inquiries at national level, using the same research tools and strategies. The original fieldwork for the project was carried out in late 1994 and early 1995, when more than 31,000 fifteen-year-old students from 27 different countries in Europe and the Middle East were interviewed using a structured questionnaire. This consisted of 48 items, with a total of 280 precoded questions, using Likert's Attitude Scales.

To ensure a real possibility of comparison of countries across Europe, it was important to have a wide variety of countries participating in the survey. The overall sample was composed of the following countries:

1. *Far North*: Iceland, Norway, Denmark, Sweden, Finland

2. *Post-Soviet* (including the Baltic republics): Estonia, Lithuania, Russia, Ukraine

3. *Central Eastern European*: Poland, Hungary, Czechoslovakia, Slovenia, Croatia

4. *South Eastern Europe*: Bulgaria, Greece, Turkey

5. *South Western Europe*: Spain, Portugal

6. Central Western Europe: Germany, Italy (including a sample from South Tyrol, consisting of all three language groups), Belgium (Flemish community only)

7. Western European countries: France, Great Britain (with an extra sample of Scotland);

8. Israel (including samples of Arab citizens and of Palestinians – West Bank, Gaza, and East Jerusalem)

The Netherlands also participated, but were not, for a variety of reasons, able to complete the fieldwork within the period that had been fixed. Data from the Netherlands are therefore not included in the main comparison of the data set[2].

European citizenship and identity versus national citizenship and identity

Analysis of the answers given to different items in the questionnaire show some findings of interest on the orientation of European teenagers' feelings and attitudes towards European integration and, more generally, on their level of political socialisation, and the relationship between this and European citizenship on the one hand, and national citizenship on the other.

Firstly, we can examine answers to those questions aimed at establishing the degree to which adolescents have developed the most general and fundamental political concepts, such as *nation*, *democracy*, or *Europe*. The first point of interest is an analysis of teenagers' views concerning European integration. Figure 9.1 shows the mean responses to the item in the questionnaire in which students were asked, 'What do Europe and European integration mean to you?'

Three of the possible statements that could be selected as a response characterised Europe as a historical-political entity. One of these was an affirmative statement (B. Europe is the birthplace of democracy, enlightenment, and progress), one was a critical statement (C. Europe is a group of white, rich countries guilty of economic and ecological exploitation of the rest of the world) and one dismissed its relevance altogether (A. Europe is a geographical expression, no more). The remaining three possible responses focused on the future role of Europe, in particular the development of European integration. One of these was a critical response and two were positive (positive: D. European integration is the only way to peace between nations that previously attempted to destroy each other; critical: E. European integration is a danger to sovereign nations, to their identity and culture; and positive: F. European integration will solve the economic and social crises of the countries in Europe).

The statement most commonly selected by students was B, the acknowledgement of Europe's role in history as the birthplace of the core values of modernity (democracy, enlightenment, progress) (Koerber, 1997, p.143). This item was slightly more likely to be chosen by students who were more interested in politics (correlating the responses to this item with answers to another item in the questionnaire that asked students how much they were engaged with and interested in politics). The second most commonly selected statement was that regarding European integration as the way to peace;

177

Figure 9.1: Responses to the question 'What do Europe and European integration mean to you?'

Responses	Mean	Standard Division
B. Europe is the birthplace of democracy, enlightenment and progress	3.34	0.92
D. European integration is the only way to peace between nations that previously attempted to destroy each other	3.27	0.96
F. European integration will solve the economic and social crises of the countries in Europe	3.23	0.91
E. European integration is a danger to sovereign nations, to their identity and culture	2.80	0.94
C. Europe is a group of white, rich countries guilty of economic and ecological exploitation of the rest of the world	2.80	1.05
A. Europe is a geographical expression, no more	2.34	1.02

Figure 9.2: Responses to the question 'What are your views on nations and the national state?'

Responses	Mean	Standard Division
B. Nations are natural entities, unified by common origin, language, history and culture	3.71	0.88
C. Nations represent a will to create a common future, despite cultural differences in the past	3.45	0.85
D. The claims of national groups for a state of their own were one main cause of wars in recent centuries	3.40	0.89
A. Nations are born, grow and perish in history, just like everything esle	3.02	1.04
F. National states should give an essential part of their sovereignty to a supranational organisation	2.88	0.91
E. National groups have the right to go to war to make their own state	2.68	1.11

the third was the item that conceives European integration as the way to solve economic and social crises. This third statement was particularly the preference of students in Portugal and in most of the Eastern European countries, that is, in those nations that in the mid 1990s saw their participation in the process of European integration as an important means of economic development.

Factor-analysis of the items of this group shows a two-factor solution: a pro- and an anti-European integration response. Analysing the correlation between these two factors and attitudes towards other political principles, the most significant finding is of a quite strong correlation between support for Europe and an affirmation of democracy: European adolescents associate the development of European integration with the development of democracy. It has been pointed out by Koerber (1997) that this finding is

> backed up by the results from the Eurobarometer standard No. 44 (October/November 1995 [taken in the same period in which the Youth and History questionnaire was administered]), which found among the adult citizens of the Union a similar picture of appreciation and critique of the European integration. Therefore, there is at least some hint that the views of the questioned students largely correspond to these of the adult citizens of the respective countries, which is an argument for considering their views and concepts as largely conventional (p.146).

The second political concept about which to consider the views of adolescents is the idea of the *nation*. The questionnaire asked: 'What are your views on nations and the national state?': the responses are shown in Figure 9.2.

In statement B we are offered as a possible response one of the classic definitions of 'nation'. This is the definition provided by Herder, which is generally seen in political theory as being opposite to the view of Renan, which is summarised in statement C. Other statements offered as possible responses focus on particular aspects of the role that the 'nation' and national states might have had in the past, or could have in the future. Some of these statements are clearly in conflict with others, but none totally contradicts the others.

As can be seen in Figure 9.2, the Herderian idea of the nation is that most favoured by European teenagers, while the Renanian interpretation of the concept is in second place. The first viewpoint is most favoured by students from the Czech Republic, Greece, Russia, Bulgaria and Turkey; the second has the highest average value in Italy, followed by France and Greece. Statement D has also a high value, coming third: this statement also positively correlates with both the acceptance of the Herderian idea of the nation and acceptance of the Renanian view. Factor analysis of this item shows that these three items appear to define a principal factor. The prevalent view of *nation* among European teenagers thus seems to be based on a blend of three fundamental principles, which are not perceived as being contradictory: nations are *both* natural entities *and* the result of the will of the people. This view of the history of nations is associated with the negative aspects of generating conflicts and wars. This shows clearly that this complex concept of the nation, held by the majority of European teenagers, must be grounded in assumptions about an objective, history-based idea of the nation. We might conclude that European adolescents are not nationalist, but that they do accept national states as an historical necessity. This interpretation appears very convincing, but is probably not quite so unanimous. In fact, examining the responses to statement F, we can state that European adolescents do not willingly accept the idea that nations should give away part of their sovereignty to a supra-national entity. This last result is of key importance to understanding the relationship between national identity and European identity: European teenagers, probably very similarly to those adults from whom they have absorbed and internalised their attitudinal models, have still a strong feeling for their nationality. In the short term it will not be easy for them to develop a new social identity in which they relate to an enlarged social group, which is much wider and has a more heterogeneous linguistic and cultural background (see below).

Interpreting the findings of the 'Youth and History' research, following Moscovici's theory of political socialisation

Thalia Dragonas and Anna Frangoudaki (1997) offer an interesting interpretation of the findings from the Youth and History research project, which aims to explain the pattern of attitudes shown by European teenagers, and in particular those concerning *European identity* as opposed to *national identity*. Their elaboration draws on the theory advanced by Serge Moscovici (1988), to develop a socio-psychological view of their attitudes. This theory suggests that explanations for occurrences, events, societal and historical problems and issues that affect individuals are not only the result of individual cognitive processes, but also the outcome of social forces. In this case, adolescents' answers to the items in the questionnaire constitute their explanation of historical issues. We can identify the origin in widely held and shared beliefs that take the form of collective values or representations. A fundamental premise of this theory is that it is only because individuals share these representations that it is possible for a social group – primarily a national group – to establish a specific identity. Moreover, it is possible for different social groups within a society to establish their identities and to come to differentiate themselves from other groups within the same society. Moscovici, and other authors who base their psycho-social theories on the social origin of attitudes, hold that every social group, irrespective of its size or geographical scope (local, regional, national, European, world) or other characteristics (language, race, ethnic and cultural background and traditions, religion, social class, ideological and political association and so on), exists only if its members *identify* themselves with the group, and this identification is based on just those characteristics.

Interpreting the findings of the 'Youth and History' research, following the social identity theory of Tajfel and Turner

Another theory that can be useful in interpreting the patterns of explanations for historical and political events and problems that are

181

shown by European adolescents is *social identity theory*, drawing on the works of Henri Tajfel and J.C. Turner (Tajfel, 1980, 1981, 1982, 1984; Tajfel and Turner, 1970, 1986). A fundamental principle of this theory is that each individual constructs an important and necessary part of his or her own identity (that is, their *social identity*) by means of a specific socialisation process, the identification process. Central to this is that the identification process is not based exclusively on absorbing the values, beliefs and other socio-cultural elements peculiar to the community or social group with which an individual identifies, but that it is also based on a process of *distinguishing* the individual from other communities or groups. Identification, in other words, acts on the basis of a *divisive* process of categorisation: I feel myself as a member of my community or group because I distinguish myself from the 'other'; thus I feel that *we* are a community because I can clearly create an image of 'them' – the 'others' from whom we are distinct. This theory holds that each individual needs to develop his or her *self-esteem*, not only in terms of a positive judgement of him or herself as an individual, but also in terms of a positive evaluation of the social group to which he or she belongs. Social identity is therefore a relevant component of one's self-esteem.

Turner (1984) held that his theory of social identification was the key mechanism of group formation, and that it also refuted both other dominant theories. The first of these focused on the 'interdependence criterion', which held that the members of a social group would be interdependent on each other in some way, for the satisfaction of needs, achievement of goals, consensual validation of attitudes and values, and that this interdependence tended to produce cooperative or affiliative interaction, mutual influence, and *social cohesion* between individuals (Sherif, 1967). The second theory was based on the 'criterion of *social structure*': according to this, social interaction between the members of a group was stabilised, organised and regulated by a system of role and status differentiations and shared norms and values. Turner pointed out that as there is in social psychology a 'reasonable descriptive consensus' about the importance of three fundamental criteria (identification, interdependence and social structure) in social group formation and their relationships, '...the accepted theory of a psychological group is that in essence it is some collection of individuals characterised by mutual interpersonal attraction reflecting some degree of inter-dependence and mutual need-satisfaction' (Turner, 1984, p.520). The most significant difficulty for this point of view, for Turner, was that

> it would seem to apply primarily and perhaps solely to small face-to-face groups whose members can interact on a personal basis. [...] These kinds of group membership may influence interpersonal interaction, but they do not seem to develop from cohesive inter-personal relationships. Nations, for example, do not emerge from friendship between individuals; they are cultural and historical givens imposed upon us by socialisation and social consensus whether or not they satisfy our individual needs. Indeed, national loyalties are sometimes at their fiercest when nationality is asso-ciated with intense deprivation and sacrifice. The members of a given nation are rarely united around some single common goal, but are normally divided by numerous issues, relevant or irrelevant to nationhood. There is not one consensual system of norms and roles: members tend to belong to numerous organisations and sub-cultures, not one of which has complete sovereignty. Finally, members do not interact with more than a small minority of their fellows and their relations are not universally amicable. Never-theless, nations can constitute psychological groups: the members tend to define themselves and be defined by others as a nation, and, under certain conditions, the vast majority will feel psycho-logically involved in the group membership, share similar emotions and attitudes and act in a relatively unitary manner towards their environment. [...] Thus, there seem to be at least some significant group memberships characterised only by the identity criterion. [...] The sufficient condition for psychological group formation seems to be the recognition and acceptance of some self-defining or self-inclusive social categorisation. (1984: pp.520-521).

On this basis, the fundamental hypothesis of the identity theory of the social group would be that group behaviour depends upon the cognitive effects of social categorisation on self-definition and self-perception (p.526).

The explanations provided by Dragonas and Frangoudaki related to Tajfel's and Turner's theory

Basing the interpretation of explanations of events and problems provided by European adolescents on the theoretical principles drawn by Tajfel and by Turner, it is perhaps possible to understand more clearly:

- which patterns are prevalent among European adolescents' understanding of national citizenship as opposed to European citizenship (including differences shown in a comparative analysis of the answers given by pupils in different countries)

- how the socialisation process of constructing European identity and citizenship works, and which different stages of development it goes through (this also appears useful in helping to understand the difficulties and obstacles that must be removed in order to facilitate this process);

- last but not least, how to translate this knowledge into effective educational strategies aimed at the educational goal of developing European identity and citizenship amongst children and young people.

According to the interpretation offered by Dragonas and Frangoudaki,

the long historical process of the formation of modern nations has been characterised by the identification of social groups to the nationalist ideal, according to which nations are seen as groups of people sharing the same past and ancestors, and having a common language and culture. All national ideologies have thus shaped the idea of belonging to a nation by means of a myth indirectly referring to the national community as to a family, and consequently describing the members of the nation mainly in terms of what their are not, that is in contradistinction to the 'other'.

The authors, developing one of the fundamental premises of the social identity theory, go on to assert that

The cultural features of [national] identity are related to economic power and social privileges, and their determination is based on differentiation, through which the categories of race or ethnic group are serving the legitimacy of social division of wealth, as well as domination. (Dragonas and Frangoudaki, 1997, pp.417-418).

To study the attitudes displayed by European adolescents on this issue of national identity as opposed to European identity, we can analyse the answers to the questionnaire about the adolescents' interests in history at different geopolitical levels (local, regional, national, European, world), and compare the mean scores we found to the two issues we are interested in for different countries. We can thus compare the degree to which young people in each country said that they were interested in either their own national history or in the history of Europe (see Figure 9.3).

This figure shows the different attitudes to national and European history shown in each country. Students from the North, Western European and some Eastern European (Estonia, Slovenia) countries show a level of interest in national history below the European average; while students of another group of countries – including most of the Eastern European countries and some South European countries (Italy, Spain, (Jewish) Israel) – show an interest near the mean of overall sample; and a third group, which includes Lithuania, Bulgaria, Greece, Turkey, Arab Israel, Palestine and Portugal, shows a very high level of interest in national history. In most of countries in this third group we find also a high level of interest in European history. So there appears to be a high degree of correlation between the general motivation for history as subject matter and specific kinds of history in terms of geopolitical contexts to which it refers (in particular, the national and the European contexts). There is also a remarkable generalised preference for an interest in the 'history of my country' over the 'history of Europe'. In every country (except Sweden, Finland and South Tyrol) the interest in national history is greater than the interest in European history; but to quite different extents: for example, in Germany and the Eastern European countries (Estonia, Ukraine and Slovenia) there is only a very small difference (Kindervater and von Borries, 1997, pp.82-83). There is also a high correlation between having an interest in these two sorts of history and having a more general interest in the value of history

Figure 9.3: National mean responses rates to perceptions enjoying the study of history – own national history and European history

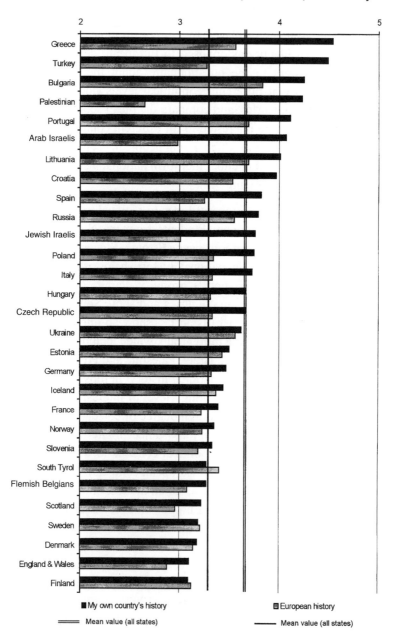

(derived from answers to other parts of the full questionnaire about the relevance of history for knowing about the past, understanding the present and for having a perspective on the future): generally, students who show a high motivation for understanding national and European history also believe that the study of history is relevant for understanding the present and considering the future (see Figure 9.4).

The first hypothesis that might be offered to interpret these results is that the students in those countries that have recently been involved in events and processes of deep change show, generally speaking, more interest in history, and particularly national history, when compared to those students from countries in which there has been a long period of stability. Movements of the present and of the recent past (often of events that they have directly experienced, and that are still vivid in their memories) stimulate an enthusiastic interest in the knowledge of the past in adolescents (Lastrucci, 1997: 346; see also Lastrucci, (1997). Related to this, and of significance, is that the degree of interest in politics shown by adolescents is strongly related to an interest in the past. In other words, because a stronger interest in history is inspired by quickly moving and changing current or recent events, which have been directly experienced, there is a consequential link to a profile that is more nationalistic than European.

A second interesting thesis comes again from the work of Dragonas and Frangoudaki. They suggest that if there is an evident preference shown for national history, as opposed to European history, this 'indirectly reveals one's desire to be tied to one's own group, i.e. an ethnocentric tendency' (Dragonas and Frangoudaki, 1997, p.418). The countries or minority groups that scored highest in the interest for local and national history were Greece, Lithuania, Israeli Arabs, Palestinians and Portugal.

Drawing from the argument that the ethnocentric attitude bolsters the positive distinctiveness of the in-group, one may claim that the adolescents' expression of an ethnocentric tendency is associated with the strong motive on their part to upgrade their sense of national belonging. They come from countries (Greece, Lithuania,

Figure 9.4: National mean response rates to perceptions of the value of studying history towards understanding the present and offering a perspective on the future

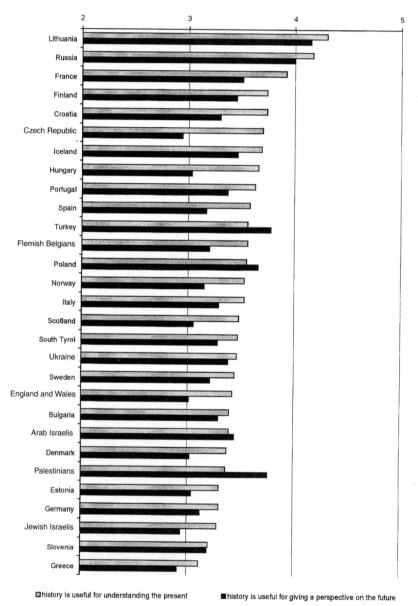

□ history is useful for understanding the present   ■ history is useful for giving a perspective on the future

the Palestine, and Portugal) or from groups (Arab Israeli) which are all, each to a different degree, and for different historical reasons, currently facing a number of social and economic problems, thus they would be ranked rather low among the rest of the countries of the so-called Western world. The adolescents find themselves being part of national groups that cannot be evaluated positively relatively to other groups. They thus respond to the identity threat by assuming an ethnocentric stance (Dragonas and Frangoudaki, 1997, pp.418-419).

The authors go on to analyse data from answers about specific interests in different extensions of the geographical area and compare these with interests in various specific periods of history (Ancient World, Middle Ages, 1500-1800, 1800-1945, 1945-today). My interpretation of their findings is that many of those same national groups which adopt an ethnocentric attitude towards history also place a stronger interest on the history of the far past than do students from the other states. Furthermore, adolescents who are more focused on the past have a stronger interest in politics.

As a rule, nations which celebrate their antiquity tend to forget their historical recency[3]. A strategy is often assumed by which identity structure is compared to a past structure that is more highly valued and is coupled with idealisation of the past. Identification with an idealised identity contributes to the formation and elaboration of an aggrandised and exalted national self which is desirable and often unattainable[4]. Many school curricula serve this idealisation of an identification with a glorious past. [...] The social identity approach argues that there is a vested interest in being associated with categories that are positive, since these can confer positive self-evaluation and create feelings of self-worth or self-esteem[5]. Europe's imperial expansion, on both the 'West and the Rest'[6], imbues the category of Europe with great symbolic power. Europe has a past of colonialism, expansionism, and violent struggles for the formation of a multitude of independent nation-states. This past shaped a particular ideology serving in legitimating territorial claims, expansion and wars, as well as dominance of 'others'. As it regards education policy, European curricular systems have been, and some still are, ethnocentric. They have been systematically over-

looking the contribution to human knowledge and progress of substantial groups of people, such as the non-majority indigenous
groups within the particular states of the EU, first and second
generation migrants representing a great range of cultures and all
those countries on the periphery of the EU whose status as Europeans is increasingly marginalised[7]. Thus following the argument
put forth by the social identity approach, as it regards one's association with positively strong categories, identifying with Europe and its
fate is likely to reflect an underlying motive to favour one's national
self. (Dragonas and Frangoudaki, 1997, pp.419-420).

The difficult process of constructing social identity: adolescence and the 'imperfect identity'

Some findings from other recent research on the development of
social identity are of interest at this point. An important inquiry
made by a group of Italian scholars has shown that adolescence constitutes the most critical stage in the process of development of
social identity (Palmonari *et al.*, 1984). The authors of this study
move away from the premise that adolescence is best considered as
a period of transition, instead suggesting that it be seen as a period
of

> a change in group affiliations, a transition from being a member of
> the group of children to being a member of the group of adults, with
> all the behavioural and emotional consequences that this entails ...
> This passing from childhood to adulthood can also be considered
> as a situation unfamiliar to the participants, representing for them a
> region of experience for which they have not had opportunity to
> build adequate cognitive structures

> [...] the simultaneous discoveries of ideal aims and of conflicts and
> contradictions sometimes create in the adolescent new enthu-
> siasm, but sometimes they drive him to doubt and, at the limit, to
> positions of complete distrust. The poor articulation of his cognitive
> field gives rise to sudden changes and 'extremes' of beliefs con-
> cerning groups and ideologies (pp.111-112).

In analysing such a question an important element is the role of
direct experience of socialisation into restricted reference groups
(such as the family, gender relationships, school and its ambience,

the first experience of work, and so on) in the process of political socialisation at the level of those wider social groups to which the adolescent belongs (such as regional and ethnic groups or minorities, the national community etc.). The decisive relevance of this phenomenon in the socialisation process, subsequently examined in depth by Lastrucci[8], was also an assumption of Palmonari *et al.* (pp.116-117).

Palmonari and his colleagues drew on the theory of the Sherifs (Sherif and Sherif 1965, 1969), whose studies showed how modifications in responsibilities, activities and modes of conduct had direct repercussions on the organisation of the self-system of each individual and on the formation of adolescent groups. They affirmed that

> the discontinuities, ambiguities and uncertainties of the adolescent period disturb the stability of the relationship previously established within the self-system, and motivate the individual to engage in an active search of new rules or guidelines of stable relations and for new ways of discovering how to leave behind present uncertainties (Palmonari *et al.*, 1984, p.119).

Based on the results of a specific research programme (pp.120-129), they formulated an explanation of the process of adolescent socialisation that offers an alternative to the Sherifs' model. They assume that 'groups of contemporaries are formed starting from a foundation of the activities of comparison, differentiation and identification in which adolescents engage in all social situations'. From this they explain the formation of adolescent groups on the basis of what Turner (1981) called the 'model of identification'. They say of this model

> it could be said that groups of contemporaries are formed when the adolescents, who are in the process of transforming their self-system, begin to perceive themselves as members of a particular social category: this implies the perception that they are different from other categories, not only those containing adults but also those including other adolescents. (Palmonari *et al.*, 1984, p.131).

The findings of this Italian group of social psychologists suggest the importance for adolescents – during the most difficult and crucial period for socialisation and the construction of social identity – to develop within their reference groups and their contexts of concrete experience (particularly the school) various specific intercultural experiences of socialisation, in order to create positive opportunities for identification within the European community, as well as within their specific national community.

Conclusion

The process of European integration is one of slow and difficult change. A real and effective integration is only possible if it is grounded in a widespread common consciousness. This consciousness consists of firstly, an historical consciousness that is founded in a view of the history of Europe as the history of a unique civilisation; secondarily, a *social identity* built on an awareness of European citizenship and on the feeling of belonging to the European community and civilisation instead to belonging to one's own national group (ultimately the sense of European citizenship must become, in the inhabitants of each member of the European Union, stronger than the sense of national belonging). In this process of changing consciousness, adolescents show the same delay as is shown by adults, and this is evidence that the educational institutions in the different European countries are still unable effectively to stimulate and promote the development of those cognitive and affective processes necessary to build a *European social identity*. The most important findings of the European survey that we have considered thus indicate the urgent need to develop in the different national curricula of Europe educational goals and strategies that are linked to this perspective of change. In order to achieve this it is urgent that we provide teachers with the professional competences and tools necessary to pursue this.

Notes

1 The chapter is a revised and extended version of the paper presented at the second Conference of CiCe Thematic Network, Athens, April 2000. That basic version of the paper has been published in the Proceedings of the Conference, Lastrucci E. (2000), History Consciousness, Social/Political Identity and European Citizenship, in A. Ross (ed.), *Developing Identities in Europe: Citizenship Education and Higher Education*, London, CiCe, pp.227-237.

2 For a general presentation of the research and its results see Angvik and von Borries (1997).

3 See Billig, 1995.

4 See Breakwell, 1986.

5 See Hogg and Abrams, 1988.

6 See Rattansi, 1994.

7 See Coulby, 1995.

8 See Lastrucci in Corda Costa (1997).

10

Young men growing up: is there a new crisis?

John Schostak and Barbara Walker
University of East Anglia, United Kingdom

Every age poses problems for its young. In particular boys have been the focus of a number of 'panics' in the British and European press. Are these problems fundamentally different today, or merely different in appearance? Based on the authors' research with young people, these issues will be explored through the experiences, understandings, explanations and hopes of boys in the context of the major social, economic and political changes taking place both locally and globally. By setting their dreams in relation to their realities, the impact on their sense of identity, agency and wellbeing is analysed in the context of social and personal expectations concerning 'maleness'. Is there a 'moral panic' about the apparent failure of boys relative to girls to succeed in education and employment? Or is there a 'real' crisis of 'maleness' going deeper than surface appearances? This chapter argues that in order to understand the experience of young people and boys in particular it is necessary to examine the differential allocation of resources to need, interests, and opportunities to develop talent to bring about the dreams, the hopes and the ambitions of young people.

Past and present

One version of the argument that little has changed can be seen in the historical evidence that the older generation have always considered lower-class boys troublesome. There is a degree of nostalgia associated with views on 'today's youth' – somehow the young were always nicer and the world better than, say, 20 years ago (Pearson 1983). Every age is able to yearn for the days when youth were more respectful. For example, in Humphries' (1981) study of working-class childhood from 1889 to 1939, the metaphors employed by con-temporaries to describe youth drew upon the images of the 'gutter', 'excrement' and 'pestilence', or of 'the jungle, with its associations of primitive sexuality, tribal savagery, bestiality and plain bovine stupidity' (p.11). Indeed,

> in moments of widespread anxiety about the disorderly behaviour of young people in the post-World War II period these two sets of images have been manipulated by the mass media to produce alarming stereotypes of rebellious youth, which have become the symbolic folk devils of their generation. Thus, for example, during the mid-sixties the media's condemnation of mods and rocker gangs as 'animals', 'dregs', 'vermin', 'rat-packs' and so on helped to create a moral panic that reinforced and legitimised repressive measures of social control by the police and the courts. (p.11)

In Britain in the 1980s and 1990s the Conservative governments under Thatcher and then Major drew upon an imagery of violence and loss of family unity and power by authority figures (for example, parents, police, teachers) to set in motion a rhetoric of a return to the values of the Victorian Age which became their stable point in a rapidly changing world. It may be argued that the judge-ment placed by each age on its youth is founded upon a political and rhetorical play of images anchored in fantasies of some previous 'golden age' that are claimed to embody the core values of those in power, or those who fear or have experienced a loss of power or security (see Schostak, 1986). These fears are revealed in many ways.

For example, some recent research has focused on contemporary peer pressure to 'be a good laugh' and its consequent effect on school performance (see, for example, Walker and Kushner, 1999). But, as Epstein *et al.* (1998) have shown, this is nothing new. Ladurie (1980) noted the same imperative amongst young men growing up in south west France in the first decades of the fourteenth century. So the phenomenon of 'boys being boys' is not novel; the question is whether these behaviours are either being interpreted as having a more deleterious effect upon the individual than in former times, or whether there is indeed some qualitative change. Thus it could be argued that, for the young peasants of Montaillou – out helping their elders mind sheep from the age of twelve or so and with schooling not an option – comic performances among peers had few if any long-term disadvantages. Even in 1970s England, Willis' (1977) working-class lads may have been condemning themselves to working-class jobs, but it might be argued that there is a sense in which they were happy to do so. Their futures were clear, with an honourable social role plus reasonable money. What changed from the late 1970s was the assumption that there was always a job. With the advent of the Thatcher government's insistence that monetarist economic strategies should replace Keynesian demand management, unemployment rocketed and even after a period of twenty years has not returned to the levels taken for granted in the 1960s and early 1970s.

Take another example: are boys and young men more violent now? Such issues were alive and well in the 1980s and early 1990s when there was rioting around the United Kingdom (Campbell, 1993; Schostak 1986, 1991, 1993). And more recently, despite well-publicised cases both in the British media (e.g. the cases of James Bulger, Stephen Lawrence, Damilola Taylor) and the French media (reported in *Times Educational Supplement* 15 December 2000), Coleman (1999) concludes that there is no great increase in youth crime, and that most of that crime relates to theft and burglary rather than to crimes against the person. In the same chapter, however, Coleman acknowledges that young people are far more likely to be the victims of violence than are adults, but noting that these attacks are most likely to be carried out by acquaintances. United Kingdom Home Office statistics on notifiable offences recorded by the police, covering the period October 1999 to September 2000, released in January 2001 (UK: 2001) show a 21 per cent increase in robbery in Britain. Such statistics as these may provoke questions but cannot provide answers.

The stories of 'panics' multiply and are tracked by the press. They produce good copy and sell papers. The way in which such a story was developed by the local press and ultimately proved to be without foundation was analysed by Davies (1991). It focused on the case of an 'arcade addict' (a person who spends a large proportion of their time and money on electronic video game machines in commercial settings) as it developed over a period of 95 days. The newspaper effectively invented a story that was well beyond the incident that gave rise to it. Rather than continuing this discussion, it has been shown clearly that 'moral panics' have always existed among the establishment when they consider young people, or working-class people, or women, or any other set of people who can be marginalised.[1] However the objects of the panics themselves perhaps typically consider themselves to gain in status by being the objects of this media concern. The media focus allows them to establish a place for themselves, an identity and indeed, a future.

What are the views of young people? Adolescence has long been viewed as a 'turbulent' age (Hall, 1904), but in the past there were desirable, and largely attainable identities to realise in the world. What if the identities to be sought are now out of reach, in flux, ambiguous? In the early years of the twenty-first century, has anything changed? In particular, what does it mean to be young and male? Have the essential characteristics changed over the years? Do the social class categorisations have meaning any more?

The identity game space
Traditional societies offered relatively stable identities for young people whether in kinship groups or feudal structures (for example, see Levi-Strauss, 1969). In Britain, the changes in the means of economic production commonly referred to as the Industrial Revolution, which gathered momentum from the late 1700s urbanised society, created the phenomenon of the 'mass' which underpins the contemporary phenomena of mass popular culture, consumerism, and the fragmentation that comes with the widespread adoption of the division of labour and specialisation that has in various forms been a feature of the nineteenth and twentieth

centuries. Similar processes followed in many parts of Western Europe and in much of the rest of Europe in the 20th Century. Furthermore, the social transformations taking place during the Industrial Revolution were associated with, or justified by, the application of scientific reasoning to solve economic, social, political and organisational problems. The scientific model largely drew its authority from its success in the domains of the natural sciences (physics, chemistry, biology and engineering) and indicated a modernist spirit that sought to rationally engineer both the material and the social or symbolic spheres of life. This rational, scientific, modernising paradigm was explicitly identified with broadly traditional male qualities and dominance. Hence, the male identity was secure under modernism to the extent that males were employed and were expected to be the heads of households and to be the 'bread winners'. For many men their identities were bound up with a particular industry, indeed, their family identities were made secure in the knowledge that they were, for example, 'steel men' in a 'steel town' that had a history of several generations. It is a pattern that has been increasingly challenged as the twentieth century progressed, whether from a feminist perspective, or through political attack (as during the Thatcher governments battles against the miners), or due to the powers of multinational companies relocating from high wage areas to low wage areas.

The game, as it were, seems to have changed. Contemporary social debate has focused attention on the claimed transitions between industrial and post-industrial or modern and postmodern. If these transitions are indeed taking place, then it would be reasonable to suppose that the experiences of young people are also changing. Do these changes make the old stable ways of finding one's bearings as a male a problem for young men? There is considerable debate in the literature on gender and on postmodernism, particularly in the field of cultural studies. These argue that the traditional dichotomies as between the essential nature and roles of male and female in society are experienced as problematic. They are perhaps game-like, perhaps tribal-like, perhaps rather like shopping for identities and styles. Rather than pursue these debates through the literature, this section introduces the experiences of two young men as points of departure for discussion. The two young men share similar social circumstances but apparently make quite different interpretations of their experiences with consequent implications for their views of the future. They each have to get their bearings in life and then build futures by identifying appropriate courses of action to achieve their desired futures. This naturally involves change, as the child becomes a teenager who becomes an adult. The question is whether individuals who are making these transitions are somehow doing it differently, or are having trouble finding ways of constructing identity because of some perceived social and cultural instability. This will require an exploration of the real circumstances faced by individuals, that either open up or close off opportunities for them to develop their sense of self in ways which realise their hopes and ambitions.

Take for example two 16-year-olds, Noel and Damien. They both attend the same school in a northern industrial city. Even local taxi drivers have difficulty in finding the school, sheltering as it does in the midst of a large council housing estate of brick-built, semi-detached houses. Although not far from a nationally renowned poor and violent area, these streets have a 'respectable' look about them. Over half of the faces in the school belong to various 'ethnic minorities', but Noel and Damien are white[2].

These two have been interviewed seven times over the last 18 months, usually in a group of the same four or five boys. The last interviews took place one to one, shortly before the boys were due to take their GCSEs (the final set of examinations for those ending their schooling at 16). The school has no provision for educating 16 to 18-year-olds, so staying on after the exams was not an option and decisions had to be made.

Eighteen months earlier both boys had been fairly optimistic. Both had part-time jobs gained through personal contacts, and saw this type of experience as useful for the future both in terms of job content – construction work for Noel, catering for Damien – but more especially in terms of local networking. In fact since both would turn 16 before taking GCSEs they were considering leaving school then, before the exams. As Damien said:

> You leave school, do whatever you're doing, get less of money. Go to college, get your paperwork, earn double the money, so... It's like that. But like you're in school, you want to leave. You want to leave, like everyone does, but you want the paperwork as well, so...

By the last interview the decision to stay on for the exams appears to have been made. These decisions are framed to some extent by the individual's sense of present circumstances, desired life style and emergent sense of identity as a young man within a given community.

The next decision point is rapidly approaching – far too soon for Noel who, already at 16, feels he has run out of options:

> That's my problem, I just don't know. I know, I just don't know what I'm going to do, I want to go to college. I've got an area what I want to study in college. I want to do something like PE, leisure and tourism, maybe something to do with English. But I don't know after that, I don't how I'm going to get a job with it, so I'm not really, I don't really know what I want to do.

He does, however, have a dream. His dream had been to play football for Manchester United but the chances are becoming slim. Despite playing for a highly successful local youth team, his talent has not so far been spotted by any of the league scouts. And time for that is running out. His second-choice option had been to go to a local college to study on a Sport and Leisure course, which he had hoped might enable him to join a minor league team as a junior coach. But he has just learned from friends already taking the course that it's 'rubbish'. There are possibilities of going to a different college and maybe doing an English A level and/or 'something to do with PE'. But he seems very vague about that option, not knowing what qualification he wants, how long he would have to study, or – most importantly for him – whether it would lead to a job:

That's what I mean. I don't know how I'm going to get a job. I've never really, since I've been to school, I've never really known, oh I'm going to do this. Like kids say, 'Oh I want to be a fireman.' I've never really said that. I've always said I want to be a footballer! But I'm going to start sending letters off to football teams, asking for trials. If you don't send letters, you're not going to get nowhere, so I'm just going to send letters.

If this tactic doesn't work, Noel will be at a loss. He talks about how all his friends appear to know what they want to do – not all of them 'brilliant' jobs in Noel's opinion, but at least they have something to work towards. He has got to a point where he wants the decision to be taken out of his hands: '[I] just want to leave school and I just want someone to be there and to say, 'Right, this is your job, you've got this job. I know what you like, this is your job.' I just want someone to say that.' Noel's face is clouded with anxiety: 'My biggest worry is what I'm going to do when I leave school. That's my biggest worry... I just want a flat, a girlfriend.'

Damien, by contrast, seems to have a strong sense of himself. In the transition from child to young adult he recognises that others will see changes in him. However, does he see a difference? 'No. Same. Well I haven't noticed have I 'cos [because] I'm myself aren't I?' He has in his own mind a fairly stable plan of development. He seems to have found a path that might lead towards his goals. He is in love with cars, and wants a job involving driving. Police work appeals to him, but he is too young to enrol with the force. So, in the meantime, he is considering a carpentry apprenticeship that appears to offer reasonable remuneration, and will furnish him with a useful skill for the future. There was one obstacle that for a time troubled his self presentation. His girl friend was the first to get a regular job and she would pay for him when they went out together. It was not something that he was comfortable with:

Interviewer: [Who pays] when you go out to a club?

I pay for her. Well like, I hadn't got a job so she's been paying most for me. Haven't been out much but she, like, pays 'cos [inaudible] but now I've got a job I'm going to pay her back what she's done for me. But she ain't going to put her hand in her pocket. Well if she wants to she will but otherwise I'll pay for her. 'Cos that's the kind of guy I am. Well you have to!

However, soon he could say:

I'm working at MacDonalds's at the moment 'Cos I just got a job last week, so I'm working there. Should give me some extra money. And hopefully I can be an apprentice. In something like carpentry – as soon as I leave school.

Getting a job enabled him to adopt the pose of the traditional male and feel confident that he is on course to achieve his ambitions.

Within the community, it is the role of friends, neighbours, people at hand to help frame a world where options become possible, are judged and potential courses of action are either outlined or dismissed. For example, Damien's brother has joined the Army. The family went up to Scotland to see him take part in an open day which impressed Damien sufficiently to encourage him to do his work experience with the Army. He did not enjoy it but was able cheerfully to write off that avenue because he had an alternative:

Well my mate, his brother's in the police. Go to the pub with him and everything. When you're in a uniform you have to have a different head on but he's still all right. Sounds good. He seems to have a good laugh.

Damien's interest in cars is sustained by a slightly older friend who already has a car which the two of them work on in their spare time. At the last interview he said he was going to get a wreck of a car himself to work on in a few weeks. Conversely there appear to be no cars amongst Noel's friends and the acquisition of one is a prospect delayed beyond the barrier of getting a job.

I'm not bothered about getting a car, not yet. When I'm older, when I've like really settled down, got a job, got everything right and I've got time to do something. I'll get driving lessons and probably buy a car, won't be buying one straight away. Don't see the point.

So there is another influence at work in the community, sometimes combining with media foci and sometimes running counter to it, and this is the stories and experiences of other young men. For instance, it is the damning accounts of those already attending the Sports and Leisure course that have persuaded Noel not to follow that route. Peer stories can run counter to advice from elders and cause confusion. Noel's older brother is 'well brighter than my sister and me', worked hard at school and was successful in exams 'but he's still only working in a supermarket'.

Their versions of 'street wisdom' also appear to be formed according to peers' experience. Soon after the first meeting, Damien said that his friends out of school tended to be older than him, often his brother's friends who included him in their group and upon whom he felt he could call if in trouble. 'Like if I got into a scuffle up that road, or wherever I am, I know that there's loads of people that would help me out.' And he proudly goes on to tell a long story of a running battle he had with a bigger boy, where his brother's presence swung an unpleasant situation in his favour.

By contrast Noel's friendship group appears to consist of boys of the same age. At one point during the research he tells stories of the group's harassment by police officers. This, he said, occurred mainly when they were 'hanging around' on street corners or outside shops ''cos they think we're going to nick something'. At the last meeting he said that he no longer socialises in his own streets, preferring to take a bus to a neighbouring area he considers to be safer. The catalyst appears to have been an incident where his brother was mugged, Noel suspects, by a group of his former friends.

Perhaps it is this distance between advice from those older and more powerful, and the experience of peers (or those just slightly older) that leads to Noel's despair. Damien has a friend who is a policeman and seems to be enjoying his job. So the messages he is hearing may be more synchronised.

In each case, the game plans for the setting and realisation of goals can be analysed. Implicit within each account are a multiplicity of subject positions which either provide access to or close off options.

This is represented in the following highly simplified diagram (Figure 10.1) which shows a range of subject positions (S_1, S_2, ..., S_n) such as, identity for self (say S_1) as distinct from identity of self as defined by others (S_2). Here S1 for Damien, signifies a strong sense of identity that persists through time and is defined in terms of his

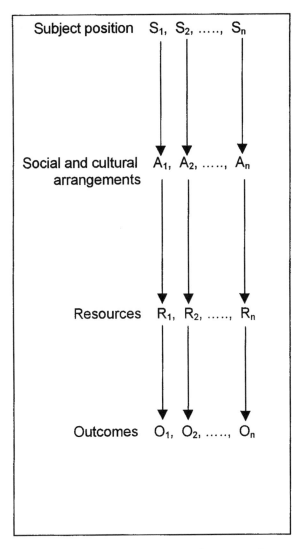

Figure 10.1: Simplified diagram of a game plan

love of cars and his attraction to the police force. For many boys, slightly older peers were role models (S_1) to a certain extent. Though the concept of a negative role model (say S_n) was much more in evidence, as in 'I don't want to end up like that' – unemployed, a drunk, seeking drug money through crime. There was the fear of becoming a member of the underclass.

Damien knows how to achieve his ambitions in a way that reinforces his strong sense of self (S_1) and hence avoids the negative possible identities (S_n). That is, he is able to draw upon knowledge, appropriate ways of behaving, skills, and social mechanisms, that is, the appropriate social and cultural arrangements, A_2, in order to move step by step (by adopting S_2, the identity as apprentice made available through social arrangements within his reach that provides relevant skills that take him) towards his goal. Noel, on the other hand, wants to have the identity of a footballer, a goal that is increasingly out of reach. The major social arrangement that would enable him to realise this goal (the college course) is problematic. His alternatives are unclear and the means (examination success) by which to achieve them are difficult. The structure of the two 'game plans' are the same but the difference is in the extent to which the social arrangements and resources are realistically within reach.

Each game plan is underpinned by a possible world that provides the rationale as to why the plan is reasonable. Damien's world is similar to those about him. Noel's world is that of the stars.

In summary, the community for each of the young men is the unit through which they conceive their world. It is largely defined in terms of geographical region, peer associations and perceived reputation. This community offers a range of potential subject positions from which to construct identities. The community thus defines what 'game structures' are possible, and the chances of being a winner or loser in these games. What is important to consider is the impact of national and global structures that impose different 'games'. At one time when the community and its identity and reputation were intimately linked to a dominant industry (the mining town, or steel town, or car town) subject positions and identities were ordered according to their function with respect to that dominant industry. As these industries declined and where no alternative work replaced them, the reputations of communities were transformed, often negatively, and new subject positions and identities appeared (unemployed, poor, shiftless, vandals, criminals) that were either adopted (willingly or reluctantly) or contested. As Noel says of his own community:

> – never feel safe on me own turf, 'cause there's people coming from like the police, they think they're patrolling Bankside and they think they're doing something good. What they don't know, they think – have you heard about all what's happening [here]? They think that the folks are just going to stay in Bankside. They're going to move, aren't they? So they're all coming to Langridge. Someone got shot in York Street.

Interviewer: Yes, so you clean up Bankside and it just –

> – yeah, that's what they've done to Bankside. They thought we'll clean Bankside up. They got all the nutters out of Bankside, and they just dump them in Langridge! That's what happens.

It is difficult for schools and teachers to abandon the mantra of 'work hard, get good exam passes, go on to further education and ensure a good job for life'. But the media, for people like Noel, provides alternative visions of a reliable world where, for example through sport or popular entertainment, people can achieve desired identities and the 'good life'. In each case, the identities, the social arrangements and the resources to attain them are made public and potentially desirable. In each case, a young man has to work out who he is, and how to be at ease with himself. He also has to learn how to operate in a group, how to make friends and contacts which ultimately, as always, are 'virtues which brought success' (Ladurie, 1980, p.329). Like any individual, in order to make decisions young people need to be able to gain access to information, analyse it and assess it. Both Damien and Noel do this, but according to different aims, principles and frameworks of judgement. However, as Furlong and Cartmel (1997, p.114) conclude their book: 'Blind to the existence of powerful chains of interdependency, young people frequently attempt to resolve collective problems through individual action and hold themselves responsible for their inevitable failure.'

Concluding remarks: social change and global games

Schooling supports a 'world' that, for those like Damien, reinforces their own world, but for many others is either obsolete and frustrating or, like Noel, does little to provide a real step towards their dreams. This world has its foundations in nineteenth-century motivations and rationales for childrearing and the reproduction of society along class, gender and occupational lines. Reforms during the first half of the twentieth-century embedded a welfare logic which in turn late twentieth-century political conservativism undermined. The motivation for this reversal drew from the increasingly powerful market logic of late capitalism and its globalising powers, reinforced by the integration of computers and telecommunications. Rather like sedimentations in the earth's crust with the ever present potential for collision and the eruption of contents from one level into another, traditional, reformist and the social impact of globalising technologies coexist in tension. Thus there are attempts to reinforce a sense of national identity, power and control at the same time that there is increasing loss of control by central governments to manage the major economic structures and events that impact upon societies.

For example, in Britain in the 1960s, following a logic of technological modernisation, there was the political ambition to reshape society for the future. One expression of this was the development of new towns. In a study by Schostak (1983) of a large comprehensive school serving a new town built in the late 1960s to re-house people from the slums of a neighbouring city, the dream of the socialist New Jerusalem had faded to become a nightmare in the late 1970s that continues to the present day. The tax breaks offered in the 1960s to the multinationals to provide employment ceased in the mid 1970s. Unemployment returned as the multinationals left to find tax breaks and low wages elsewhere in the world. The impact upon the communities was devastating. The stories of violence, theft, and hopelessness mingle with those of ambitions and hopes for the future just as much in Schostak (1983, 1991) as in the voices of Noel and Damien. There is little they can do as individuals to change the circumstances they face in their communities. Indeed, the games played at a local level all have the sense of 'reality' and are within the bounds of common sense. Through the interview transcripts of each boy one can analyse the range of things they need to manage, to know about, to find evidence to ground their judgements about what to do. However, although the global means of making desires public impact on their expectations of what the world is like and what identities are possible, the global structures and mechanisms through which resources are allocated to individuals, organisations, and communities are substantially hidden from the boys. This is not something dramatically new. It is a complaint often expressed by those who would wish to change social circumstances, that individuals do not understand the real circumstances of their lives. The worlds of everyday life, are in effect, imaginary (Anderson, 1983). And they are not unitary, but rather multiple (James, 1890; Schutz, 1967; Kuhn, 1970).

The issue is not whether globalisation or Europeanisation is having an effect on young people and boys in particular, but whether within their communities young people are any better able to effect change and influence their futures today than they were in previous decades and centuries. Have the defining features of their communities through which they construct their identities changed? Yes, as always there is change. The most significant changes have to do with

• the social status and position of women on the social and economic stage

• the decline of old mass industries defining whole communities

• the rise of the global market place underpinned by media and information technologies.

Nation states are grudgingly recognising and adapting to these changes. As authors such as Haseler (2000) point out, the governments of nation states are increasingly unable to make more than symbolic changes in policy. Global multinationals are forcing nations to compete with each other to attract investment. This means bidding down the cost of employment, which places an emphasis on reducing taxes which in turn means less to spend on welfare and the core issues relating to poverty and the need for economic regeneration. On the other hand, where the influence of the nation state is dwindling, the significance and perhaps the power of regions appears to be increasing. Particularly, within the European Union, emphasis is being placed on regional funding for development. What then might this mean for young people and in particular boys like Damien and Noel? At one level, very little. They are no closer to the means of power than were their parents, grandparents, great-grandparents and so on.

At another, more institutional and political level, with the dwindling of national power there has been a change in regional or local power. How this may impact on the identities of individuals and their felt sense of community and ability to shape their futures is perhaps still too early to say. There is no unambiguous impact as revealed in the voices of the young people who were the subjects of the research reported in this chapter. Their sense of self is fundamentally influenced by the people in their vicinity, the people they interact with, the people who have social status in the eyes of their friends, family and neighbours. However, their life chances are now being defined by structures and processes that happen at a global level and impact locally. This would suggest that any focus for reforms should aim at this local–global relationship. Schooling in Britain has been reluctant to do so. Indeed, at the very same time that Britain was locked into the development of a national core curriculum, a return to 'basic' skills and core 'Victorian values', Finland (Norris et al., 1996) initiated curriculum reforms (National Board of Education, 1994) that moved from a core national curriculum towards a flexible curriculum focusing on regions and their communities. They considered that a 'curriculum is an expression of the local decision-makers' political will' (p.18). They envisaged a world where:

> The realm of knowledge is growing with leaps and bounds, which means that it is difficult to master it all through the traditional means the school has to offer. What is important is on what grounds the

contents of the matters to be studied are chosen so that one's studies would lead to an organised structure of knowledge. (p.11)

In short, the Finnish national curriculum looked ahead towards the new global–local relations and began the task of allowing communities to review their traditional strengths in relation to the new economy based upon 'knowledge' and the new information technologies. The individual became not a standardised unit for assessment but a creative centre for the personal and social organisation of knowledge. Of course putting policies into practice is always problematic, because practices have to change, new skills and philosophies need to be learned and previous social arrangements have to be, at least in part, replaced as described in our evaluation report of these reforms (Norris et al 1996). What is important is rather that European models are beginning to emerge that are genuinely responsive to contemporary needs rather than locked into nineteenth-century views of the world.

Unless educational and community models appropriate to the new conditions facing young people emerge, people like Noel and Damien will have no basis upon which to construct a sense of identity that is creatively attuned to the online globalised worlds of the twenty-first century. Bhaskar (1986) has provided a strong philosophical case for the political and ethical imperatives that can be drawn from research. Far from research being a neutral, value-free activity 'it always consists in a *practical intervention* in social life and it sometimes logically entails value and practical judgements.' In summary terms the conclusion to the argument is that if research shows that a particular belief about the way the world works is false, then the social reasons why people continue to hold that belief need to be removed so that they can have access to 'true' beliefs about the world. For individuals and communities to act in their own best interests they should have access to knowledge about their circumstances in relation to the ways in which resources are currently allocated to individuals and communities. If national structures no longer hold the key to reform and to the enhancement of life chances, then alternative structures need to be developed. These alternatives may be found in such emergent phenomena as

Europeanisation, regionalisation, and community action. Unless researchers can develop the new models needed, there will be no local mechanisms that can be used to ensure that resources actually meet real local needs. Unless Damien, Noel and all the others in communities like theirs find a way of creatively engaging with the new social realities, there will be little hope for those communities.

Notes

1   Although the term 'moral panics' was developed in the early 1970s by the criminologist Stan Cohen in examining the media's responses to the violence between Mods and Rockers in the 1960s (Cohen, 1973)

2   During the research, race did not figure in the ways the boys talked about their experiences.

11

On the development of education for democracy and citizenship in the Czech Republic

Pavel Vacek

University of Hradec Králové, Czech Republic

In this chapter I discuss the possibilities and the prognosis for education for democracy and citizenship in the Czech Republic. I consider particularly the time between 1989 and the present, and will approach this systematically from the position of the psychology of morality, following Piaget and Kohlberg. My focus is thus more social psychological and sociological, but I also consider economic and political explanations of the period.

Although I base this chapter on specifically Czech experiences, I also consider the fundamental features of social development – and generally the same is true also of educational development – as being very similar in all those countries of Central and Eastern Europe that were once members of the Soviet block.

The starting position of all these countries was very similar: an economic life was that centrally planned, isolated from the reality of the laws of the market, economic rules, the ownership relationship, a banking system that was biased and distorted, and the lack of such institutions as a stock-exchange, and so on. The massive and extremely fast transfer of vast amounts of property that belonged to 'nobody' (the so-called nationalised property) to real individual owners in the process of privatisation was not well managed, and caused extremely high economic losses.

The change of orientation, in both the political and the legal sphere, back to parliamentary democracy was not easy. In the Czech Republic at present we are in a phase of stabilisation. When we started, we knew nothing about the free competition of political parties, and only through practice – and our own painful experience – did we realise the meaning of words that are common and widely understood in the west – words like *coalition, opposition, majority* or *minority government*, and so on. We had to create new laws, including a constitution, establish or re-establish new democratic institutions, such as the Constitutional Court and the office of ombudsman. We found that we had totally new phenomena in our society, such as independent mass media – with all their pros and cons, and with all their mighty influence on public life. With these changes came other social movements, such as charities, ecological and civic groups, all of which have had a constantly increasing influence on our social life.

Together with our neighbouring post-communist countries, we have found that the world of democratic countries around us has opened up for people from the Czech Republic. We can now travel abroad, not only to see new countries but also to study or work there. In this particular case, there are some major differences between particular post-communist countries. The former German Democratic Republic, with its exclusive position, is at one end of the range and some of the countries of the former Soviet Union (particularly the Ukraine and Belarus) are at the other.

Another issue is the differences between post-communist countries in the field of religious groups and nationalities or ethnic groups. For example, there are significant variations between some highly secularised regions, such as in the Czech Republic or the former German Democratic Republic, and the highly religion-focused situation in Poland, which has a population deeply committed to Catholicism. Some countries have an even more complicated situation, where there may be complex structures that interconnect various national minorities and religious groups. For example, Slovakia has a significantly large Hungarian minority, but the beliefs of this minority do not substantially differ in their affiliations from those of the Slovakian majority. When nationalistic tendencies combine with religious differences the situation is obviously at its most complicated. The dissolution of the former Yugoslavia and the dramatic events that followed – namely the war in Bosnia and present tension in Kosovo – are sad examples arising from such complicated situations.

In analysing and commenting on these aspects of nationalism, it is necessary to point out that this problem was not solved in totalitarian states, and was usually repressed, and only silenced with the use of force. This meant that many of these nations only experienced national or state sovereignty at the very moment they turned to democracy: their first opportunity for a long time. The division of Central and Eastern Europe into a string of smaller countries at the beginning of the 1990s was not only a natural process, but also a very necessary precondition for the possibility of further integration on a qualitatively higher level.

There are other phenomena that are new for the people from the post-communists countries, some of which are not easy to get used to. For example, there is evidence of gradually growing social differences in society, a phenomenon we refer to as 'the inner diversification of society'. There is growing unemployment, which in our societies is understood as a near-fatal situation: unemployed people – mainly men – explain their situation either as one of personal failure or as an example of a fundamental lack and insufficiency of the social system – a further disappointment of democracy.

This scene-setting should make it obvious that any consideration of education for democracy and citizenship in the countries of Central and Eastern Europe will only be meaningful if we also take the broader social context into consideration.

The broader social context

The broader social context in the Czech Republic affects education for democracy and citizenship in a number of ways: I have grouped these under six headings.

1. The short period of development for democracy

We have only had a little over ten years for developing democratic institutions, following a period of almost 50 years of political totalitarianism. In the Czech Republic, as in the other post-communist countries, the first decade of democratic development has come to an end. The social changes that have occurred in the field of bringing up children and education have been moderate, even slow, and very specific. Although the year 1989 represented an important line dividing our national history, it did not bring a full discontinuity with the past: this would have been impossible in the context of social processes. Democratic changes were more easily applied in formal economic and social structures in general (though some limitations have been mentioned above); but on the other hand, it has been rather more difficult to introduce change in those informal relational structures that are connected to customs and traditions. The stereotypical thinking and behaviour of individuals represent another barrier to change. In education, this has meant that while there was hardly any problem in removing the former ideology from the school system and replacing it with an education grounded in the principles of democracy, there was, and still is, a problem in changing individual teachers' personalities and stereotypical behaviour.

2. Immaturity in the political and social scene

In traditional democracies advancement up the political career ladder is usually step by step: future social leaders get checked, assessed by the electorate, and approved (or not) on the lower rungs as they move through their political career. The swift way up the system is much rarer than in our country. After 1989 and the Velvet Revolution many people, who were sometimes lacking in the basic qualities of citizenship and morality, achieved very fast advancement in their careers. Others, perhaps usually more honest, were not able to cope with the great responsibilities that came with so suddenly and easily obtained power. I do not include in this those people with a weak character who had previously held important posts in the communist period and were now able to continue in positions of power, and to reassert and even strengthen their position. Similar patterns of development – with similar results – happened also in Poland, Slovakia and other countries. Of course, not all of those who were connected with the last regime were necessarily lacking in professional, human or moral qualities. The presidents of both Poland and Slovakia held important political positions before 1989, and both are today regarded as highly renowned people in their countries.

This situation strongly influenced changes in the area of upbringing and education. Firstly, we have no rules of so called 'political culture'. We lack those standards that one would expect people, especially those working in social and civil services and administration, to follow naturally. These standards amount to an implicit culture, something not written, but understood, agreed and accepted. Standards like this are probably created over many years or even decades.

Secondly, we commonly tolerate the many misdemeanours, lapses or simply wrongdoings of our politicians: lies, broken promises, vulgarisms, arrogant behaviour, taking unauthorised advantages, and so on. Our citizens are tolerant of these shortcomings in the wrong way. The result of such misplaced tolerance is a weak belief in democracy as such, and a general refusal to consider seriously politicians and their policies. In consequence, many people now are only concerned with taking care of their own business, and are not concerned with matters of common interest or of wider importance.

Thirdly, there are few models of the behaviour and way of life one would expect of honest leaders, which could be accepted and promoted in educational circles. For example, we do not have examples of leaders who have resigned because of their moral failure, or for telling lies.

3. Doubts about the basic principles of democracy

Some people think that current social problems and economic uncertainty (such as those created by unemployment), our imperfect laws, our scandals, the increased criminality that is evident, and so on, are all connected with the new democratic system. This contributes to their doubts about the basic principles of democracy: so much so that one third of Czech citizens now consider that the previous totalitarian system was better when compared with today's system. In other post-communist countries there appears to be a similar, or even greater, sense of disappointment in democracy, often in a larger portion of the population (for example, in Poland, Slovakia, Romania and Bulgaria). Of course, a scandal may occur anywhere in any form of society, but in traditional democracies virtually nobody doubts the basic principles of democracy because of these scandals: instead, they look for the culprits and take the necessary steps to rectify the situation.

4. Czech society nationally homogeneous

After the displacement of the large German minority (which amounted to a third of the total population), and after the division of Czechoslovakia, the Czech Republic became, to certain extent, a nationally unique country, because it does not have a large national or ethnic minority of any significant size. The largest minority is the Slovak people, who are not perceived as being foreign. The next largest ethnic group is the Gypsies. While this lack of substantial minorities minimises the potential for conflicts based on nationalistic or xenophobic grounds, it also, on the other hand, slows down our development as a multicultural European state. Most Czechs lack any real personal experience of contact with members of other ethnic groups, cultures or nations. In some Western European countries, part of society appears to becoming more racialist, because of the subjective perceptions of negative experiences with immigrants: people in the Czech Republic, though they usually have not shared such experiences, are no less xenophobic. Ultra-right nationalistic groups of young people cry out 'patriotic' slogans, such as 'The Czech country to the Czech people' although the people whom they address are very few. One might predict that the increasing level of immigration into the Czech republic not only will be desirable and lead to an enriching multiculturalism, but at the same time, for many of our citizens, will not be easily acceptable. At present we are not prepared for this, and this is particularly important for our children and youth.

5. The preference for material needs, and the decline of interest in spiritual and cultural values

Democracy offers choice, but this is accompanied by an increased degree of uncertainty. People in post-communist countries are still not self-reliant: they show a significant lack of independence and expect that 'someone' will help them, as was the case in past times. Many people gain, or regain, this lost feeling of certainty through a paradoxical, simple and one-sided preference for money and for material property. Materialism also stems from the fact that:

- for many years West European countries, unreachable and admired, were associated with high standards of living, freedom of travel and exclusive goods, but were connected much less frequently with spiritual values

- after many years of self-denial, there is a tendency towards over-compensating with those material goods which used to be so difficult to obtain

- our societies are still less resistant to commercial manipulation: crafty advertisements can be very successful in our countries. The next generation may be able to leave this historical burden behind, and naturally accept the combination of high standards of living with freedom and democracy as part of their everyday lives.

On the other hand, the contribution made by the countries of Central and Eastern Europe to the rather uniform and culturally static model of western civilisation might be very stimulating.

6. A strong aversion to the use of terms that were discredited in the totalitarian period (seen as ideological contamination)

Many terms used to describe widely-accepted human values became discredited during the period of the totalitarian state, because of their misuse: a phenomenon known as ideological contamination. For example, if the term 'democracy' was mentioned, the only correct way to use this was in 'socialist democracy'; the word 'morality' was always qualified as 'communist morality', and in a similar manner, socialist patriotism and citizenship. Having rejected communist ideology, we have pushed aside issues of citizenship and ethics because of their previous associations and usage.

To find ways of presenting topics such as these is particularly difficult for ordinary teachers in the schools. All the ideological discourse has been removed from schools, which is a good thing, but at the same time our schools have become apolitical, so that there is very little, if any, reflection on contemporary events – and this is not a good thing. Because of this, to talk about freedom, patriotism, love and pride in our own nation often seem to us pathetic and improper: it is as though we were ashamed of such feelings and attitudes.

The Czech school system and education for democracy

The Czech school system and the extent and level of education in the country has a long and rich tradition which is attributable in part to the contribution of J.A.Komenský. Compulsory school attendance was introduced as early at 1774, within the framework of the former Austro-Hungarian empire. The level of literacy of the Czech and Moravian people was one of the highest in Europe. Since the nineteenth century, the education of teachers has developed from the traditions and ideas of Komenský. Modernising tendencies influenced the system between the world wars, during the period of Czechoslovakia. This movement effectively combined American pragmatism and the European reform movements. This promising development was then interrupted by the Second World war and the following period of communist totalitarian rule.

In general one can say that the Czech and Slovak school systems (and those of Poland and Hungary) are closer to the Austrian and German school systems than to the more liberal Anglo-Saxon systems. The era of totalitarianism managed to deeply imprint many common features into the school systems of the countries of the former Soviet block, and many of these have outlasted the era of totalitarianism. A basic feature of the period was a form of unification that had an international character, and this was found in the educational systems of all countries of the Soviet block. This unification was based on an ideology of an educationally firm and fixed framework and a unified syllabus that determined the contents of what was taught. The school system was completely in the hands of the state bureaucratic administration, which controlled not only the content of the curriculum but also the teaching methods employed in the classroom. The development of alternative school programmes, in the way that is common in the west, was simply not possible for ideological reasons. In the final resort, nothing but the state school could exist before 1989. My own personal experience confirms that there was very little difference between the Czech, German, Soviet and Polish school systems. The system was based on the mechanism of control from outside, and this control checked and diminished the autonomy and the self-regulative and self-control mechanisms of teachers, and led to their lack of independence, as will be described below.

There are some obvious problems, discussed later in the chapter, but apart from these, visiting pedagogues from western countries tend to praise highly the behaviour and discipline of our students, the sense of order in schools and classrooms, the well organised teaching, the high qualifications of teachers, and the fixed and firm organisational structure of the Czech school system. But all of these apparently meritorious aspects can also, under certain circumstances, be counterproductive. This is particularly the case in teaching and education for citizenship, or in similar programmes that aim to influence the character or morals of pupils. In other words, problems in education will appear not when pupils are learning information and knowledge, but when teachers are attempting to influence and develop desirable human qualities and attitudes. I have identified a number of characteristics in this, which I suggest apply not only in the Czech Republic, but also – and for the same reasons – more or less in all the other countries of the former Soviet block.

Education for democracy and broader citizenship has not really yet moved to become of central interest to our schools.
I have indicated some of the causes of this situation.

- The development of the policy that schools should not be political agents has led to another extreme: that schools are now kept separate and aloof from contemporary social events. This is caused partly by fear, and partly by the lack of training for our educators to handle sensitive social issues in class. The prevailing educational method is to put to students the only possible and correct solution, and if the teacher does not know this, or there is no 'correct' solution, then the topic is avoided and never tackled.

- There remains a strong and persistent general dislike of all topics that used to be associated with an ideological dimension (identified above as ideological contamination). A major reason that any discussion about issues like freedom, personal courage and self-respect is avoided is that many of us who were working in the earlier period were forced to be loyal: we were anxious to keep our own jobs and positions (as well as the jobs and positions of our relatives) and we did and said things which were not in any sense expressions of personal courage. Habit and careerism drove many of our decisions. The courage to explain and confess our past weaknesses is a form of bravery today, which might for our pupils and students serve as advice about the importance of protecting democracy and freedom in the future.

- There is over-reliance on the belief that topics related to democracy and citizenship, such as values, leadership, character and similar concepts, can be 'taught' within appropriate subjects in the curriculum, such as civics and history. There is still a strong prevailing opinion that democracy and citizenship can be taught 'by heart'.

- The prevailing teaching style tends to be authoritative, where the teacher is the source of all knowledge and opinion: there is very little, if any, space for any dialogue and discussion with pupils and students.

- Teachers show a lack of independence in deciding what to teach in the classroom, and in what way to teach. There is an almost servile sticking to the curriculum, which is not in fact compulsory in its detail.

- It is clear that our school system is now unwittingly and dangerously selective. The previous regime created an illusion of social equality based on an ideological conviction that the most progressive, and thus the most important, part of society was the working class. Despite the spurious character of such statements, it was true that in this period the social position, the financial standing, and the self-esteem of people from working-class and agricultural backgrounds was higher than it is now. While democracy offered many new opportunities to young people, it seems that in practice only those students and pupils who are more gifted, heading towards secondary schools and universities, are able to take advantage of these opportunities and to use them. This is not a problem. But less successful students and pupils, who do not have such predispositions and aspirations, and who aim more towards blue-collar jobs, are now more threatened by unemployment, have weaker self-confidence and a lower competence in language. These young people experience frustration; the advantages of a democratic society do not work for them in these respects. This is probably the basis of future problems around the extreme radicalisation of this part of the population.

To summarise this: while we are able to educate quite well the elite elements of our society we cannot do this with average or less able students and pupils. We do not seem able to develop their potential. My view is that there are parallel developments in the countries around us, and there is a degree of danger of social exclusion connected with the lack of achievement in the levels of general education and broad literacy in this sector of our societies.

Education for democracy is very often given in the form of abstract principles, as a proclamation.

In the curriculum, particularly in civics, concepts such as values, democracy, human rights, morals, and the virtues of citizenship are usually taught to pupils in the form of complicated and demanding comments. Pupils try to memorise abstract terms and ideas and then to repeat them mechanically. For example, some topics in civics allow teachers to influence pupils' attitudes, and to use enactive and cooperative methods, but so many other fragments of knowledge are required to be taught that there is not enough time to attempt the work on attitudes. It is in any case highly questionable whether teaching any abstract moral principle can be an effective approach to education for developing these sorts of qualities. Abstract nouns are particularly difficult to pin down at the concrete level. As Bull says: '... Honesty is a vague, blanket, intangible abstraction. An honest boy is far more meaningful. But an honest boy will only be recognised through his actions' (Bull, 1973, p.134).

Education for democracy and citizenship is deductive rather than inductive.

General maxims that are unconnected to reality or to the recent experiences of pupils may be very wise, but their influence is not strong. Maxims of this kind are bound to be soon forgotten.

Pupils and students are passive and show little independence.

Unfortunately, the ideal pupil for many Czech teachers is one who is submissive, passive and obedient. Czech pupils are not expected to express their opinions or start a dialogue with their teachers or amongst each other. Teachers have not been prepared for teaching methods that would allow for and build on such independent behaviour. Teachers often suppress pupils' opinions, and directly or indirectly avoid dialogue, saying that there is insufficient time for it. In civics lessons in the past, the parroted repetition of abstract and ideological dogmas was quite common. Today the content has changed, but the methods are the same: children repeat by heart other – possibly better – maxims.

Our form of education makes a minimal appeal to the mind.
In the Czech Republic pupils and students often refuse to accept –
and sometimes even reject – rules and constraints which they have
not been able to discuss and which they do not understand. Piaget's
and Kohlberg's work shows that it is the ability to understand a rule
and accept it that is the principal factor leading to respect for the
rule. If pupils have had the opportunity to participate in the creation
of common rules at school and in the class it is helpful. Our research
focused on the analysis of internal rules and regulations of primary
and secondary schools, and this showed that it is only rarely (8.9 per
cent) that students or pupils were able to participate in the process of
creating school or class regulations and rules in forms of self-
government (Vacek, 2000b, p.52).

***The authoritarian tradition of our education tends to be negative
in character.***
Our schools prefer to teach students what they should *not* do. The
path to positive personal behaviour is often vague and nebulous. In
our research on school regulations and rules, the prevailing forms
were duties, prohibitions and various limitations over students' and
pupils' rights. Only in 3.8 per cent of cases (n=79) were the ratio of
rights and duties in balance (Vacek, 2000b, p.48).

Schools ignore contemporary conflicts.
There are plenty of topics on freedom, democracy, humanism, etc. in
our school curricula, but on the other hand there are very few
teachers who manage to reflect contemporary events of local,
national or international importance in their teaching. Bull points
out that an education which ignores the conflict of values found in
real-life situations is a threat to the development of students' and
pupils' characters. 'Blind adherence to any value is totally inadequate for moral living; and hence the weakness of blanket principles' (Bull, 1973, p.137).

Outlooks of education for democracy and citizenship

Projects which focus on supporting education for democracy, citizenship and European values in the countries of Central and Eastern Europe must take into consideration not only the cultural and national differences but also those wider social contexts which have been mentioned above.

There are some more general presuppositions for the successful implementation of education for democracy and citizenship into educational programmes in the Czech Republic.

- Firstly, there needs to be some strengthening of the technical infrastructure for information transfer: in the context of the education of children and young people for democracy the Internet is a very strong and influential tool.

- Secondly, we need to improve language learning to the level where it allows full working communication. The quality of foreign language teaching in our primary schools is not adequate, and students who complete these language courses are often not able to communicate properly in the language. A minority of our young people (those who study at secondary schools and later at universities) do not have problems in acquiring at least one foreign language, but the majority of students and pupils from secondary vocational schools do not acquire a good working knowledge of a foreign language. A useful step forward would be the introduction of a general state certificate of proficiency in a foreign language. This is planned and already in progress. There are also some older teachers who are 'communicationally handicapped' in that they can speak only Russian. Alongside the introduction of new modern information technologies we must also strengthen in-service teachers study of languages.

- Thirdly, projects on education for democracy and citizenship should also become the focus of study by future teachers, and also be a part of their continuing professional development and education. Good examples here would be multidisciplinary,

226

complex and long-term school projects. Moral education and education for democracy and citizenship should become priorities in all educational institutions.

What are the actual conditions necessary for the introduction of education for democracy into school programmes? I suggest two factors are essential:

1. We must concentrate on the preparation of teachers. They must not simply be supplied with knowledge, but also with the skills of how to *realise* education for democracy and citizenship, which means mastering the necessary pedagogic methods and techniques to do this. We must pay attention to further educating teachers in their practice, so that traditional (and ineffective) methods of influencing attitudes and opinions are replaced with (effective) active and experiential methods.

2. We must prepare a well-rounded programme of education for democracy and citizenship, for both primary and secondary schools, which would be universal, complex, flexible (so that it is easily adaptable for use in any school or class) and simple.

During 1999 and 2000 in the Department of Pedagogy and Psychology, Pedagogical Faculty, at the University of Hradec Králové, we developed a long term project offered to primary and secondary schools in the Czech Republic. This programme may also have applications in other countries, such as Slovakia, Poland and Hungary.

The Programme of Education for Democracy and Morals is based on several sources:

• A respect for cultural and national traditions (which is mirrored in the choice of topics and in the methods of application)

• Active and experiential methods and procedures (using drama in education, experiential pedagogy, and so on). These techniques have a long tradition in our region outside the school system; and we have also used and studied British experiences in this area, through frequent contact with many outstanding specialists on drama in education in various workshops (J.Neelands, D. Warvick, T.Goode and others). (See Neelands, 1992)

- Moral psychology and a project based on moral education (Kohlberg's 'just community'), and projects focused on character and values education (Lickona, Berkowitz, Murphy).

- National and international programmes focused on the development of citizenship, democracy and European identity (our main source here is the CiCe project). (Ross, 1999)

Our programme is based on four elements of education for democracy identified by Berkowitz (1998):

1. *Building a foundation for the capacity to function democratically* – to gain strong and wide support for the programme, from schools and other institutions

2. *Providing knowledge about democracy for education* – to offer a wide range of topics (varying according to the type of school, age of pupils, etc.), which will be used in the programme to establish the necessary knowledge for the consequent active teaching methods.

3. *Practising democracy* – through school and class parliaments, participating in the creation and modification of school and class rules, using pupils' questionnaires, magazines, activities and projects that start dialogues and discussions, finding objective solutions and using simulations of local problems as well as broader problems in society.

4: *Building a democratic character* – the most complicated and long-term part of the project. Berkowitz suggests two possible approaches to designing a character for democracy, the first generic, the other targeted. We believe that a combination of the two approaches can be most effective.

Education for Character or How our Schools can Teach Respect and Responsibility (Lickona, 1992) was a complex project that advocated respect and responsibility as the central values. 'Character' here consists of the three elements of moral knowing, moral feeling and moral action.

To fulfil this aim, Lickona set out twelve strategies, nine of which are performed in the classroom, and three within the whole-school framework.

Class: 1. The teacher as a provider of care, a model and a mentor

2). A moral classroom community

3. Moral discipline

4. A democratic classroom environment

5. Teaching values through the curriculum

6. Co-operative learning

7. Conscience of craft

8. Moral reflection

9. Teaching conflict resolution

School: 10. Caring beyond the classroom

11. Creating a positive moral culture in the school

12. Schools, parents, and communities as partners.

We modified Lickona's original twelve-fold model and Murphy's project (1998), and relating these to our own specific context, we created the following ten strategies:

1. The teacher in the role of a protector, a care provider, a mentor and a model of behaviour, who supports students' pro-social behaviour and corrects unsuitable behaviour.

2. The creation of a moral and democratic community in the class. Helping pupils/students to know and respect each other, offering pupils/students possibilities to make decisions and to carry the responsibility for creating a social environment in the class as one that is good for life, work and study.

3. The application of a discipline based on the creation and application of rules (norms), using these as the means to develop moral thinking, self-control and respect for others.

4. Teaching values within the framework of the curriculum, and using the contents of subjects to examine ethical topics, con-

necting together the formal curriculum, the informal curriculum and the hidden curriculum.

5. Using cooperative teaching for the development of skills and habits which will help others and support working in a team.

6. Stimulating moral reflection through reading, writing, discussions, debates and practising decision-making.

7. Teaching students to solve conflicts, so they find fair and non-violent solutions and outcomes.

8. Stimulating and supporting useful and helpful student activity out of school, using the models and possibilities offered by the school and municipal community.

9. Creating a positive moral culture within the framework of the whole school, starting with school management, encouraging good relationships between teachers and other adults, relations with students and pupils, effective students' or pupils' self-governments, and including time for activities with a high moral content and values.

10. Cooperating with parents and others in the community to support schools to educate for values and morals, and working to support parents as first teachers of morals to their children. (Adapted from Lickona, 1992, pp.78–79).

The project also offered teachers and schools a wide range of topics and of worked-out examples of methods and of presentation (Vacek, 2000c). We continue to work on checking the efficiency of our project on a larger scale. These examples of topics are oriented towards democracy, citizenship and European identity:

the perception of Czech society by the young generation ten years after the Velvet Revolution

understanding (and not understanding) the principles of democracy

the notion of the freedom of the individual, and its actual operation bringing together personal and social perspectives

where is my home: locality, the Czech Republic, Europe

what personal perspectives do I see in a unified Europe

European states and nations that we prefer and believe to be good (and why)

patriotism and nationalism today

how to understand the dissolution of Czechoslovakia

emigrants and immigrants in Central Europe

international law and the international courts (Nuremberg, den Haag)

the role of minorities and multicultural influences on society

space for children and young people to exercise democracy

The project has been structured in three planes. Firstly, we wanted teachers not only to accept the idea of education for democracy and citizenship and education of moral values as a good and useful thing, but to accept and understand it as a priority in their work, regardless of the subject they teach and regardless of the school or the class they teach.

Our next step was to offer our wide range of topics – which included economic, ethical, ecological and social-psychological themes. We also included topics that are attractive to students and pupils, and at the same time socially very important, such as drug and alcohol abuse.

Our third step, taken in parallel with the second, was the introduction of different models for the implementation, and various forms for the presentation, of each of these topics. We preferred to introduce active methods and those that led to team and individual work – a collection of various discussion methods (such as those aimed at the solution of moral dilemmas, presentation of speeches, 'parliamentary' discussions and so on) and other methods used mostly in drama in education. We also highlighted the importance of interdisciplinarity, because many of the topics we selected could not be classified simply as belonging to one particular subject. This inter-disciplinary character of topics was considered most important, because it helped to establish and maintain cooperation between teachers of various subjects, which is today not very usual.

Conclusion

This chapter has analysed some of the reasons for the present situation, and also various perspectives of education for democracy and citizenship in the Czech Republic. Some overview of the similarities between these developments and those in other post-communist countries has been provided. I hope that this will help, at least in part, to deepen our understanding of the field, and will contribute to the process of unification in Europe.

Notes on Contributors

Anna Emilia Berti is Associate Professor of Developmental Psychology at the Faculty of Developmental Psychology and Socialisation at the University of Padova (Italy). The focus of her research interest is children's societal understanding. She has carried out several studies on three to fourteen year old children's understanding of economic and political institutions, such as buying and selling, employment, banking, firms, government, and the judicial system. She has also conducted several intervention studies on elementary school children's understanding of economic and political notions before and after teaching. She is CiCe National Coordinator for Italy.

Christina von Gerber is a researcher and psychologist at Linköping University (Sweden). Her main research interests are children and families. She has studied unemployment and the economy of everyday life from a child's perspective using qualitative approaches. She also works as a consultant specialised in stress, coping with crises and supervision.

Merryn Hutchings is Reader in Education at the University of North London (UK). Her PhD thesis, Children's Constructions of Work, was winner of the British Educational Research Association's Dissertation Prize for 1997. Her research interests continue to focus around careers and inequalities, and include social class and widening participation in higher education, and teacher supply and retention.

Márta Fülöp is a senior research fellow in the Institute for Psychology of the Hungarian Academy of Sciences, Budapest (Hungary) and a Széchenyi Professor of Social Psychology in the Department of Psychology of the University of Szeged. Her main research interest is the psychology of competition with a special attention to adolescents and young adults and cross-cultural aspects. She has carried out research on competition in Japan, the USA, Canada, Costa Rica and Great Britain. She is a member of the CiCe Steering Group and chairs the Network's working party on eleven to eighteen year olds.

Riitta Korhonen is a senior lecturer at the University of Turku in the Department of Teacher Education in Rauma (Finland). She lectures on teaching in pre-school and primary education and on special education. Her particular research interests are in the areas of pre-school teaching, play and learning. She is a member of the CiCe Steering Group and chairs the Network's Data group.

Beata Krzywosz-Rynkiewicz is a psychologist and a senior lecturer in Department of Psychology, in University of Warmia and Mazury in Olsztyn (Poland). She is a member of two international educational projects co-ordinated by University of Exeter and the University of North London. She is involved in creating of private, alternative primary school and is its director. Author and co-author two of books and several articles mainly about children; their social lives, their attitudes towards other and teachers; and solving social problems in the school. She is a member of the CiCe working party on seven to eleven year olds..

Emilio Lastrucci is Professor of Pedagogy at the University of Basilicata and the University of Rome 'La Sapienza' (Italy). After a university degree in philosophy, took several master's degrees in philosophy, experimental psychology and educational sciences; in 1990 he obtained the PhD at the University of Rome in educational sciences with a dissertation on history teaching and the development/socialisation processes. He has participated in many international educational surveys (IEA 'Written Composition', IEA 'Literacy', 'Youth and History', TSER – 'Effective School Improvement' and others). His main interests are in history teaching and learning, civic education, evaluation and school effectiveness. A councillor of the Italian Ministry of Education, he is member of several committees at national and international level. He is member also of the Steering Group of the CiCe network.

Elisabet Näsman is professor in social and cultural analysis at Linköping University (Sweden). Her main research interests are children, childhood, families and the generational order. From the child's perspective, she has studied work-life conditions, unemployment, everyday life economy and level of living standards. She is also leading a project on participation and democracy at school. She is a member of the CiCe Steering Group.

Alistair Ross is Professor of Education and Director of the Institute of Policy Studies in Education at the University of North London (UK). He is International Coordinator of the CiCe Thematic Network Project. As well as a long-standing interest in children's political and social understanding, he has interest in social class and participation in higher education and in teachers' careers and teacher supply.

John Schostak is Professor and Director of the Centre for Applied Research in Education, University of East Anglia (UK). He has been involved in over 40 funded research projects. His general research areas are research and evaluation of institutional change, professional development, strategies for inclusion, learning environments, the impact of information technology on the personal, social, cultural and political life of people, and the development of qualitative research methodologies.

Pavel Vacek is an pedagogical psychologist and teacher in the Faculty of Education at the University of Hradec Králové (Czech Republic). His research interests are in the areas of moral development, moral education, character education, education for democracy and citizenship. He has published Ke krizi mravní výchovy v současné škole (on the crisis of moral education in contemporary schools) in Výchova k evropskému demokratickému občanství in 1998, and. Morální vývoj v psychologických a pedagogických souvislostech (on moral development in a psychological and pedagogical context.) in 2000.

Barbara Walker is a Senior Research Associate at the Centre for Applied Research in Education at the University of East Anglia (UK). For the last six years she has been researching and publishing widely in the areas of sex education and the acquisition of gender identity. She is currently evaluating a project designed to involve young people in community music activities.

Aigli Zafeirakou is Assistant Professor in Education at the Democritus University of Thrace (Greece). After taking her master's and Ph.D. in Education at the University of Nanterre, she consulted for OECD and EU programs and worked as a Fulbright Scholar at the Institute of Early Childhood Education and Development, Department of Education, Washington D.C. (1998). Her research interests include social representations and interactions of teachers, pupils and museum educators; pedagogical practices in the classroom and museums; educational policies for pre-primary school education and school failure.

Bibliography

Acock, A.C. (1984) 'Parents and their children: the study of inter-generation influence', *Sociology and Social Research* 68, 151-171

Adelson, J. and O'Neil, R. (1966) 'Growth of political ideas in adolescence: the sense of community', *Journal of Personality and Social Psychology*, 4, 295-306

Agazzi, A. and Berti, A.E. (1995) 'La comprensione del concetto di democrazia in studenti di V elementare, III media, I anno di Università' [The understanding of the concept democracy by fifth and eighth graders and freshmen], *Scuola e Città*, 45(7), 290-301

Ahier, J. (1988) *Industry, Children and the Nation*, Lewes: Falmer

Ahier, J., and Ross, A. (Eds.) (1995) *The social subjects within the curriculum*, London: Falmer Press

Aho, S. (1996) *Lapsen minäkäsitys ja itsetunto* [A Child's Self-image and Self-esteem], Helsinki: Edita

Aho, S. and Heino, S. (2000) 'Itsetunnon vahventaminen päiväkodissa' [The Reinforcement of self-esteem in the Kindergarten], *Julkaisusarja* A :191, Turun yliopiston kasvatustieteiden laitos, University of Turku

Ajello, A. M., Bombi, A. S., Pontecorvo, C. and Zucchermaglio, C. (1986) 'Children's understanding of agriculture as an economic activity', *European Journal of Psychology of Education*, 1, 67-80

Ajello, A. M., Bombi, A. S., Pontecorvo, C. and Zucchermaglio, C. (1987) 'Teaching economics in the primary school: the concepts of work and profit', *International Journal of Behavioural Development*, 10, 51-69

Alanen, L. (1992) *Modern Childhood? Exploring the 'Child Question' in Sociology*, Jyväskylä: Jyväskylä University

Amann-Gainotti, M. (1984) 'Quelques données sur l'évolution de la representaiton du monde social chez des enfants de differents milieux socio-culturels', *Archives de Psychologie*, 52, 17-29

Anderson, B. (1983) *Imagined Communities: Reflections on the Origin and Spread of Nationalism*, London and New York: Verso

Andorka, R., Healey, B. and Krause, P. (1994) A Gazdasági és a politikai követelmények szerepe a rendszerváltozásban: Magyarország és Kelet-Németország 1990-1994, *Szociológiai Szemle*, 4. 61-82

Angvik M. and Von Borries, B. (1997) *Youth and History*, Hamburg: Koerber Stiftung (2 vol. and a CD-ROM)

Antonovsky, A. (1987) *Hälsans mysterium*, Stockholm

Aronsson, K. (1997) *Barns världar-barns bilder*, Stockholm

Baltes, P.B. and Baltes, M.M. (1990) 'Psychological perspectives on successful ageing: the model of selective optimization with compensation', in P.B., Baltes and M.M. Baltes (eds). *Successful Ageing: Perspectives from Behavioral Sciences*, New York: Cambridge University Press, pp.1-34

237

Beck, I. L., and Mc Keown, M. G. (1994) 'Cognitive construction of knowledge', *Educational Psychologist*, 33 (2/3), 109-128

Beck, I. L., Mc Keown, M. G. and Gromoll, E. (1989) 'Learning from social study text', *Cognition and Instruction*, 6, 99-158

Berend, I. (1993) 'The role of non-economic and external factors in East Central European economic transformation', in: Schonfeld. R. (ed.) *Transforming Economic Systems in East Central Europe*, Munich: Sudosteuropa-Gesellschaft

Berger, P. and Berger, M. (1972) *Sociology: A Biographical Approach*, New York: Basic Books

Berger, P. and Luckman, T. (1992) *La construction sociale de la réalité*. Paris: Meridiens Klincksieck.

Berkowitz, M. R. (1998) 'Educating for character and democracy: a practical introduction'. (a paper prepared for Ciuadadana, Bogota, Colombia)

Berti, A. E. (1994) 'Children's understanding of the concept of the state', in M. Carretero and J. F. Voss (eds.): *Cognitive and Instructional Processes in History and the Social Studies.* Hillsdale, NJ: Erlbaum, 49-75

Berti, A. E., and Griolo, A. (in press) 'Third graders understanding of core political concepts (law, nation-state, government) before and after teaching', *Genetic, Social, and General Psychology Monographs*

Berti, A. E., and Vanni, E. (2000) 'Italian children's understanding of war: a domain-specific approach', *Social Development*, 9(47), 478-496

Berti, A. E., Bombi, A. S. and Lis, A. (1982) 'The child's conception about means of production and their owners', *European Journal of Social Psychology*, 12, 221-39

Berti, A. E., Guarnaccia, V. and Lattuada, R. (1997) 'Lo sviluppo della nozione di norma giuridica' [The development of the concept of law], *Scuola e Città*, 48(12), 532-545

Berti, A. E., Mancaruso, A. and Zanon L. (1998) 'Lo sviluppo della conoscenza del sistema giudiziario' [The development of knowledge of the judicial system], *Scuola e Città*, 49(1), 3-18

Berti, A.E. (1988) 'The development of political conceptions in children between 6-15 years old', *Human Development*, 41, 437-446

Berti, A.E. (1991) 'Capitalism and socialism: how seventh graders understand and misunderstand the information presented in their geography textbooks', *European Journal of Psychology of Education*, 6, 411-421

Berti, A.E. (1992) 'Acquisition of the concept of shop profit by third-grade children', *Contemporary Educational Psychology*, 17, 1-7

Berti, A.E. (1999) 'Knowledge restructuring in an economic subdomain: banking', in W. Schnotz, S. Vosniadou, and M. Carretero (eds.) *New Perspectives on Conceptual Change*, Oxford, UK/Elsevier Science Publishers

Berti, A.E. and Benesso, M. (1998) 'The concept of nation-state in Italian elementary school children: spontaneous concepts and effects of teaching', *Genetic, Social, and General Psychology Monographs*, 120(2), 121-143

Berti, A.E. and Monaci, M. G. (1998) 'Third-graders' acquisition of knowledge of banking: restructuring or accretion?' *British Journal of Educational Psychology*, 68, 357-371

Berti, A.E. and Ugolini, E. (1998) 'Developing knowledge of the judicial system: a domain-specific approach', *Journal of Genetic Psychology*, 159(2), 221-236

Berti, A.E., and Bombi, A.S. (1988) *The Child's Construction of Economics*, Cambridge: Cambridge University Press

Berti, A.E., and Ferruta, A. (1999) 'Il sistema economico: le concezioni dei bambini e le nozioni proposte dai programmi per la scuola elementare e dai sussidiari' [The economic system; children's conceptions compared with the notions provided for by elementary school syllabus and textbooks], *Scuola e Città*, 50 (7), 276-287.

Bhaskar, R. (1986) *Scientific Realism and Human Emancipation*, London: Verso

Bikont, A. (1988) 'Tozsamo's'c spoleczna – teorie, hipotezy, znaki zapytania', in M. Jarymowicz (ed.), *Studia nad spostrzeganiem relacji ja-inni*, Warszawa: Ossolineum

Billig M. (1995) *Banal Nationalism*, London: Sage

Blyth, A. (1992) 'A British view of American assessment of young children's economic understanding', in M. Hutchings and W. Wade (eds.) *Developing Economic and Industrial Understanding in the Primary School*, London: PNL Press

Boden, M. (1979) *Piaget*, London: Fontana

Boehnke, K. (2001) 'Parent-offspring value transmission in a societal context', *Journal of Cross-Cultural Psychology*, 32(2), 241-255

Borba, M. (1989) *Esteem builders: A K-8 Self-esteem Curriculum for Improving Student Achievement, Behaviour and School Climate*, Torrance, California: Jalmar Press

Borba, M. (1993) *Staff Esteem Builders*, California: Jalmar Press

Boski, P. (1992) 'O byciu Polakiem w ojczy'znie i o zmianach tozsamo'sci kulturowo-narodowej na obczy'znie', in P. Boski, M. Jarymowicz and H. Malewska-Peyre (eds) *Tozsamo's'c a odmienno's'c kulturowa*, Warszawa: Instytut Psychologii Polskiej Akademii Nauk

Bradley, B. S. (forthcoming) *The New Psychology: Poetics for a New Vision of Mental Life*.

Bratt, N. (1977) *Den tidiga jagutvecklingen*, Stockholm

Breakwell, G. (1986) *Coping with Threatened Identities*, London: Metheun

Bronfenbrenner, U. (1979) *The Ecology of Human Development: Experiments by Nature and Design*, Cambridge, MA: Harvard University Press

Bruszt, L. and Simon, J. (1991) *The Change in Citizen's Political Orientations to the Transition to Democracy in Hungary*, Budapest: Institute for Political Science of the Hungarian Academy of Sciences

Bull, N.J. (1973) *Moral Education*, Trowbridge: Redwood Press Limited

Burman, E. (1994) *Deconstructing Developmental Psychology*, London: Routledge.

Burr, V. (1995) *An Introduction to Social Constructionism*, London: Routledge.

Burris, V. (1976) 'The child's conception of economic relations: a genetic approach to the sociology of knowledge', (unpublished doctoral thesis), Princeton University, Princeton, NJ.

Carbone, F. (2000) 'La comprensione del denaro e il suo valore in bambini di I elementare prima e dopo l'insegnamento', [First-graders' understanding of money and its value before and after teaching] (unpublished dissertation)

Carey, S. (1985) *Conceptual Change in Childhood*, Cambridge, MA: MIT Press

Certeau, De M. (1990) *L'invention du quotidien*, Paris: Gallimard, Folio

Chi, M. (1988) 'Children's lack of access and knowledge reorganization: an example from the concept of animism', in F. Weinert and M. Perlmutter (eds.) Memory Development: Universal Changes and Individual Differences, Hillsadle, NJ: Erlbaum, 169-194

Chombart De Lauwe, M.J. (1987) *Espaces d' enfants*, Fribourg: Suisse Delval

Christensen, E. (1994) *Når far og mor drikker...*, Copenhagen: Socialforskningsinstitutet

Citron, S. (1989) *Le mythe national: L'histoire de France en question*, Paris: EDI

Cohen, S. (1973) *Folk Devils and Moral Panics: The Creation of Mods and Rockers*, London: Paladin

Coleman, J. (1999) *Key Data on Adolescence*, Brighton: Trust for the Study of Adolescence

Conger, K.J., Rueter, M.A., Conger, R.D. (2000) 'The role of economic pressure in the lives of parents and their adolescents: the family stress model', in L.J. Crockett, R.K. Silbereisen (ed.) *Negotiating adolescence in times of social change*, Cambridge: Cambridge University Press. 201-223

Connell, R.W. (1971) *The Child's Construction of Politics*, Carlton, Vic.: Melbourne University Press

Corda Costa, M. (ed) (1997) *Formare il cittadino: Laboratorio di educazione civica per la scuola secondari*, Firenze; La Nuova Italia

Corona, J. (1999) 'La formacion de nociones politicas en niños tepoztecos', (paper presented to second meeting of Alpha Network, Queretaro (Mexico) June 7 1999)

Coulby D. (1995) 'Ethnocentrity, postmodernity and European curricular systems', *European Journal of Teacher Education*, 18(2/3), 143-153

Crockett, L.J. and Silbereisen, K. (2000) 'Social change and adolescent development: issues and challenges, in L.J. Crockett and R.K. Silbereisen (eds.) *Negotiating Adolescence in Times of Social Change*, Cambridge: Cambridge University Press, 1-13

Curt, B. C. (1994) *Textuality and Tectonics: Troubling social and psychological science*, Buckingham: Open University Press

Dahlberg, G. (1993) 'Modern barnuppfostran och modernt familjeliv – en komplex och sofistikerad förhandlingsprocess', in *Om modernt familjeliv och familjeseparationer, Stockholm: Socialvetenskapliga forskningsrådet*, 87-98

Dahlberg, G., Holland, J., and Varnava-Skouros, G. (1987) *Children, Work and Ideology: A Cross-Cultural Comparison of Children's Understanding of Work and Social Division of Labour*, Stockholm: Almqvist and Wiksell

Dalhouse, A.C. and Frideres, J.S. (1996) 'Intergenerational congruency: the role of the family in political attitudes of youth', *Journal of Family Issues*, 17, 227-248

Danziger, K. (1958) 'Children's earliest conception of economic relationships', *Journal of Social Psychology* [Australia], 47, 231-40

Dasen, P. (1972) 'Cross-cultural Piagetian research', *Journal of Cross-Cultural Psychology*, 3(1), 23-39

Dasen, P. and Heron, A. (1981) 'Cross-cultural tests of Piaget's theory', in H. Triandis and A. Heron (eds.) *Handbook of Cross-Cultural Psychology* 4, Boston: Allyn and Bacon

Davies, I., Fülöp, M. Hutchings, M., Ross, A., Berkics, M. and Floyd, L. (2001) 'Education and enterprising citizens: what is to be done?', in A. Ross (ed.) *Learning for Democratic Europe*, London: CiCe

Davies, R. (1991) 'That obscure object of inquiry: the story of a problem', in Schostak, J. F. (ed.) Youth in Trouble: Educational Responses, London: Kogan Page

Delval, J (1994) 'Stages in the child's construction of social knowledge', in M. Carretero and J. F. Voss (eds.) *Cognitive and Instructional Processes in History and the Social Studies*, Hillsdale, NJ: Erlbaum, 77-102

Dennis, J. (1985) 'Foreword', in S. W. Moore, James Lare, and K. A. Wagner, *The Child's Political World: A Longitudinal Perspective*, New York: Praeger

DES (1984) *Initial Teacher Training: Approval of courses* (Circular 3/84), London: Department of Education and Science.

Deschamps, J-C. and Devos, T. (1998) 'Regarding the Relationship Between Social Identity and Personal Identity', in Worchel, J. F. Morales, D. Paez and J. C. Deschamps (eds.) *Social Identity: International Perspectives*, London: Sage Publications

Donaldson, M. (1978) *Children's Minds*, London: Fontana

Doumas, D., Margolin, G. and John, R.S. (1994) 'The intergenerational transmission of aggression across three generations', *Journal of Family Violence*, 9(2), 157-175

Doverborg, E. and Pramling, I. (1988) *Att förstå barns tankar*, Stockholm: Liber

Dragonas T. and Frangoudaki, A. (1997) 'National identity among European adolescents: a psychosocial approach', in Angvik, M. and Von Borries, B. (eds.) *Youth and History*, Hamburg: Koerber Stiftung, 417-423

Duit, R. (1999) 'Conceptual change approaches in science education'. in W. Schnotz, S. Vosniadou, and M. Carretero. (eds.) *New Perspectives on Conceptual Change*, Oxford, UK: Elsevier Science Publishers

Dunn, J. (1988) *The Beginnings of Social Understanding*, Oxford: Basil Blackwell.

Elder, G.H., JR. (1974) *Children of the Great Depression: Social Change in Life Experience*, Chicago: University of Chicago Press

Elvstrand, H. (forthcoming) 'Children's reflections on income and savings', in M. Hutchings, M. Fülöp and A. M. Van Den Dries (eds.) *Young People's Understanding of Economic Issues in Europe*, Stoke on Trent: Trentham

Emler, N. and Dickinson, J. (1985) 'Children's representations of economic inequalities: the effects of social class, *British Journal of Developmental Psychology*, 3, 191-8

Emler, N., Ohana, J., and Moscovici, S. (1987) 'Children's beliefs about institutional roles: a cross-national study of representations of the teacher's role', *British Journal of Psychology of Education*, 57, 26-37

Encyklopedia PWN (1999) Warszawa: Wydawnictwa Naukowe PWN

Epstein, D., Elwood, J., Hey, V. and Maw, J. (1998) *Failing Boys? Issues in gender and achievement*, Buckingham, Philadelphia: Open University Press

Erikson, E. H. (1962) *Lapsuus ja yhteiskunta*, Jyväskylä. Gummerus.

Erikson, E. H. (1950) *Childhood and Society* (1962) [Lapsuus ja yhteiskunta], Jyväskylä: Gummerus

Erikson, E.H. (1968) *Identity: Youth and Crisis*, New York: W.W. Norton

Erikson, E.H. (1987) 'Psychosocial identity', in *Selected Papers from 1930 to 1980, Erik Erikson* (edited by S. Schein) New York: W.W. Hutton

Etzioni, A. (1988) *The Moral Dimension*, New York: The Free Press

Feldman, R. S. (1982) *Development of Nonverbal Behavior in Children*, Heidelberg: Springer

Fitzgerald, T. K. (1993) *Metaphors of Identity*, New York: State University of New York Press

Foucault, M. (1972) *The Archaeology of Knowledge*, London: Tavistock

Frangoudaki, A. and Dragonas, T.H. (1987) (in Greek) *'What is our Patrie?' Ethnocentricity in Education*, Athens: Edition. Alexandreia

Fülöp, M. (1995) 'A versengésre vonatkozó tudományos nézetek I: A versengő magatartás eredete', *Pszichológia* 15(1), 61-111

Fülöp, M. (1999) 'Students' perception of the role of competition in their respective countries: Hungary, Japan and the USA, in A. ROSS (ed.) *Young Citizens in Europe*, London: University of North London 195-219

Fülöp, M. (2001) 'Teachers' ideas about the role of school in preparing students for competition in life', (unpublished manuscript)

Fülöp, M. (2001) 'Teachers' perception of the role of competition in their respective countries: Hungary, Japan and the USA', *Children's Social and Economic Understanding* (in press)

Furlong, A. and Cartmel, F. (1997) *Young People and Social Change: Individualization and Risk in Late Modernity*, Buckingham: Open University Press

Furnham, A. (1984) 'Getting a job: school-leavers' perceptions of employment prospects', *British Journal of Educational Psychology*, 54, 293-305

Furnham, A. and Gunter, B. (1989) 'Young people's political knowledge', *Educational Studies*, 13. 91-104

Furnham, A. and Lewis, A. (1986) *The Economic Mind: The Social Psychology of Economic Behaviour*, Brighton: Wheatsheaf

Furnham, A. and Shiekh, S. (1993) 'Gender, generation, and social support: correlates of mental health in Asian immigrants, *International Journal of Social Psychiatry*, 39, 22-33

Furnham, A. and Stacey, B. (1991) *Young People's Understanding of Society (Adolescence and Society)*, London: Routledge

Furnham, A. and Thomas, P. (1984) 'Pocket money: a study in economic education', *British Journal of Developmental Psychology*, 2, 205-231

Furth, H. G., Baur, M. and Smith, J. E. (1976) 'Children's conceptions of social institutions: a Piagetian framework', *Human Development*, 19, 351-374

Furth, H.G. (1980) *The world of grown-ups*, New York: Elsevier

Gallatin, J. (1980) 'Political thinking in adolescence', in J. Adelson (ed.) *Handbook of Adolescent Psychology*, New York: Wiley

Geertz, C. (1973) *The Interpretation of Cultures*, New York: Basic Books

Gergen, K. J. and Gergen, M. M. (1986) 'Narrative form and the construction of psychological science', in T. R. Sarbin (ed.) *Narrative Psychology: The Storied Nature of Human Conduct*, New York: Praeger

Giron, C. (2001) 'In search of social representations of unemployment', in C. Roland-Lévy, E. Kirchler, E. Penz and C. Gray (eds.) *Everyday Representations of the Economy*, Vienna: WUV

Glass, J. and Bengston, V.L. (1986) 'Attitude similarity in three-generation families: socialization, status inheritance or reciprocal influence', *American Sociological Review*, 51(5), 685-698

Goldstein, B. and Oldham, J. (1979) *Children and Work*, New Jersey: Transaction Books

Goodnow, J.J. and Warton, P. (1992) Contests and cognitions: Taking a pluralist view, in P. Light and G. Butterworth (eds) *Context and Cognition: Ways of learning and knowing*, Hemel Hempstead: Harvester Wheatsheaf

Greenberg, J., Simon, L., Pyszczynski, T., Solomon, S. and Chatel, D. (1992) 'Terror management and tolerance: does mortality salience always intensify negative reactions to others who threaten one's world view?' *Journal of Personality and Social Psychology*, 63, 212-220

Gumpel, W. (1993) 'The mentality problem in the transition process from centrally planned economy to market economy' in: R. Schonfeld, ed., *Transforming Economic Systems in East Central Europe*, Munich: Sudosteuropa-Gesellschaft.

Halbwachs, M. (1968) *La mémoire collective*, Paris: PUF.

Hall, G. S. (1904) *Adolescence: Its Psychology and its Relation to Physiology, Anthropology, Sociology, Sex, Crime, Religion and Education,* vols. I and II, New York: D. Appleton

Harré, R. (1974) 'The conditions for a social psychology of childhood', in M. Richards (ed.) *The Integration of a Child into a Social World*, Cambridge: Cambridge University Press

Harré, R. (1983) *Personal Being*, Oxford: Basil Blackwell

Harris, P. and Heelas, P. (1979) 'Cognitive processes and collective representations', *Archives européenes de sociologie*, 20, 211-241

Harrison, R. (2001) 'Records of achievement: tracing the contours of learner identity', in C. Paechter, R. Edwards, R. Harrison and P. Twining (eds.) *Learning, Space and Identity: Gateshead*, Paul Chapman Publishing Ltd; Open University Press

Haseler, S. (2000) *The Super-Rich: The Unjust New World of Global Capitalism*, Basingstoke: Macmillan Press Ltd; New York: St Martin's Press

Haste, H. and Torney-Purta, J. (1992) 'Introduction', in H. Haste and J. Torney-Purta (eds.) *The Development of Political Understanding: a New Perspective*, San Francisco: Jossey-Bass 1-10

Henriques, J., Hollway, W., Urwin, C., Venn, C. and Walkerdine, V. (1984) *Changing the Subject: Psychology, Social Regulation and Subjectivity*, London: Methuen

Hobbs, S. and McKechnie, J. (1998) Children and work in the UK: The evidence, in B. Pettit (ed.) *Children and Work in the UK: Refocusing the debate*, London: Save the Children Fund and CPAG.

Hoffman, M. (1981) 'Perspectives on the difference between understanding people and understanding things: the role of affect', in J. Flavell and L. Ross (eds.) *Social Cognitive Development*, Cambridge: Cambridge University Press

Hogg, M. and Abrams, B. (1988) *Social Identification*, London: Routledge

Holstein, J. A. and Gubrium, J. F. (1995) *The interactive interview*, London: Sage

Holt, S. (1996) 'Reflecting light and shade: psychodynamic thinking and educational psychology in the 1990s', in J. Carmel and E. Kennedy (eds.) *The Reflective Professional in Education: Psychological Perspectives on Changing Contexts*, Melksham: Jessica Kingsley

Hong Kwang, R. T. and Stacey, B. G. (1981) 'The understanding of socio-economic concepts in Malaysian Chinese school children', *Child Study Journal*, 11, 33-49

Hujala, E., Parrila, S., Lindberg, P., Nivala, V. Tauriainen, L. and Vartiainen, P. (1990) *Laadunhallinta varhaiskasvatuksessa* [Quality in early childhood education], Oulun yliopisto, Varhaiskasvatuskeskus

Hujala, E., Puroila, A-M., Parrila-Haapakoski, S. and Nivala, V. (1998) '*Päivähoidosta varhaiskasvatukseen*' [From the day care to early childhood education], Varhaiskasvatus 90 Oy, Jyväskylä: Gummerus

Humphries, S. (1981) *Hooligans or Rebels? An Oral History of Working-Class Childhood and Youth 1889-1939*, Oxford: Basil Blackwell

Hutchings, M. (1997) 'Children's constructions of work', (unpublished Ph.D thesis, University of North London)

Hytönen, J. (1992) *Lapsikeskeinen kasvatus* [Child-centred Education], Juva: WSOY

Ingleby, D. (1986) 'Development in social context', in M. Richards and P. Light (eds.) *Children of Social Worlds*, Cambridge: Polity Press

Inglehart, R. (1990) *Culture shift in advanced industrial society*, Princeton, NJ: Princeton University Press.

Inhelder, B. and Piaget, J. (1955) *De la logique de l'enfant à la logique de l'adolescent*, Paris: PUF

Inhelder, B., Sinclair, H. and Bovet, M. (1974) *Learning and the Development of Cognition*, Cambridge, MA: Harvard University Press

Iverson, J. M. and Goldin-Meadow, S. (1998) *The Nature and Functions of Gesture in Children's Communication*, San Francisco: Jossey-Bass,

Jahoda, G. (1964) 'Children's concepts of nationality: A critical study of Piaget's stages', *Child Development*, 35,1081-1092.

Jahoda, G. (1979) 'The construction of economic reality by some Glaswegian children', *European Journal of Social Psychology*, 9, 115-127

Jahoda, G. (1981) 'The development of thinking about economic institution: the bank', *Cahiers de Psychologie Cognitive*, 1, 55-73

Jahoda, G. (1983) 'European 'lag' in the development of an economic concept: a study in Zimbabwe', *British Journal of Developmental Psychology*, 1, 113-20

Jahoda, G. (1984) 'The development of thinking about socio-economic systems', in H. Tajfel (ed.) *The Social Dimension*, Cambridge: Cambridge University Press.

Jahoda, G., and Woerdenbagch, A. (1982) 'The development of ideas about an economic institution: a cross-national replication', *British Journal of Social Psychology*, 21, 337-338

James, A. and Prout, A. (1990) 'Re-presenting childhood: time and transition in the study of childhood', in A. James and A. Prout (eds.) *Constructing and Reconstructing Childhood: Contemporary Issues in the Sociological Study of Childhood*, London: Falmer

James, W. (1890) *Principles of Psychology*, 2 vols., New York: Henry Holt

Jarymowicz, M. (1992) 'Tozsamo´s´c jako efekt rozpoznawania siebie w´sród swioch i obcych. Eksperymentalne badania nad procesem róznicowania Ja-My-Inni', in P. Boski, M. Jarymowicz and H. Malewska-Peyre (eds.) *Tozsamo´s´c a odmienno´s´c kulturowa*, Warszawa: Instytut Psychologii Polskiej Akademii Nauk

Jarymowicz, M. (1994) 'O formach umys_owego ujmowania My i ich zwi_zku ze spostrzeganiem Innych', in M. Jarymowicz (ed.) *Poza egocentryczna perspektywe widzenia siebie i ´swiata*, Warszawa: Instytut Psychologii Polskiej Akademii Nauk

Jenkins, R. (1996) *Social identity*, London and New York: Routledge

Jennings, K.M. and Niemi, R.G. (1982) *Generations and politics: a panel study of young adults and their parents*, Princeton NJ: Princeton University Press

Jodelet, D. (1987) 'The study of people–environment relations in France', in Stokols, D. and Altman, I. (eds.) *Handbook of Environmental Psychology,* New York: John Wiley.

Justegard, H. (forthcoming) 'Earning money of your own: paid work among teenagers in Sweden', in M. Hutchings, M. Fülöp and A. M. Van Den Dries (eds.) *Young People's Understanding of Economic Issues in Europe*, Stoke on Trent: Trentham

Keltinkangas-Järvinen, L. (2000) *Tunne itsesi, suomalainen*, Juva: WS Bookwell OY

Kildevang, H. (1990) *Ti stille når du taler til de voksne!* Copenhagen: Förlaget Sociologi

Kindervater, A. and von Borries, B. (1997) Historical Motivation and Historical-Political Socialisation, in Angvik, M. and von Borries B. (eds.) *Youth and History*, Hamburg: Koerber Stiftung, 62-105

Knafo, A. and Schwartz, S.H. (2001) 'Value socialization in families of Israeli-born and Soviet-born adolescents in Israel', *Journal of Cross-Cultural Psychology,* 32(2), 213-228

Knight, G.P. and Kagan, S. (1977) 'Acculturation of prosocial and competitive behaviors among second and third generation Mexican-American children', *Journal of Cross-Cultural Psychology*, 8(3), 273-284

Koerber, A. (1997) 'Knowledge, associations and concepts', in M. Angvik and B. Von Borries (eds.) *Youth and History,* Hamburg: Koerber Stiftung, 1, 106-152

Kofta, M. and Sedek, G. (1999) 'Stereotypy duszy grupowej a postawy wobec obcych: wyniki bada´n sondazowych', in B. Wojciszke (ed.) *Rozumienie zjawisk spolecznych*, Warszawa: Pa´nstwowe Wydawnictwo Naukowe

Kohlberg, L. (1976) 'Moral stages and moralisation: the cognitive developmental approach', in T. Lickona (ed.) *Moral Development and Behaviour*, New York: Holt Rinehart and Winston

Kohn, M.L. (1983) 'On the transmission of values in the family: a preliminary formulation', in A.C. Kerchoff (ed.) *Research in Sociology of Education and Socialization* (vol.4) Greenwich, CT: JAI, 3-12

Kourilsky, M. L. and Carlson, S. R. (1996) 'Mini-society and Yess! Learning theory in action', *Children's Social and Economic Understanding*, 1(2), 105-117

Krzywosz-Rynkiewicz, B, Topczewska, E. and Derkowska, M., (1999) 'Children's tolerance for different cultures from the perspective of their educational background', in A. Ross (ed.) *Young Citizens in Europe*, London: CiCe Publications

Kuhn, T. (1970) *The Structure of Scientific Revolutions* (2nd edition), Vols. I and II, Foundations of the Unity of Science, Chicago: University of Chicago Press

Ladurie, E. (1980) *Montaillou*, Harmondsworth: Penguin

Lamer, K. (1991) *Du får inte vara med!* Studentlitteratur, Lund

Lassarre, D., Ludwig, D., Roland-Lévy, C. and Watiez, M. (1987) *Education du Jeune Consommateur: Les sources d'information économiques des enfants de 11-12 ans*, Paris: Paris University Press.

Lastrucci E. (1997) 'Specificities of historical consciousness in Italian adolescents', in M. Angvik and B. von Borries (eds.) *Youth and History*, vol. 1, Hamburg: Koerber Stiftung 344-353

Lastrucci, E. (1997) 'Alfabetizzazione civica e civismo', in Corda Costa, M. (ed), *Formare il cittadino: Laboratorio di educazione civica per la scuola secondari*, Firenze; La Nuova Italia, 3 - 54

Lastrucci, E. (2000) 'History consciousness, social/political identity and European citizenship', in A. Ross (ed.), *Developing Identities in Europe: Citizenship Education and Higher Education*, London: CiCe Publications, 227-237

Lave, J. (1988) *Cognition in Practice: Mind, Mathematics and Culture*, Cambridge: Cambridge University Press

Lave, J. and Wenger, E. (1991) *Situated Learning: Legitimate Peripheral Participation*, Cambridge: Cambridge University Press

Lea, S. E. G., Tarpy, R. M. and Webley, P. (1987) *The Individual in the Economy*, Cambridge: Cambridge University Press

Leiser, D. (1983) 'Children's conceptions of economics: the constitution of a cognitive domain', *Journal of Economic Psychology*, 4, 297-317

Leiser, D., Sevon, G. and Lévi, D. (1990) 'Children's economic socialisation: summarising the cross-cultural comparisons of ten countries', *Journal of Economic Psychology*, 11, 591-614

Levi-Strauss, C. (1969) *The Elementary Structures of Kinship*, (trans. James Harle bell, John Richard von Sturmer and Rodney Needham), Boston: Beacon Press

Lewis, A., Webley, P. and Furnham, A. (1995) *The New Economic Mind: The Social Psychology of Economic Behaviour*, Hemel Hempstead: Harvester Wheatsheaf

Lickona, T. (1992) *Educating for Character: How Our Schools Can Teach Respect and Responsibility*, New York: Bantam Books

Linton, T. (1990) 'A child's-eye view of economics' in A. ROSS (ed.) *Economic and Industrial Awareness in the Primary School*, London: PNL Press

Livesley, W.J. and Bromley, D.B. (1973) *Person perception in childhood and adolescence*, London: Academic Press

Lukaszewski, W. (1998) 'Tozsamo´s´c narodowa mlodych Niemców i mlodych Polaków a stosunek do narodów Europy', *Czasopismo Psychologiczne*, 4(1), 7-19

Lukaszewski, W. (1999) 'Mlodzi Polacy o narodach Europy' in B. Wojciszke (ed.) *Rozumienie zjawisk spolecznych*, Warszawa: Pa´nstwowe Wydawnictwo Naukowe

Lunt, P, and Furnham, A. (1996) *Economic Socialisation: The Economic Beliefs and Behaviours of Young People*, Cheltenham, UK: Edward Elgar

Lynch, K. (1971) *L'image de la ville*, Paris: Dunod

Malewska-Peyre, H. (1992) 'Ja w´sród swoich i obcych', in P. Boski, M. Jarymowicz, H. Malewska-Peyre (Eds.) *Tozsamo´s´c a odmienno´s´c kulturowa*, Warszawa: Instytut Psychologii Polskiej Akademii Nauk

Marshall, J. (2000) 'Teenage killings fuel wave of anxiety' *Times Educational Supplement*, 15, December 2000, p.12

McGurk, H. (ed.) (1978) *Issues in Childhood Social Development*, London: Methuen

Meadows, S. (1993) *The Child as Thinker: The Development and Acquisition of Cognition in Childhood*, London: Routledge

Mercer, N. (1992) 'Culture, context and the construction of knowledge in the classroom', in P. Light and G. Butterworth (eds) *Context and Cognition: Ways of learning and knowing*, Hemel Hempstead: Harvester Wheatsheaf.

Metais, J.L. (1999) 'Values and aims in curriculum and assessment frameworks: a 16 nation review', in B. Moon and P. Murphy (eds.) *Curriculum in Context*, London: Paul Chapman Publishing/Open University

Moore, S. W., Lare, J., and Wagner, K. A. (1985) *The Child's Political World: A Longitudinal Perspective*, New York: Praeger

Morin, M. (1984) 'Représentations sociales et évaluation des cadres de vie urbains', *Bulletin de Psychologie*, 366, 823-832

Morss, J. R. (1996) *Growing Critical: Alternatives to Developmental Psychology*, London: Routledge

Moscovici, S. (1984) (sous la dir.) *Psychologie Sociale*, Paris: PUF

Moscovici, S. (1984) 'On social representations', in R. Farr and S. Moscovici (eds.) *Social Representations*, Cambridge: Cambridge University Press

Moscovici, S. (1988) 'Notes towards a description of social representations', *European Journal of Social Psychology*, 18(3), 211-250

Murphy, M. M. (1998) *Character Education in America's Blue Ribbon Schools*, Lancaster: Techbomic

Näsman, E. (1995) 'Vuxnas intresse av att se med barns ögon', In L. Dahlgren and K. Hultqvist (eds.) *Seendet och seendets villkor: En bok om barns och ungas välfärd*, Stockholm: HLS förlag

Näsman, E. and Von Gerber, C. (1996) *Mamma pappa utan jobb*, Stockholm: Rädda Barnen förlag

Näsman, E. and Von Gerber, C. (1998) *Arbetslös- Berätta för barnen*, Norrköping

Näsman, E. and Von Gerber, C. (forthcoming) 'Pocket money, spending and sharing: young children's understanding of economy in their everyday life', in M. Hutchings, M. Fülöp and A. M. Van Den Dries (eds.) *Young People's Understanding of Economic Issues in Europe*, Stoke on Trent: Trentham

Neelands, J. (1992) *Learning through imagined experience*, Suffolk: Hodder and Stoughton

Ng, S.H. (1983) 'Children's ideas about the bank and shop profit: development stages and the influence of cognitive contrasts and conflict', *Journal of Economic Psychology*, 4, 209-21

Nikitorowicz, J. (2000) *Mlodziez pogranicza kulturowego Bialorusi*, Polski, Ukrainy wobec integracji europejskiej. Bialystok: Trans Humana

Nordström, G. Z. (1996) *Rum Relation Retorik*, Stockholm

Norris, N., Aspland, R. Macdonald, B., Schostak, J. and Zamorski, B. (1996) *An Independent Evaluation of Comprehensive curriculum Reform in Finland*, Helsinki: National Board of Education

Olson, D. (ed.), *The Social Foundations of Language and Thought: Essays in Honor of Jerome S. Bruner*, New York: Norton.

Pahl, R. (1984) *Divisions of Labour*, Oxford: Blackwell

Palmonari, A., Carugati, F., Ricci Bitti, P.E. and Sarchielli, G. (1984) 'Imperfect identities: a socio-psychological perspective for the study of the problems of adolescence', in Tajfel H. (ed.), *The social dimension*, vol. 1, Cambridge: Cambridge University Press, 111-133

Papastergiou, N. (1998) *Dialogues in the Diasporas: Essays and Conversations on Cultural Identity*, London and New York: Rivers Oram Press

Pearson, G. (1983) *Hooligan: A History of Respectable Fears*, London and Basingstoke: Macmillan

Piaget, J (1924) *Le jugement et le raisonnement chez l'enfant*, Neuchatel: Delâchaux et Niestlé

Piaget, J. (1926) *The Language and Thought of the Child* (originally published 1923), London: Routledge and Kegan Paul.

Piaget, J. (1926) *The Language and Thought of the Child*, New York: Harcourt Brace

Piaget, J. (1929) *The Child's Conception of the World* (originally published 1926), London: Routledge and Kegan Paul

Piaget, J. (1948) *La représentation de l'espace chez l'enfant*, Paris: PUF

Piaget, J. (1963) *La construction du réel chez l'enfant*, Neuchatel: Delâchaux et Niestlé

Piaget, J. (1967) *Six Psychological Studies* (originally published 1964), New York: Random House

Piaget, J. and Inhelder, B. (1969) *The Psychology of the Child* (originally published 1966), London: Routledge and Kegan Paul

Piaget, J. and Weil, A.M. (1951) 'Le développement, chez l'enfant, de l'idée de patrie et des relations avec l'etranger', *Bulletin International des Sciences Sociales*, Paris, UNESCO, 3, 605-621

Pollack, D. (1997) 'Das Bedürfnis nach sozialer Anerkennung. Der Wandel der Akzeptanz von Demokratie und Marktwirtscahft in Ostdeutschland', *Politik und Zeitgeschichte* (Beilage zur Wochenzeitschrift 'Das Parlament'), 13, 3-14

Potter, J. and Wetherell, M. (1987) *Discourse and Social Psychology: Beyond Attitudes and Behaviour*, London: Sage

Prout, A. and James, A. (1990) 'A new paradigm for the sociology of childhood? provenance, promise and problems', in A. James and A. Prout (eds.) *Constructing and Reconstructing Childhood: Contemporary Issues in the Sociological Study of Childhood*, London: Falmer

Quortrup, J. (1990) *Childhood as a Social Phenomenon: An Introduction to a Series of National Reports*, Eurosocial Report 36, Vienna: European Centre

Rattansi, A. (1994) 'Western racism, ethnicities and identities in a post-modern frame', in A. Rattansi and S. Westwood, (eds.) *Racism, Modernity and Identity on the Western Front*, Cambridge: Polity Press

Reitzle, M. and Silbereisen, R.K. (1997) 'Adapting to social change: adolescents' values in Eastern and Western Germany', paper presented at the Biennial Meeting of the Society for Research in Child Development, Washington DC

Reykowski, J. (1995) 'Kolektywny system znacze'n', in W. Lukaszewski, *W kregu teorii czynno'sci*, Warszawa: Instytut Psychologii Polskiej Akademii Nauk

Rich, J. and Devitis, J.J. (1992) *Competition in Education*, Charles C. Thomas Publisher

Rogoff, B. (1990) *Apprenticeship in Thinking: Cognitive development in social context*, New York: Oxford University Press.

Roland-Lévy, C. (forthcoming) 'Economic socialisation: how does one develop an understanding of the economic world?', in M. Hutchings, M. Fülöp and A. M. Van Den Dries (eds.) *Young People's Understanding of Economic Issues in Europe*, Stoke on Trent: Trentham

Rose, N. (1989) *Governing the Soul: The Shaping of the Private Self*, London: Routledge

Rose, R., and Mishler, W.T.E. (1994) 'Mass reaction to regime change in Eastern Europe: polarization or leaders and laggards', *British Journal of Political Science*, 24, 159-182

Ross, A. (ed.) (1999) *Young Citizens in Europe*, London: CiCe

Ross, A. (ed.) (2000) *Developing Identities in Europe*, London: CiCe

Sani, F., Bennett, M., AgostinI, L., Malucchi, L. and Ferguson, N. (2000) 'Children's conception of characteristic features of category members', *The Journal of Social Psychology*, 140(2), 227-239

Schaffer, H. (1989) 'Joint involvement episodes as context for cognitive development', in H. Mcgurk (ed.) *Contemporary Issues in Childhood Social Development*, Lonon: Routledge

Schaffer, H. and Crook, C. (1978) 'The role of the mother in early social development', in H. Mcgurk (ed.) *Issues in Childhood Social Development*, London: Methuen

Schlenker, B. R. (1985) 'Identity and self-identification', in B. R. Schlenker (ed.) *The Self and Social Life*, New York: McGraw Hill

Schönpflug, U. (2001) Introduction, 'Cultural transmission: a multidisciplinary research field', *Journal of Cross-Cultural Psychology*, 32(2), 131-135

Schönpflug, U. And Silbereisen, R.K. (1992) 'Transmission of values between generations in the family regarding societal keynote issues: A cross-cultural longitudinal study on Polish and German families' in S. Iwawaki, Y. Kashima, K. and Leung (eds), *Innovations in cross-cultural psychology*, Lisse, The Netherlands: Swets and Zeitlinger.

Schostak, J. (1993) *Dirty Marks: The Education of Self, Media and Popular Culture*, London: Pluto Press

Schostak, J. F. (1983) *Maladjusted Schooling: Deviance, Social Control and Individuality in Secondary Schooling*, London, Philadelphia: Falmer

Schostak, J. F. (1986) *Schooling the Violent Imagination*, London, New York: Routledge and Kegan Paul

Schostak, J. F. (ED) (1991) *Youth in Trouble: Educational Responses*, Kogan Page: London

Schutz, A. (1945, 1967) *Collected Papers I, The Problem of Social Reality*, The Hague: Martinus, Nijhoff

Scribner, S. (1984) 'Studying working intelligence', in B. Rogoff and J. Lave (eds.) *Everyday Cognition: Its Development in Social Context*, Cambridge: Harvard University Press

Sherif, M. (1967) *Group conflict and cooperation: their social psychology*, London: Routledge

Sherif, M. and Sherif, C.W. (1965) *Problems of Youth: Transition to Adulthood in a Changing World*, Chicago: Aldine

Sherif, M. and Sherif, C.W. (1969) 'Adolescent attitudes and behaviour in their reference groups', in J.P. Hill (ed.) *Minnesota symposia on child psychology*, vol. 3, Minnesota: Minnesota University Press

Shotter, J. (1992) 'Getting in touch: the meta-methodology of a post-modern science of mental life', in S. Kvale (ed.) *Psychology and Postmodernism*, London: Sage

Shotter, J. (1993) *Conversational Realities: Constructing Life through Language*, London: Sage

Siegler, R.S. and Thompson, D.R. (1998) 'Hey, would you like a nice cold cup of lemonade on this hot day?': children's understanding of economic causation', *Developmental Psychology*, 3(1), 146-160

Sierens, S. (ed) (2000) *Us Them Ours: Points for attention in designing interculturally sound learning materials*, Gent: Universiteit Gent/Steunpunt Intercultureel Onderwijs

Silbereisen, R.K. (2000) 'German unification and adolescents' developmental timetables: continuities and discontinuities', in L.J. Crockett and R.K. Silbereisen (eds.) *Negotiating adolescence in times of social change*, Cambridge: Cambridge University Press, 104-122

Simmons, C. (1996) 'Cross-cultural concepts of adolescence in Europe, the United States and Japan', *Asia Pacific Journal of Education*, 16(2), 53-66

Simmons, R. and Rosenberg, M. (1971) 'Functions of children's perceptions of the stratification system', *American Sociological Review*, 36, 235-49

Slomczynski, K., Janicka, K., Mach, B.W. and Zaborowski, W. (1999) *Mental adjustment to the post-communist system in Poland*, Warshaw: IfiS Publishers

Sommer, D. (1977) *Barndomspsykologi*. Utveckling i en förändrad värld, Runa: Hässelby

Sommer, D. (1996) *Barndomspsykologi*. Utveckling i en förändrad värld, Runa: Hässelby

Stacey, B.G. (1978) *Political Socialisation in Western Society*, London: Edward Arnold

Stacey, B.G. (1982) 'Economic socialisation in the pre-adult years', *British Journal of Social Psychology*, 21, 159-73

Stainton Rogers, R. and Stainton Rogers, W. (1992) *Stories of Childhood: Shifting Agendas of Child Concern*, Hemel Hempstead: Harvester Wheatsheaf

Stern, D. N. (1991) *Spädbarnets interpersonella värld*, Stockholm: Natur and Kultur

Stevens, O. (1982) *Children Talking Politics*, Oxford: Martin Roberston

Tajfel, H and Turner, J.C. (1986) 'The social identity theory for intergroup relations', in W.G. Austin and F. Worchel (eds.) *Psychology of Intergroup Relations*, Monterey: Brooks/Cole, 7-24

Tajfel, H. (1969) 'The formation of national attitudes: A social-psychological perspective', in Sherif, M. (ed) *Interdisciplinary Relationship in the Social Sciences*, Chicago ILL: Aldine

Tajfel, H. (1972) 'La categorisation sociale' in S. Moscovici (ed.) Introduction à la Psychologie, Paris: Larousse. (Referred to by Emler and Dickinson, 1995)

Tajfel, H. (1980) 'The 'New Look' and Social Differentiation: a semi-Brunerian perspective', in Tajfel, H. and Bruner, J.S. (eds), *The Social Foundations of Language and Thought*, New York: Englewood-Cliffs.

Tajfel, H. (1981) *Human Groups and Social Categories*, Cambridge: Cambridge, University Press

Tajfel, H. (1982) 'Social psychology of intergroup relations', in *Annual Review of Psychology*, 33, 1-39

Tajfel, H. (ed.) (1984) *The Social Dimension: European Developments in Social Psychology*, 2 vols., Cambridge: Cambridge University Press

Tajfel, H. and Bruner, J.S. (1964) *Cognitive Risk and Environmental Change*, New York: Englewood-Cliffs

Tajfel, H. and Turner, J.C. (1970) 'An integrative theory of intergroup conflict', in W.G. Austin and F. Worchel (eds.) *The Social Psychology of Intergroup Relations*, Monterey: Brooks/Cole, 33-48

Tajfel, H., and Turner J.C. (1970) 'An integrative theory of intergroup conflict', in W.G. Austin and F. Worchel (eds) *The Social Psychology of Intergroup Relations*, Monterey, Ca: Brooks/Cole, pp 33 - 48.

Tallandini, M. A., and Valentini, P. (1995) *La scuola è una grande casa* [The school is a big house], Milano: Raffaello Cortina

Tapp, J. L. and Kohlberg, L. (1977) 'Developing senses of law and legal justice', in J. L. Tapp, and L. Kohlberg (eds.) *Law, Justice, and the Individual in Society*, New York: Holt, Rinehart and Winston

Tizard, B. and Hughes, M. (1984) *Young Children Learning: Talking and Thinking at Home and at School*, London: Fontana

Torney-Purta, J. (1994) 'Dimensions of adolescents' reasoning about political and historical issues: ontological switches, developmental processes, and situated learning', in M. Carretero and J. F. Voss (eds.) *Cognitive and Instructional Processes in History and the Social Studies*, Hillsdale, NJ: Erlbaum 103-122

Trommsdorf, G. (2000) 'Effects of social change on individual development: The role of social and personal factors and the timing of events', in L.J. Crockett and R.K. Silbereisen (eds.) *Negotiating Adolescence in Times of Social Change*, Cambridge: Cambridge University Press 58-68

Trommsdorf, G. and Chakkarath, P. (1996) 'Kindheit im Transformationsprozess (Childhood in the process of transformation)' in S.E. Hormuth, W.R. Heinz, H-J. Kornadt, H. Sydow, and G.Trommsdorff (eds.) *Individuelle Entwicklung, Bildung und Berufsverlaufe. Berichte zum sozialen und politischen Wandel in Ostdeutschland*, KSPW Bd. 4, Opladen: Leske and Budrich 11-77

Trommsdorff, G. (1999) 'Social change and individual development in East Germany: a methodological critique', in R.K. Silbereisen and A. Von Eye (eds.) *Growing Up in Times of Social Change*, Berlin: Walter de Gruyter 171-199

Turner J.C. (1984) 'Social identification and the psychological group formation', in H. Tajfel (ed.) *The Social Dimension: European Developments in Social Psychology*, Vol. II, Cambridge University Press 518-538

Turner, J.C. (1981) 'Towards a cognitive redefinition of the social group', *Cahiers de Psychologie Cognitive*, 1981(1), 93-118

UK (2001) *Home Office: Statistics on Notifiable Offences Recorded by the Police*, October 1999-September 2000, London: HMSO

Urwin, C. (1984) 'Power relations and the emergence of language', in J. Henriques, W. Hollway, C. Urwin, C. Venn, and V. Walkerdine *Changing the Subject: Psychology, social regulation and subjectivity*, London: Methuen

Vacek, P. (2000a) 'Education for Democracy and Citizenship in the Czech Republic', in A. Ross (ed.) *Developing Identities in Europe: Citizenship Education and Higher Education*, Second European Conference of CiCe, Athens: University of Athens, 169-174

Vacek, P. (2000b) 'Anal´yza školních řád°u a její pedagogicko-psychologické souvislosti', *Pedagogická orientace*, 1, 45-55

Vacek, P. (2000c) '*Morální v´yvoj v psychologick´ych a pedagogick´ych souvislostech*', Hradec Králové: Gaudeamus

Van Hoorn, J.L., Komlósi, Á., Suchar, E. and Samelson, D.A. (2000) *Adolescent Development and Rapid Social Change*, Albany: State University of New York Press

Venn, C. (1984) 'The subject of psychology', in J. Henriques, W. Hollway, C. Urwin, C. Venn, and V. Walkerdine *Changing the Subject: Psychology, social regulation and subjectivity*, London: Methuen

Venn, C. and Walkerdine, V. (1978) 'The acquisition and production of knowledge: Piaget's theory reconsidered', *Identity and Consciousness*, 3, 67-94

Vikan, A. (1987) 'Barns forståelse av sosiala årsaksforhold', *Barn* 4, 35-45

Virág, T. (2000) *Children of Social Trauma: Hungarian Psychoanalytic Case Studies*, Jessica Kingsley Publisher

Vosniadou, S. (1991) 'Designing curricula for conceptual restructuring: lesson from the study of knowledge acquisition in astronomy', *Journal of Curriculum Studies*, 23, 219-237

Vygotsky, L. (1986) *Thought and Language* (trans. A. Kozulin, originally published 1934), Cambridge, MA: MIT Press

Walker, B. & Kushner, S. (1999) 'The Building Site: an educational approach to masculine identity', *Journal of Youth Studies*, Vol 2 (1) pp.45-58

Walkerdine, V. (1984) 'Developmental Psychology and the child-centred pedagogy: the insertion of Piaget into early education', in J. Henriques, W. Hollway, C. Urwin, C. Venn, and V. Walkerdine *Changing the Subject: Psychology, social regulation and subjectivity*, London: Methuen

Walkerdine, V. (1993) 'Beyond developmentalism', *Thought and Psychology*, 3, 451-469

Walkerdine, V. (1994) 'Reasoning in a post-modern age', in P. Ernest (ed.) *Mathematics Education and Philosophy*, London: Falmer Press

Walkerdine, V. and Lucey, H. (1989) *Democracy in the Kitchen*, London: Virago

Webley, P. (1983) 'Economic socialisation in the pre-adult years: a comment on Stacey', *British Journal of Social Psychology*, 22, 264-5

Webley, P. and Wrigley, V. (1983) 'The development of concepts of unemployment among adolescents', *Journal of Adolescence*, 6, 317-28

Weigl, B. (1999) *Stereotypy i uprzedzenia etniczne u dzieci i mlodziezy*, Warszawa: Instytut Psychologii Polskiej Akademii Nauk

Wellman (1990) *The Child's Theory of Mind*. Cambridge, Ma: Bradford/ MIT Press.

Wellman, H. M, and Gelman, S. (1998) 'Knowledge acquisition in foundational domains', in D. Kuhn and R. S. Siegler, (eds.) *Handbook of child psychology*, Vol. 2, Cognition, Perception, and Language (5th edn.) New York: Wiley, 523-574

White, M. (1993) *The Material Child: coming of Age in Japan and America*, Berkeley: University of California Press

Willis, P. (1977) *Learning to Labour: How Working Class Kids get Working Class Jobs*, Farnborough: Saxon House

Wojciszke, B. (1991) *Procesy oceniania ludzi*, Pozna'n: Nakom

Wong, M. (1989) 'Children's acquisition of economic knowledge: understanding banking in Hong Kong and the USA', in J. Valsiner (ed.) *Child Development in Cultural Context*, Norwood, NJ: Ablex

Wood, D. (1988) *How Children Think and Learn*, Oxford: Blackwell

Youniss, J. (1978) 'Young children's understanding of society', in H. Mcgurk (ed.) *Issues in Childhood Social Development*, London: Methuen

Zavalloni, M. and Louis-Guerin, C. (1984) Identité sociale et conscience, Introduction à l'ego-écologie, Montreal: Les Presses de l'Université de Montréal.

Index